Fierce Tenderness

MARY E. HUNT

Fierce Tenderness

A Feminist Theology of Friendship

CROSSROAD • NEW YORK

1991
The Crossroad Publishing Company
370 Lexington Avenue, New York, NY 10017

Printed in the United States of America
Typesetting output: TEXSource, Houston

Library of Congress Cataloging-in-Publication Data

Hunt, Mary E., 1951–
    Fierce tenderness : a feminist theology of friendship / Mary E.
Hunt.
      p. cm.
    Includes bibliographical references and index.
    ISBN 0-8245-1078-X
    1. Feminist theology. 2. Friendship—Religious aspects—
Christianity. 3. Lesbianism—Religious aspects—Christianity.
I. Title
BT83.55.H85 1991
241'.676'082—dc20   90-41832
                                           CIP

For my friends,
especially Diann Neu,
who embody fierce tenderness.

Contents

We gratefully acknowledge permission to quote from the following works:

"love & friendship," from *Movement in Black*, by Pat Parker. Ithaca, N.Y.: Firebrand Books, 1983.

"Vulnerable," from *Omega*, by Patricia Ryan. Berkeley, Calif.: Carmarthen Oak Press, 1983.

"Song of Community" by Carolyn McDade. Words and Music by Carolyn McDade, Womancenter at Plainville. Copyright 1979 Surtsey Publishing.

Zami: A New Spelling of My Name by Audre Lord. Trumansburg, N.Y.: The Crossing Press, 1982.

"They Have Threatened Us with Resurrection," from *Threatened with Resurrection*, by Julia Esquivel. Elgin, Ill.: The Brethren Press, 1982.

The lines from "An Observation" are reprinted from *Collected Poems (1930–1973)* by May Sarton, by permission of the author and W. W. Norton & Co., Inc. Copyright © 1974 by May Sarton.

The lines from "AIDS" are reprinted from *The Silence Now: New and Uncollected Earlier Poems* by May Sarton, by permission of the author and W. W. Norton & Co., Inc. Copyright © 1988 by May Sarton.

"Every Woman" by Bernice Johnson Reagon. Copyright © Songtalk Publishing Co.

The quote from *Georgia O'Keeffe* by Georgia O'Keeffe. Copyright 1987 by Juan Hamilton.

Acknowledgements

My theological reflections on friendship are informed by countless people. I consider our exchanges to be important data for this book. In talks with friends, counselling sessions with people struggling to be friends, and especially in the nurture and loss of my own friends, I have learned more than most books can ever convey. My task is to filter these perceptions through a theological lens and invite readers to do the same.

I am grateful to the participants at workshops and lectures where the ideas that have taken root in this book were first offered and always enriched. It was my privilege to share the earliest version of this work some years ago with the Women's Ordination Conference in Boston, Mass. Later it was refined at a seminar on friendship organized by Anne Stewart with Rustum Roy at Wesley Theological Seminary in Washington, D.C. I have let the ideas simmer and steep since then, but those early considerations were formative. I hope that this book is equal to their inspiration.

Women's groups shaped this work. First, my own friends at the Women's Alliance for Theology, Ethics and Ritual (WATER) in Silver Spring, Md., reacted favorably to it in early form. Then women of faith in Albany, N.Y., Claremont, Calif., and Roanoke, Va., as well as the Conference for Catholic Lesbians meeting in California, gave me their input. The Company at Kirkridge and students at Colgate University made me aware that "fierce tenderness" is not for women only. I appreciate their frank, critical, and constructive responses.

I shared some aspects of this work with groups in Mendoza, Córdoba, and Buenos Aires, Argentina. There I learned that "fierce tenderness" works for Latin American friends as well. I discussed parts of this work at an international conference in Amsterdam, The Netherlands, where Dutch theological students and other participants gave it their enthusiastic and careful attention. In these international settings, as well as with friends of racial/ethnic groups different from my own in the United States I was taught that one cannot make blanket assumptions without putting relationships in context. At the same time, I learned that friendship is friendship. This tension remains problematic for me, and I remain indebted to these friends for their forthright clarity.

I am grateful to Tish Jaccard and Laura Bernstein for technical assistance in the preparation of this manuscript, and to Carol Scinto for copy editing. I thank Robert Canavello, Clare Fischer, Susan Phillips, Mary Lou Randour, and Kathy Shorter for their useful comments on the text. Justus George Lawler intuited the importance of this book from the beginning and wisely let it ripen. He encouraged its development and brought a keen mind to the finished product. My thanks to him are, appropriately, in the form of feminist friendship. I have no words to express my appreciation to Diann Neu for muse-like inspiration and deep friendship as I pondered. I appreciate the Research Assistance Grant from the American Academy of Religion that supported the preparation of the manuscript.

Friendship is a tricky subject. I try to approach it personally, without self-indulgence or privatization. I try to approach it politically, without dissection or sterilization. The art of theologizing is to achieve this delicate balance. I am fortunate that my art is a communal one, and that there are so many others who accompany me in this work.

Introduction

love

        &   friendship

are words of

people

telling

people

trust is

a word

for

bankers

me

       & you

   &

You

are

words

for

us.

—Pat Parker, "Love and Friendship"
from *Movement in Black*

Everyone has friends, but by reading contemporary theology one would never know it. Relational patterns are shifting all around us and theology hardly seems to notice. My aim is to explore friendship in all of its theological splendor from a feminist perspective. While women's friendships with women form the skeleton of my work, I am equally concerned about female-male and male-male relationships. They deserve attention both as they bear on female-female friendships

1

and as all friendships participate in the divine-human cooperation called creation.

I envision this book as especially useful to people who want to teach the next generation by example how to love well. It is a kind of feminist theological primer for those who seek new models for ethical reflection, new lenses through which to filter their own experiences. Women as well as men will find challenges to old assumptions as the revolution in relationships that began in the 1960s takes root in the twenty-first century. This book is meant as a stimulus for those who hope that such changes portend greater inclusivity, richer community, and deeper self-awareness.

It would be interesting to begin this analysis with a review of the theological literature on the topic of friendship. But as Sallie McFague understated, the concept of friend is "found in the tradition, though sparingly: in Irenaeus of Lyons,...the medieval mystics; and a variation of it in A.N. Whitehead's metaphor for God as 'fellow-sufferer.'"[1] Unfortunately these sources only distract since they are rooted in patriarchal worldviews that systematically pass over the particular experiences of women. Using them as starting points only reinforces what needs to be replaced, although it is comforting to know that somebody paid attention to these matters. What remains a puzzle is why more attention has not been paid by theologians. The solution to the puzzle begins here. Further, I question whether A. N. Whitehead's metaphor, the closest analogue to ours both in time and intent, would ever emerge from women's experiences. While it is true that suffering is as common a human happening as friendship (a feminist theological perspective on suffering is properly the subject of another study that needs to be done), my sense is that women would rarely choose to lift it up as paradigmatic of anything positive. By contrast, human friendship serves as a useful paradigm of right relation for the whole of creation. Friendship is the model of healthy relating and the goal of human community.

Suffering tends to divide the sufferer from those who do not suffer. In this sense it is the antithesis of relationship. It tends to emphasize that over which we have limited control as opposed to those choices that evidence our agency. In short, it is not a close cousin, though the very difference points out the value of using friendship from women's perspectives if relationality and religious agency are primary. That they are and that they are defining characteristics of a new theo-ethical approach is central to this book.

Naming the New

The most obvious and for some the most startling aspect of this work is the assumption that women's friendships include physical, sometimes genital expression and that such friendships are good. Since this is a provocative claim in some circles (albeit an obvious and welcome one in others), I address it head on as a way to defuse any attention that may distract from the larger project at hand. Fierce tenderness is not for lesbian women only. It is not even for women only, though it is written by a lesbian woman.

One reading that I expect from right-wing religionists, but conceivably from liberal colleagues as well, is that a feminist theology of friendship is simply an apologia for same-sex relationships, especially those between women. As such it may be said to trivialize other forms of friendship and to imperialize a lesbian choice over the heterosexual marriage norm, replacing one form of ethical tyranny with another. Likewise such a critique could write off the deeper insights of friendship here for fear of accepting anything that starts from premises that are not shared.

To this I respond that same-sex love needs no apology. Nor unfortunately is it necessarily any better or worse than any other form of right relation even though it is made more difficult in a patriarchal, heterosexist society. Finally this neither increases its virtue nor decreases its challenge. The potential for friendship and the willingness and conditions to actualize it are simply part of creation. Women loving women are a wonderful part of creation that has been passed over socially as well as in the theological work that shapes so much of Western culture. As we lift up that reality to public expression, as we sacramentalize it like any other good, its true value is revealed.

What is new, and to some controversial, is taking a previously marginalized, often ignored, and usually condemned experience and making it the center of a theo-ethical framework that is not for lesbian women only but at least implicitly for all. This takes ethical boldness. The aim is to lift up within the Christian theo-ethical tradition a longstanding mistake and use it constructively to reshape that tradition. The point is to use it as a resource among the very people who have erred, including Christian women, since women's friendships express value and meaning that resonates with the better instincts of that community.

Much more than making the theo-ethical world safe for women's friendships of all stripes is going on here. Critics will rightly pick this out as innovative, though wrongly interpret it as the major move.

That is to take the most narrow view of what is a much wider effort to begin to transform nothing less than the theo-ethical landscape for all kinds of friends. A Copernican revolution in relationship is underway.

The major move that this book represents is from an individual ethic based on limited experiences to a collective ethic that grows organically out of the many relational possibilities that good people choose to live in right relation. As such, lesbian women's friendships are an attractive and persuasive possibility, though one among many. It is not necessary to prioritize them over all other types. It is simply my point that they have been passed over as a rich and suggestive model for all friendships in favor of heterosexual marriage. This has produced an unworkable ethic. I understand how dangerous my suggestion is to those who wish to maintain the status quo. But for others who wish that Christian theo-ethics would catch up with how good people live well, this will be a welcome contribution.

An old feminist adage was that "feminism is the theory and lesbianism is the practice." Tempting as it may be to some to affix this to my analysis, I reject both the form and the content of the assertion. In fact, feminism is neither pure theory nor is lesbianism pure practice. The overwhelming evidence of fierce tenderness as the motivation for social change, of love with politics, reveals that such an assertion is so mired in patriarchal dichotomy as to impede progress. We are moving from "either/or" to "both/and" thinking in our theo-ethical approach, so there is no reason to reinforce an outmoded model in this way.

Rather, I suggest that friendship, beginning with the kinds of friendships that women have with one another, whether sexually explicit or not, is paradigmatic of the unity of theory and practice that feminists live out. Women friends, both lesbian and heterosexual, know that collective survival and the choices we secure depend on bonding and on friendly actions for structural change. They do not depend ultimately on sexual preference but on justice-seeking actions.

Ironically, although my analysis of fierce tenderness is predicated on individual women's experiences, it ultimately rests on the many relational possibilities women and men face. The fact that some women develop strong friendships with men is not to be trivialized nor ignored. It can be incorporated as part of the collective wisdom and celebrated with an eye toward duplicating the experience a million-fold. Men may have parallel experiences of fierce tenderness with other men though much of this remains to be articulated by them. It will be a welcome addition to the larger theo-ethical conversation.

Discussion of women's friendships will be a springboard for that kind of consideration as well.

The fact that women and men are learning new ways to relate is very much in keeping with this analysis. In fact, for further study these female-male and male-male friendships will produce new models and new insights that will complement this work. Meanwhile, the revolution in relationships goes on and those of us who value reflection on it as a way to shape the results can start here.

· 1 ·

Fierce and Tender

To move among the tender with an open hand,
And to stay sensitive up to the end
Pay with some toughness for a gentle world.

—May Sarton, "An Observation"
in *Collected Poems (1930–1973)*

Friendships Explored

All relationships are not friendships, but certain significant human efforts to love and be loved qualify. There are far more friendships around than we acknowledge. Friendship is available to everyone, at least potentially. The tiny baby who is befriended by her mother is learning friendship. The elderly person around whom a community gathers when she is dying is capable of teaching friendship. Friendship, by its nature, assumes that persons live in relationships, and that relationships are good. Of course not all relationships are friendly, but for my purpose I will focus on those that are in the hope of evoking more of them.

Friendships do not all work or last over time. Some do, but quality, not quantity, is the measure of their value. There is some luck involved, and, as I will argue, there are skills for building, keeping, and leaving friendships that can be learned and taught. In each friendship we are brought face to face with ourselves, with one another, and with a larger world in which the mysterious forces of attraction work beyond our ultimate control.

Friendship is a useful theological construct. Friendship illuminates questions of ultimate meaning and value. This is what friends strive

7

for and desire for one another. But not even theology and ethics can pierce the elusive dimensions of friendship. Nor should they pretend to do so. Theology can hold up friendship as something to be analyzed critically, and ethics reminds us that friendship is ultimately important. In the final analysis friends are sufficient in themselves of course, but there is much to be learned through the lens of friendship that theology and ethics have all but ignored.

I write about friendship first of all as a friend, and then as a feminist theologian. My effort to report and reflect on experience, even to propose new ways in which it might be understood, is filtered through my friendships. It cannot be otherwise. I have had my share of friends, and I have lost enough to know that fierce tenderness comes in many guises, usually when one least expects it and rarely without complexity.

Friendship is not just ephemeral experience that cannot be analyzed. In fact, it is a foundational way in which we orient our lives. As such it demands careful, critical theo-ethical analysis both to understand it and to "do" it better. In this work my presupposition is that friendship is, finally, not only a personal relationship but also a political activity. It is political insofar as it is a public activity for which friends assume mutual responsibility. It is political because each friendship is part of the constellation that is a society. It is never enough to say, "We're just friends."

Nothing defeats the purpose of feminist theology faster than an obscure, abstract treatment of some phenomena "out there." The task of a theologian is to look critically at the data of human experience in light of a faith tradition and to make claims that invite the whole community to new insights. I invite the reader to theologize as well, to bring her/his experiences to bear, and to contribute those insights to a wider community of friends.

Readers may find it helpful to discuss this work in groups, testing my claims against the myriad experiences of friendship that they have. Such an approach will round out the insights and make for creative theologizing.

Doing Theology

The patriarchal theological enterprise has wandered far from its original roots in a community of friends, when theologians ponder issues alone as has been the twentieth-century Western Christian approach. Latin American liberation theologians insist that *hacer teología*, to make or to do theology, is a communal responsibility, an activity of justice-seeking friends who do theology in order to right injustice. Feminist theologians seek to reorient the tradition by using a compass set to a true center and taking women's experiences seriously. These two theological traditions have shaped my methodology in a decisive way. I am indebted also to black (now called African American), Asian, and African liberation theologians for insights into how oppression shapes our worldviews. I look hopefully to womanist theologians in the United States as well as to women around the world who are working out theological agendas from their unique perspectives as women to complement and challenge my work.

Feminist theology finds its roots in women's experiences of marginalization and in efforts to move from the margin to the center.[1] It is not only women who need to move to the center. Persons who are economically poor, members of racial/ethnic groups that are discriminated against, lesbian and gay people, elderly, physically and mentally handicapped persons, all who have been systematically cast aside in favor of the prevailing powers are moving, with a little help from their friends, toward justice. Feminist theology helps groups to articulate and clarify what is meaningful and valuable in this search and to communicate it to a wider community.

Mine is a political vision of fierce tenderness in action. My conviction is that theology, far from retarding progress, as has often been the case with much of the mainstream, anti-body Christian approach, can motivate the deep reflection and personal conversion that sustain efforts at political change. Otherwise I would abandon theology as self-indulgent and counterproductive, and simply set my sights on more strategic purely political goals. To the contrary, I find that only by attending to the divine-human nexus in all of its diversity and complexity can I approximate a theo-political strategy deep enough to make change.

Friendship has been discussed rarely in Christian theological literature. This strikes me as peculiar in a faith tradition where laying down one's life for one's friends is lauded. Instead, certain assumptions are made about the moral normativity of coupled, heterosexual relationships that move toward marriage. These norms function to downgrade or leave aside entirely the vast, rich experiences of friendship that are actually more common. Such norms function to obscure the reality of friendship as the true human relational norm and to deny the validity of friendship as the foundational relational experience, of which heterosexual marriage is but one example.

Women's friendships in particular are virtually ignored as data for theological reflection. They are passed over, as is women's experience in general, in the few examples of noteworthy friends that one finds in theological sources. Given the poor track record of heterosexual marriage in contemporary Western society, it seems that the Christian tradition is missing the ethical boat by limiting its scope of acceptable and replicable relationships to marriage. Taking women's relationships seriously should seem natural in a tradition based on the imperative to love one another. At the very least it will open up new possibilities, and at the very most it will redefine what it means to love.

Doing Feminist Theology

Friendship is a challenging starting point for fresh theological reflections by women who have been excluded from most theologizing in the past. Rather than invite women to reflect on the now tried and often untrue theological categories of God, creation, salvation, and the like, I suggest that when women (and other previously excluded people) enter theological debates, the issues under consideration will shift. For example, women experience friendships as a plural experience including other human beings, ourselves, and the divine. The personal/communal split is meaningless. Multiple friendships are a simultaneous, not a competing, experience.

I consider friendship to be the ultimate political act. To go and make friends in all nations is a common calling for people of good will. The healthiest, most generative friendships are set in the widest possible context. Indeed we can say that the world is better for these friendships. While patriarchal Christian theology has emphasized laying down one's life for one's friends, a feminist approach focuses on sharing and enjoying life with friends, a common, accessible experience. The task for feminist theology is to look in this new way at what are really new data of revelation and to make sense of them by communal theologizing. Thus it is not simply that my friends are important to me, but that many women, when invited to reflect on what is ultimately meaningful and valuable for them, say that friendship is key. Of course we have different experiences due to different situations. But this convergence in claims says something important about remaking society. Feminist ethics can find no more foundational concept.

A feminist approach contrasts sharply with the one-dimensional and often vertical understanding of divine-human friendship that has been the hallmark of patriarchal theology. Even the "I-Thou" model of Martin Buber or the "friend as soul mate" of the ancient Greeks seem weak by comparison. While these have been among the more useful sources that have shaped Western ways of being friends, they are inadequate to encompass most women's experience. These notions, and many other equally limited ways of living and understanding friendship, were based on men's experiences, touching little if at all on women's often very different starting points. With the advent of feminist consciousness in our time, the data of women's experiences can no longer be ignored if a claim is made about the human condition.

My effort is to lift up women's experiences of friendship, not because turning the tables is fair play, but because these simply have not seen the light of theological day. I do not intend to complement men's experiences of friendship. I intend to refresh friendship in general by starting with women's lives. I aim to resurrect it literally as the basic relational goal of those who live in "right relation."[2] By doing so I invite women to articulate and celebrate what we know. I invite men to learn something new about relating and to name previously unnamed parts of their own experience.

I focus this book on women's female friends. Of course most women have male friends. What distinguishes my starting point is that it *begins with women's experiences on their own terms*. In many circles currently, though I hope not forever, this is done most clearly and easily without men. Of course women's experiences are not monolithic. Differences in race, ethnicity, class, age, and sexual preference condition women's experiences in significant ways. It is impossible to include all of them but it is necessary to limit one's claims accordingly.

My starting point is as a white, Catholic, U.S.-based, middle-class, upper-educated lesbian feminist woman with access to travel, study, and meaningful work. This conditions my choice of the topic of friendship and my basically positive view of it. I realize that there are limits to how far I can generalize even interest in the theme. Still I find some commonality insofar as all women's experience as women has included some form of marginalization. Gender is, admittedly, but one of many factors. While it unites women at one level, it can never mask the deep differences that race, class, ethnicity, and sexual preference provide. Nonetheless, I advocate pursuing solidarity on gender lines where it is found, knowing that at other junctures differences will dictate distance. It is only good strategy to use what is readily available.

I look forward to reflections on this theme by other women, especially those who live in circumstances that are very different from mine. In fact I have been encouraged in my explorations by the writings of other theologians, for example, Ada Maria Isasi-Diaz and Carolyn Lehmann, whose starting points are distinct from my own, but whose focus on the topic leads me to claim some, however small, commonality.[3]

I hope that this analysis will be helpful for men as well as for women since starting points are simply starting points. Obviously as women's starting points join men's in the center of the theological project, some men will feel threatened. I can only urge that we operate out of the assumption of plenty and not of scarcity. There is plenty of meaning and value to go around as long as one perspective does not need to hold sway to the exclusion of others. So male readers are urged to relax and absorb women's perspectives, to be instructed by the parts that apply to them and to rejoice in what women are learning for our common good.

Theological Method Enhanced

I am employing new ways of doing theology in this exploration. I am using the insights of liberationists of many kinds, especially Asian, African American, feminist, Latin American, and womanist. I am proposing that only by starting with particularity, naming it and insisting that we limit our claims on the basis of it, can we hope to make adequate and meaningful theological statements. I am inviting readers to subject those statements to scrutiny and to repeat the process endlessly without fear of circularity, as we create a friendlier world. Some will find my ease with process over product unacceptable. But I find that if I have to choose between a carefully crafted theological project and a community empowered to theologize on the basis of its own experience, I can have both most of the time. High expectations yield high results.

My reflections emerge from a particular set of experiences for which I neither apologize nor boast. My work is no more nor any less valuable than any other. But some aspects of my particular life experience, especially my feminist and lesbian perspectives, shape and mold my theologizing in ways that have not been part of the theological mix until now. I do not insist that everyone share them, only that they be respected and taken seriously like any other.

By the same token, I expect that my work will be evaluated for what it is and without prejudice. The point is that *all theology is partial, limited, and contextual.* Some theologians refuse to admit this and prefer to maintain the status quo that privileges a white, mostly male, heterosexual, Euro-American starting point. I on the other hand consider diversity to be a methodological strength.[4]

Others would, I believe mistakenly, purport to do theology for everyone. That is simply impossible without riding roughshod over different experiences. The history of theology is replete with examples of such treatment. Liberation approaches emerged to counter this assumption that any one set of experiences could be drawn upon to represent the whole. The demands of particularity and participation no longer permit this approach to be considered adequate and meaningful. I claim that everyone can do theology insofar as we seek to ask and answer questions of ultimate meaning and value. Some people, like myself, who are professional theologians, do this on a regular basis as our life's work but always in collaboration with a community of accountability. Our success is measured in part by how effectively we animate and facilitate others in the process. The goal of my theological model is to help a theological chorus to sing, even if some have a hard time carrying the tune, rather than empowering one brilliant soprano to reach her highest note while the rest listen. This reflects placing a value on the community over the individual. It is a deliberate theo-political choice, but one that I think needs no defense. It is an advisable option from a liberationist perspective. This community-based approach to theology is an alternative to what I call a corporate approach.[5] In the latter one seeks to theologize simply as a means "to the greater glory of God," the theological equivalent of profit. Someone is the chief executive officer, the theologian for the group, and others are middle managers, for example, clergy. They parrot the company line to customers, the so-called faithful, and offer few alternatives.

I am suggesting that none of the lofty ideals that define the corporate model need be left aside. Rather, with the best interests of the people of God as the primary goal, we can shape cooperative, community-based ways of doing theology that empower people to be theological agents for themselves while paying attention to the needs and aspirations of one another. It is a model that begs for creativity, patience, and the willingness to experiment. It shifts gears and assumes that the best answers are partial, limited, contextual, and arrived at together. Fortunately, liberation theologies in many arenas have helped to make such a model increasingly prevalent throughout the world, theo-political power structures notwithstanding. My intention is that this study of friendship be part of that tradition emerging from the North American context.

Ethical Implications

My primary theological purpose is to contribute to the transformation of the prevailing patriarchal ethical tradition. I want to underscore and encourage the shifts in relationships. I want to lift up new ways of loving well from women's experience and make them accessible as models. Insofar as Western Christian ethical norms have been based on men's experiences and have reflected a theological model that excludes most people from the development of ethics, I am proposing nothing less than a reshaping of the ethical framework in which most Western Christians operate. These norms involve assumptions about all forms of relationships, especially dating, marriage, and family life, that beg for redefinition in light of emerging patterns of love and common life. A friendship norm implies new patterns of relating that reflect values of love and justice lived out not two by heterosexual two, but in many combinations of genders and in threes, fours, and dozens as well. This is what it means to call for a new relational ethic based on friendships, lots of them. It assumes that we will be just as rigorous in our evaluation of friendship as others have been dogmatic in their condemnation of anything that did not approximate their coupling. Such rigor, I believe, serves to inform us about the subtleties of love and caring, and the difference these make in our search for a just, participatory society.

Implications of such a shift reach far beyond ethics. Models of church and community that are based on coupling (whether homosexual or heterosexual) and on limited notions of family need to be re-examined. The celebration of marriage, for example, comes under scrutiny as but one of many ways in which human commitment and community can be sacramentalized. Images of the divine must be rethought in light of the fertile symbol system that comes with friendship. Our relationship to the earth needs to be re-evaluated in light of the friendship extended by both humans and other living parts of the cosmos. In short, changing one element in the theological equation shifts everything else. This is what it means to do theology contextually and systematically.

All of this can be seen as purely intellectual work. I certainly strive to convince readers of new ideas and even of new ways of thinking. But before all of that, it can and must be done as practical work, for example, showing children how important friends are to us. We live into new patterns and values, and the children live with us. Then we reflect on our experiences and pass them on, not as ethical imperatives to be followed mindlessly, but as historical examples of faithful life, of right relation. From here, our children are on their own, invited to bring the best of what we have created to bear on their new situation. This is what it means to be part of a tradition.

Sources

One of the methodological shifts that this book represents is the move away from starting theologizing with philosophical categories. I assume that the preconditions for friendship are not found in philosophy, but in an openness to and experience of relationships. This does not mean that certain theoretical constructs are not helpful. To the contrary, I use feminist and other critical forms of history, philosophy, anthropology, psychology, political theory, and economics to inform my arguments. But I begin with the data of real lives, people struggling to love well and act justly. Only then does the theoretical work have an appropriate context; only then is it helpful and not prescriptive.

Other sources for this work include the recent spate of popular books on friendship that make it clear that feminist theological reflection on the theme is long overdue. These books include Lillian B. Rubin's *Just Friends*, Letty Cottin Pogrebin's *Among Friends*, and Luise Eichenbaum and Susie Orbach's *Between Women*.[6] These and many other books provide invaluable clues to the topic. But in no case do I find serious grappling with the religious or spiritual dimensions of friendship. I do not find an in-depth theological treatment of the issue. Little if anything has been done with an appreciation for the insights of feminist theology. My book is intended to fill this gap at a time when feminist theory is increasingly dependent on feminist theology and vice versa.

An essential contribution in feminist philosophy, the closest analogue to my work, is Janice Raymond's *A Passion for Friends*.[7] The author traces the history of what she calls Gyn/affection, claiming that women have always been one another's most trusted friends, lovers, and companions. She demonstrates convincingly how a vision of female friendship can provide insight into living "in a world as men have defined it while creating the world as women imagine it could be."[8] Janice Raymond's book is a breakthrough in the field, coming on the heels of so little substantive philosophical treatment of the topic. Once again philosophy has preceded theology. I intend my treatment of friendship to complement Raymond's insofar as we both take as a given women's exclusion from the patriarchal traditions over against which we write. Likewise, we both assume that the most important insights needed now stem not from female-male relations, but from female-female friendship. Finally, we both favor a woman-identified perspective as essential to the full exploration of female friendship. That we work from philosophical and theological perspectives respectfully only means that Janice Raymond and I are pushing horizons with different emphases. Both are necessary.

Structure of the Book

My exploration of what I call "fierce tenderness" proceeds from experience to analysis, to application and critique, then back to new experiences of praxis. This represents a hermeneutic circle that includes the basic elements of a useful theology while at the same time keeping the critical/self-critical edge that distinguishes the feminist liberation theological approach from some of its cousins.

I begin with concrete experiences of women's friendships. Several stories suffice to give the flavor of the variety and depth of caring and commitment, bereavement and betrayal that characterize an honest appraisal of friendship. Dozens of women have shared with me their exhilaration and pain at being friends. Yet no one, myself included, has a full bearing on why some of these relationships flower and why others wilt. In addition to the usual complex of personal and social factors, there is obviously some mystery involved. But there is not so much mystery that we cannot analyze and change our ways of relating if we understand something of the process and its implications.

Acknowledging mystery is not an excuse for leaving things unexplored. It is an invitation to look more deeply at what historical, social, economic, psychological, and even theological factors attend friendship. It is an impetus to understand the ins and outs of human relationships without the burden of finally explaining it all away in some mechanized model. Naming mystery where it exists is also a caveat against reducing human experience to a set of easy factors. It is a subtle sanction against believing that hard and fast rules guide where sometimes only love and luck tread. Friendship defies description but has predictable parameters. It is revealed in a peculiar way.

"Theo-politics" is the most ample rubric under which to evaluate friendship as revelation. By theo-politics I mean that the claims that are made about ultimate meaning and value reflect power dynamics as well as faith positions. In this case, women's friendships have been hidden under the bushel of patriarchy and heterosexism. Just as important, they have been held captive by powerful ideologies that negate them without exploration. My task is to free these for future use.

Women's friendships contain previously unexplored and unappreciated elements that reveal something about the human condition. They literally unveil for us what has been obscured. I find that these new data are interesting and useful not only for social scientists, but also for theologians and communities of faith. These data have theological significance insofar as they can help us to live in right relation with ourselves, one another, with the earth, and with the divine. If women's friendships remain obscured we have no access to this rich store of revelation. Improving the quality of our collective life lends urgency to this undertaking.

In Western, and especially Christian, societies women's friendships have been downgraded, denied, and in some cases painfully destroyed by those who seek to maintain control and assert power. This is a milieu in which women are not taken seriously as moral or religious agents.[9] I do not mean to create a few women theologians who function as agents for the whole community. Rather, by this community-based approach I endeavor to empower all women (1) to name their experiences on their own terms, (2) to make decisions on the basis of their experiences, and (3) to live in relationships and to form communities of accountability on the basis of those choices. This is what it means to be a religious agent. Friendship is a common starting point for that effort. Theologizing about friendship gives women practice at being religious agents and invites men to evaluate their own agency as well.

Friendships are sacramental in ways that I will describe later. I want to lift friendships to public expression on their own terms in order to analyze and celebrate them. This is what religious agents do by naming the holy, making choices about how to live it out, and then fostering that experience in communities of accountability.

I propose a model for doing so that includes love and power, sexuality and spirituality as four components of friendship. There may be other dynamics at play, but these four in this configuration encompass what most of us experience. I do not claim that such a model will solve power problems, much less make anyone friends. In fact, I welcome refinements of the model. But I do believe that having a heuristic device for seeing some of the complicated dynamics of friendship is a first step toward being able to identify the next steps necessary to make friendship the relational norm within the Christian community.

The creation of a model marks my effort as constructive. My approach is not simply a critical look at friendship from a feminist perspective in order to show up the weaknesses of a patriarchal view. It is a move into the new with some theoretical help along the way. The creation of a model may also facilitate friendship since it has practical roots and reaches. Such a side effect would be a happy outcome. At least it provides us with ways of talking together, even when we disagree. From those conversations we can build even more helpful models. For now I offer my model as a stimulus, not as an answer.

The next step is to apply my model. First, I show how often only the loss of friendship makes much of what I am explaining clear. My point is to stem this tide, to try to provide some basis for understanding the dynamics of friendship before the relationship is over. Sometimes the end cannot be prevented, nor should it be. But at least it can be understood more clearly, if only in hindsight, since every friendship is part of another one. Applying this to friendships that issue in commitments such as marriage or covenant, some clarity along the way can help to avoid breakups and/or make sense of these when they happen.

Second, I suggest that celebrating friendships, really bringing them to public expression in the sacramental sense, will be a boon for human community. Here I acknowledge that for many of us friends have replaced family as our primary relational referent, as our "significant others." I show how to reinforce the bonds of friendship between and among people by intentional rituals. I touch on commitment, breakup, and death as moments that often go unheralded but that, if acknowledged, might make obvious how central friends are for us. Both loss and celebration are occasions when the symbolic demands of communities meet the ethical demands of friendship. We are responsible for our own people. If we do not mourn and marvel, who will? When we mourn and marvel we are acting like good friends. None of it is easy but it must be done.

Then I push the application to larger circles, claiming that friendship, especially within the Christian tradition, is often based on the mutual search for justice. This is what the Christian community has historically done best. The Christian tradition began with the disciples and members of the Jesus movement who were, if nothing else, friends seeking ways to express their faith in a hostile environment. It continues through our day when groups of justice-seeking friends unite to overturn unjust rulers and to conduct political refugees to sanctuary, for example.

Such friendly action is not limited to Christian communities. Secular political groups and people of other faith traditions do the same work, often with better results. But justice-seeking friends who unite in unlikely coalitions are what I mean by "church." These are friends who strive to be a "discipleship of equals," as Elisabeth Schüssler Fiorenza has called those who seek equality in the tradition of the Jesus movement.[10] It is a good model for friends who take their relationships beyond the privatized level of greeting cards to the theo-political level of commitment and action as a faith community.

I explore this in my own experience with friends in other countries, drawing on "Women Crossing Worlds," an effort by WATER, the Women's Alliance for Theology, Ethics and Ritual, and other women's groups to "promise a permanent presence" with our friends in the Southern Cone. I understand the importance of cross-cultural friendships as a route to political awareness and sustained political commitment for change. Far from being an overly personal approach to systemic change, activists are finding that it is *because of* deeply rooted friendships that we are able to sustain the energy necessary to make substantive social change in an often unfriendly world. Ideology alone is simply not a sufficient motivator when times get tough. But acting because of and with friends is a powerful, sustainable force.

I am wary of putting too much weight on friendship, considering it a theological cure-all. But I am equally reluctant to permit myself a theological failure of nerve by leaving these more amorphous matters by the wayside.

My theological treatment of friendship concludes in the tradition of systematic theology as well as of ethics. It is not an effort to create a full system as such, using friendship as the guiding metaphor. Yet it is sufficiently embedded in that line of thinking to involve consistency and to include the most far reaching ramifications of a thoroughgoing analysis. I repeat, experience sharing is no substitute for rigorous analysis.

Theology is not simply about responding to other theologians, nor only an effort to ground human efforts in transcendent claims. It is about the divine-human relationships that we struggle to understand and enrich. Thus I draw some feminist theological conclusions, assuming of course that they are necessarily tentative and always open to clarification.

I look at some of the implications of calling the divine "friend." It is a step in the right direction, but one fraught with the same tendencies to anthropomorphize and project onto the divine that other linguistic conventions like "Lord" and "comforter" contain. I maintain that it is an improvement though not a final answer to a linguistic conundrum for which there is, finally, no answer. And that is the answer.

I mention the importance of cultivating a friendly stance toward the whole of creation, especially in a nuclear age when unfriendly actions are not simply rude, but potentially deadly. This is perhaps the most practical suggestion in the whole book, challenging us to develop new attitudes that may spell the difference between a friendly environment and no environment for our descendants.

The challenges to this perspective are many. I begin with some obvious ones that emerge from the rich reflections of womanist theology. The word "womanist" comes from the work of Alice Walker, who distinguishes between feminist, the theory and praxis of change based on sexual equality that has emerged primarily from white women's experience, and womanist, which describes the struggle for survival that African American women know best. Calling womanist a kind of "black feminist or feminist of color" approach, she distinguished it by writing: "Womanist is to feminist as purple is to lavender."[11] Delores S. Williams is a womanist theologian and poet who has given profound theological shape to this insight, though others are doing important work as well.[12] Asian and Latin American women, while not claiming a womanist perspective as such, are posing their own challenges to the work of white feminists.[13] Now white feminists are obliged to relativize our claims, cease using universalizing language, and place our contributions alongside those of women from other racial ethnic groups.[14]

I consider all of this to be part of the constructive moment as theology is done on many women's terms. Other women theologians' work is the first and most interesting place I look for challenges that push the horizons of my own thinking. I eagerly await the work of my sister theologians around the world as they explore friendship from their various vantage points. I suspect that we will find friendship even more central than previously thought when now silenced voices speak. But that is for others to confirm. In my own country the womanist challenge is central.

One of the most salient features of a womanist perspective is the focus on the survival needs of women and their dependent children. Another is the need to live and work with men as part of the praxis of liberation. Both of these elements offer useful rejoinders to my work. I believe that my work is consistent with these claims insofar as many women have learned that we would not survive if it were not for our friends, both women and men. Nor would our children thrive if friends did not pitch in and help. Likewise, I know few women who want to live in a world without men, and even fewer, if any, who really do so. It is not my preferred future to deal only with women, though there are days when the unyielding pressures of patriarchy make it a fleeting fantasy! The point is not to ignore men friends but to lift up women friends as they have been the sustainers of generations of struggling people.

Justice involves making friends, lots of friends, many kinds of friends. Friendship in this sense is not a cheap effort to buy freedom with flattery or treachery, pretending to be friends for personal gain when in fact some structures and conditions make friendship impossible. Rather, justice is the fundamental relational goal that issues from communities of accountability where change takes place. Justice is the reason for personal nurture. Justice-seeking friends empower one another to keep making change when the work is hard. In fact, the job is so massive that we need all the friends we have, of whatever gender or nationality, to get it done.

I applaud this womanist insight and I claim it as my own. Yet I do not call my theology "womanist" but rather "feminist influenced by womanist" out of respect for the hard wrought knowledge that many women of color have gained. I look forward to the day when feminist and womanist will be synonymous in content while always distinct in history. Until then, I believe that more is gained by respecting and preserving the integrity of our historical starting points than urging a premature collapsing of the terms.

I conclude with a practical approach to friendship, almost a how-to section. Of course no one can follow a recipe for friendship, but it is exciting to consider how specific acts of solidarity and celebration can make love and justice more than nice words. A theology that begins in experience concludes in practice only to produce renewed experiences that form the basis of future theological reflection.

Fierce and Tender

My hope is that this book will revitalize friendships insofar as it invites attention and discussion. Simone Weil wrote that attention to people and to the divine is all of a piece. It is a focus that is not forced so much as willed. It is a way of being present that is at the same time being detached. She writes:

> Those who are unhappy have no need of anything in this world but people capable of giving them their attention. The capacity to give one's attention to a sufferer is a very rare and difficult thing; it is almost a miracle; it is a miracle.[15]

Ellen Goodman, a popular columnist, had a similar thought when she wrote about the harried husband racing to the candy store on Valentine's Day for the obligatory heart filled with chocolate to take home to his wife. Ellen Goodman observed that the wife would be grateful, but went on to say that what most women want is not simply Valentine's candy but attention every day of the year.

Attention is what friends provide even if we are not in touch very regularly. Attention to friends is at once interesting and frightening. We want it but we fear what it will reveal. Attention is a hallmark of spirituality. We want it but we shy away, uncomfortable with the intensity. I intend this book to serve a spiritual function as well. We attend to the quality of our lives and the lives of those we love. That is sufficient spirituality for me.

I call friendships "fierce" because of the intensity of attention. It can be hard to be known so well, to be understood and transparent to friends who pay attention. Likewise, we all crave the tenderness that only those who love us can offer. Tenderness does not affect the ferocity, but it is the quality of care and nurture that only friends share. Of course a care giver can be tender in touch, but only friends are tender in feeling.

I hope to compel readers to try out some new norms that are based on friendship and not coupling. I do not expect an ethical revolution overnight. However, I do think that constructive suggestions are often all we need to move from inadequate, constricting counter-intuitive rules to liberating common agreement that we embrace willingly because it works. At the very least, friendship is something virtually everyone likes to talk about. Lots of people can feel like experts. This is a hint about the methodological shift that I hope will be obvious in this book. I am calling on this expertise as a way to get and to keep the conversation going. My commitment is to participatory theologizing and ethics. Beginning with an accessible, easily discussed topic is a sure way to encourage widespread participation.

The dangers, of course, are that those who participate shape the outcome. Or worse, ethics can become a kind of "majority rules" enterprise. This is not my intention. I try to avoid these problems by suggesting that friendship is a cross-cultural, cross-generational, interdisciplinary experience that can be plumbed fruitfully in many corners. I am not selling a recipe for friendship as much as focusing attention on what exists.

Likewise, there is some shared wisdom coming from the Christian ethical tradition, albeit with certain fundamental corrections for its patriarchal roots. The bottom line is that we are not starting from scratch in this work, but neither should we take anything on the skewed faith we have received.

Children can be guided to reflect on their friends, whom they love and why. They can be taught about friends who went before them. Genealogies of friends, like family trees, thanks to Janice Raymond's work, are part of our histories. It is amazing how rapidly people will talk about their friends, how clear many of us are about what we believe constitutes friendship, and how pained we are when it disappears. Why not tap this wellspring and channel it toward ethical clarity? This is my proposal, for children as well as for adults.

Some Ways to Utilize This Book

This book is meant for general readers as well as for students of theology and ethics. It is written with a minimum of technical jargon so that it is easily accessible. However, some may wish to pass over the methodological details in favor of the basic materials on friendship, the stories and reflections. Some theological and ethical intricacies come with the territory if one wants to make change in these fields, but the experiences are the heart of the matter. I urge readers to use the book as a stimulus for discussion. Friends can read and react to it as a way of examining their own relationships. Theologians can ponder the concepts since I am making some claims about friendship and ethics that deserve critical attention. Groups can literally play with the model to see if and how it illuminates their experiences. Counselors and ministers/rabbis will find the model an aid for their work, perhaps recommending that friends or couples use it to evaluate and/or change their behavior.

Base communities will find the section on unlikely coalitions geared to their experiences. A full treatment of ecclesiology is beyond the scope of this project, but I hope to encourage some concrete ways of moving from hierarchical, bureaucratic styles of being church to the women-church model where friends gather in small groups, mindful of belonging to something larger.

Other white feminists have things to say on this topic, but I await a womanist treatment of friendship since African American, Asian, and Latin American women in theology have important insights to contribute. I hope that my refusal to claim universality, my insistence on limiting claims, will be read as an invitation to others to take up where I have left off, making the particularity of their experience a new starting point. Then we can all get on with more effective ways of being friends in deed.

A Word about the Title

Often when I lectured on parts of this book I would mention its title. People reacted with delight at first, then often with puzzlement. It was powerful somehow, but they were not always sure why. "Fierce tenderness" seems to capture the both/and experience that friendship usually is. The Spanish translation, *la ternura feroz*, is equally expressive. In fact, there is a different quality to the phrase when the *ternura*/tenderness comes first.

In any case, friendship is both fierce and tender. Witness: the first flush of attraction, the fury of a divorce, the exuberance of love making on a spring afternoon, the depths of loss when death comes. Witness: the caress of a baby at her mother's breast, the attempt to deliver a present unseen, the embarrassment of being more vulnerable than desired, the need to let go when a move is inevitable. These are fierce tenderness on the personal level. Political dimensions, like people choosing to send humanitarian aid to their friends abroad or countries agreeing to a cease fire for everyone's sake, still need to be recognized and articulated as friendship.

The title was inspired by May Sarton's poem "An Observation," in which she describes her mother's gloveless hands as she worked in her garden. I picture hands gnarled with arthritis (May Sarton mentions this in a later essay) tending tiny shoots in fresh soil. Over and over in friendships I have seen this same juxtaposition, and every time it seems to be held together as naturally and successfully as the gardener's efforts help to bring forth flowers.

Enough of hierarchical dualism, of either/or, I decided. On to the expression of complex human experiences in simple if seemingly contradictory terms. Hence "fierce tenderness" has found its way into my vocabulary, and maybe into others', with no hint of contradiction. Fierce tenderness simply evokes the "ah ha" of realizing that linear thinking notwithstanding, "both/and" is the way that right relation is lived.

We never know how fierce a friendship can really become, nor how tender a person is capable of being, until quite far into the experience. Sometimes we do not know until loss or celebration brings us up short and invites us to reflect. Likewise, a theological work of this sort is open-ended. It needs the input of those who read it to test out, modify, and deepen the work begun by the author. I invite you to do just that.

·2·

The Power
of Women's Friendships

Every woman who has ever loved a woman
You oughta stand up and call her name
Mama — sister — daughter — lover
Every woman who ever loved a woman
You oughta stand up and call her name

—Bernice Johnson Reagon
"Every Woman"

Women's friendships have always intrigued me. I could never understand why no one talked about what seemed to be so obvious. Instead, dating and marriage were touted as the "normal" way in which adolescent and adult relationships would move. I mentioned to my mother once that I loved Susy. My mother, an excellent elementary school teacher, corrected me by saying that I "liked" Susy and that I would "love" John or Bill or Bob. I repeated that I loved Susy. My mother reiterated the "grammar" of friendship. Somehow she did not convince me. Now I know that English verbs like "love" and "like" are not gender inflected. But then the message was clear: a girl can like girls but will love a man, a boy can like boys but will love a woman. My mother did not make it up. She thought that she was fulfilling her parental responsibility to teach her child the ways of relationships, especially the ways that her church and the larger culture had taught her.

Ironically, it was her own friendships with women that were my proof that something was wrong with her logic. My parents "married late" for their era (both in their mid-thirties), so my mother had had significant years of teaching and living away from home before she married and had children. She taught in a small town where single women lived together in a proper rooming house. Her women friends were paramount — especially during World War II when most young men were overseas. Friday night was their time together. Even after she moved, married and began her family, the same friends, some married, and some single, persisted in their Friday evening gatherings. They did not play cards nor go to the theater that night; they did not watch television or even listen to the radio. They simply got together for drinks and conversation. They just wanted to be together and catch up on the week's activities, although most of them lived in the same small town and taught in the same school. They simply acted like friends. They attended to one another.

My mother travelled several times a year to be with them. She always timed her visits to include a Friday night. Such dedication to one another caught my attention as a child. I knew that these friends were special even though my mother had countless others. I knew I had heard her use the term "love" about one or two of them, so why couldn't I say it about Susy? Children often pick up nuances when parents least expect it.

I have come to realize that my mother's experience was not unique. Adele Logan Alexander reports an almost identical experience of her mother in Washington, D.C., with a group of African American women who attended Dunbar High School in the 1920s and have met monthly for more than sixty-five years.[1] My white mother had all of the trappings that her society expected — a husband, children, a home to care for, and volunteer activity. In her era middle-class white women did not work outside the home if they did not need the money. Personal fulfillment through work and work-related relationships did not enter the equation. But I detected that what gave her an extra measure of meaning was her friends, namely, her women friends. In this way I am my mother's daughter. Adele Logan Alexander, while different from me, is undoubtedly her mother's daughter as well.

The power of women's friendships is amazing in a cultural context that makes them a relational also-ran. With heterosexual marriage touted as every woman's goal, friendships with other women become way stations on the road to the perfect match with Mr. Right. Fortunately the development of feminist theory and the construction of more socially acceptable ways to be in relationships other than marriage have eased this pressure. But friendship is still far from the relational norm and society is not constructed as if friends matter.

In fact, the teachings of most Christian churches and other major shapers of Western culture have not encompassed friends at all. People like my mother might have a powerful experience of friendship. But most people do not have the stimulus to shift their own perceptions and patterns nor the encouragements necessary to think anew. They might feel that they are odd or unusual, even sick or inadequate. That is how normative assumptions work to maintain the status quo. Of course certain exceptions are permitted, but they are just that, exceptional cases that reflect idiosyncrasies or limitations. The norms prevail and so strongly so that significant data are passed over.

The development of feminist analyses has brought to public attention the bonds between women. It has named them, called them important, and begun to restructure certain social institutions on the basis of new insight into their value. Such progress stirs backlash. Western Christian culture makes the social price high for women who love women in more explicit ways than my mother did. And the so-called "requiem for the women's movement" has been rehearsed several times, a sure sign that progress has been made and must be stopped lest the very foundations of family, sex roles, and power relationships be shifted. My intention is to name and encourage the shift.

A word about definitions is in order. Lines blur between friendship, love, eros, romance. What is clear is that friendship has been downplayed in favor of romance on the assumption that friendship was for buddies and romance for heterosexual married couples (or at least those who could be). Intimacy is measured by degrees, with some cultures and languages expressing those degrees by different words. For example, the *tu* and *usted* forms for "you" in Spanish clearly differentiate between levels of intimacy.

Many cultural distinctions represented by such language are falling away. False formality, like false intimacy, distorts human community. The point of this book is to rethink some of the categories, to rethink friendship not as a catchall for people one likes but, looking particularly at women's experiences, as a word that represents the most desirable human relationship.

For a working definition at the outset I mean by friendship those voluntary human relationships that are entered into by people who intend one another's well-being and who intend that their love relationship is part of a justice-seeking community. Much more needs to be said about how this happens. But for now this working definition will at least point to and limit what I am examining. It is a task for another study to evaluate various kinds of friendships — co-workers, lovers, colleagues among others — in order to distinguish those that are most worthy of the term. I reject that task, at least for now, because my aim is to show the extent to which all such relationships are friendships albeit of varying kinds. Women's experiences make this obvious and provide clues for further analysis.

Some Friendships

Before proceeding to an analysis of the power of women's friendship let me offer six examples that illustrate the transformative potential of seeing friendship as the central relational experience for most people. These are chosen from the many experiences that have been shared with me. In some instances the names have been changed to assure privacy where the cost of clarity is more than the individuals should have to pay. Data from these examples will help us to explicate what is meant by fierce tenderness. These examples in no way exhaust the possibilities but are meant to illustrate some aspects of friendship that are seen best in the concrete rather than in theory.

Deborah and Sandra
Deborah is a North American student who was doing research in Latin America in order to develop a solidarity project. Her mother-in-law, Sandra, is active in a church-based group that supports Latin American women by selling their crafts. The two decided to travel together to Latin America though they had never done so before. Between them they could manage the language and find their way. They looked similar enough to evoke the soap commercial of which was the mother and which was the daughter. After several weeks on the road they participated in a women's conference where friendship was a central theme. The mostly Latin American women gathered there shared experiences of friends who helped each other through labor, who found each other jobs, and who took care of each other's children. When they introduced themselves, Deborah and Sandra said that they were daughter-in-law and mother-in-law.

When they were ready to leave they shared with the group what had been their prime learning. They had come thinking of each other in the categories that society provided, but feeling uneasy because their relationship through Deborah's husband and Sandra's son was only a small part of their connection. Somehow the labels were not enough. Even using them obscured something important. But they could not quite put their fingers on it. They said finally that they were leaving as friends. The delight with which they shared this insight made it obvious to everyone that they had learned something new and been emboldened to proclaim it. I was reminded of Ruth and Naomi, friends in the Hebrew Scriptures who were also related by a marriage but whose friendship was far more transformative than the marriage. How have we missed such an obvious social clue? Better, why have we missed it in the spate of mother-in-law jokes that keep such love at bay?

Coca and Julia

At the same meeting two Argentine women from a very poor *barrio* came to share their lives. A feminist anthropologist had done an interview and a video of the life of Coca. She is a powerful person, full of energy and activity. She has brought up a family and taken on all of the responsibilities as head of her household. It would be hard to find a more able agent of change. Julia is quiet, reserved, almost withdrawn. She too has a family and the daily pressures of making ends meet. In fact the two are neighbors, but the more important fact is that they are the closest of friends. Julia, even though she never spoke during the video presentation and discussion, would not have dreamed of letting Coca meet with a group of strangers without going with her. Coca made it clear that even though Julia did not seem to contribute much to the event her presence was indispensable. "We are friends," she said, and Julia's smile confirmed the obvious.

Two Chilean women, from equally marginal circumstances, who were at the meeting recognized in Coca and Julia something of their friendship. Each is the *comadre*, or godmother, of the other's child. When asked exactly what this meant, they replied, "She is at one with me in the mothering of my child. I trust her like myself." As the four women hugged one another I had a flash of the commandment to love the neighbor as the self, and was thankful for its concretion in these fine women friends. Note that the commandment is not to love one's spouse, but one's friends or would-be friends.

Susan and Adrian

Susan is a nun who works as an architect in a well-respected Midwestern firm. She has been in her community for twenty years, so the roots are deep enough to keep her connected. Her boss, George, quickly recognized her exceptional ability both as a professional and as a person. When they became acquainted he said, "You must come home and meet my wife. You'll just love her." And she did.

Adrian had been married to George for ten years. Things were decent, not great. Five children took up most of her time and George's career was on the rise so their time together was limited. Adrian and Susan hit it off immediately. They both liked to ride bikes, which they did together as exercise and a chance to get away from the kids and the telephone.

As time went on their relationship became more and more precious to them. Neither of them had ever been so deeply involved with a woman before. It caught them both off guard. They even talked briefly about what it would be like to leave the community and the family and live together. The prospect excited and frightened them. How would they explain it? Mostly they just dreamed. One day they were out riding when a motorcyclist pushed Adrian off the road in a freak accident. She died instantly. Susan was left, grief stricken and without friends who understood the depth of her loss. She got though the funeral and the sorting of Adrian's personal effects. She even survived the tasteless sympathy that issued in suggestions that now perhaps she and George could marry and raise the children. Heaven forbid. But the gaping loss of Adrian left her devastated for some time afterward.

She had a hard time looking at the children's pictures because of how much they reminded her of Adrian. She felt in communication with Adrian in a strange way, as if they could still be friends even beyond death. I suggested that she had been robbed of the chance to say goodbye, something that friends always want to do. I understood her strong sense of her friend's presence and her conviction that friends remain even after they are dead. This must be what eternal life is about, I thought. Maybe the so-called communion of saints are our old friends. Why not? I cannot imagine a better definition.

Catherine and Her Significant Multitude
Catherine worked for an ecumenical agency on a variety of justice fronts. Her contribution to Latin American people, despite her rather rudimentary knowledge of Spanish, was a testimony to the transforming power of friendship. Her premature death was a shock and a loss to many people.

The wake and funeral service were attended by as motley a crew as ever assembled: street people and heads of Catholic religious orders, United Nations representatives and community organizers, priests in black suits and women-church adherents in colorful Central American embroidered blouses. It was the gathering of an unlikely coalition, a kind of old-home week for friends who had worked with

Catherine for justice. Although the pastor of the church made clear that only Catholics were invited to receive communion, virtually everyone in the church, Catholics and non-Catholics alike, received "in memory of her." Friendship permitted it, better, friendship demanded it.

When her obituary appeared it included an infamous line, "No immediate survivors," a blatant lie when her life is considered. Many and varied friends survive and keep their memories of her alive. Survivors need not be blood relatives or a relative by marriage. This was repeated on the death of Robert Joffrey, founder and guiding spirit of the Joffrey Ballet. In the same newspaper that detailed his impact on the world of dance, his generosity to so many people, and his popularity as a mentor and animator of innovative choreography, it was pointed out that there were "No immediate survivors."

Catherine's cat was probably her best friend. Sophisticated newspapers are not prone to taking pets seriously, though they might report more accurately if they did. Still, Catherine's human friends, whose numbers were legion, survive her in the most immediate way, to continue the good work that she began. Such invisibility is a cruel irony in the case of a woman who took seriously the imperative to go and make friends in all nations.

Peg, Jane, and Karen
Peg, Jane, and Karen are three doctors who have been friends since medical school fifteen years ago. They live in different cities but vacation together for a week every winter. They discuss the difficult cases they have faced that year — now their concern is pediatric AIDS — but they keep plenty of time for a full rendering of each one's personal life. One winter, cozily nestled in a ski lodge, Peg broke the news to the group that she would no longer continue the custom of the annual holiday together. She announced her engagement to a male physician who was about to take a job abroad. The other two were supportive of her impending marriage but deeply disappointed by the notion that anything would stand in the way of their annual outing. Money, it turned out when they offered to share the cost of travel, was no problem. The fact was that Peg's future husband takes a dim view of separate vacations, and she realized that he would not be welcome in the all-female group.

The three enjoyed their skiing but kept returning to this difficult topic every time they had any serious discussion. What they realized was that their friendship, the three of them together, meant a great deal to them. It was not only that they had shared the rigors and ridiculous demands of life at the bottom on the medical heap. Of course they rehearsed those memories from their now more prominent places in the medical establishment; they could laugh at their youthful adventures. But something deeper held them together: a commitment, albeit unspoken until this week, to accompany each other for the long haul. Peg's decision threatened that. None of them wanted the change.

Jane and Karen, although they would continue to get together, intuited that it simply would not be the same. Dynamics are different with three; conversation is more varied and there is never a lack of a partner. Patterns get set, and even though things usually work out two and one there is something about this threesome that works nicely. Of course other friends who envied their annual get-together would have joined them in an instant if they were invited. But it simply would not be the same.

In the end Peg told Jane and Karen more about her fiancé, a likeable if insecure man. She decided that she could have her friendship with these women as well as with him. She went home committed to informing him that the annual week with her friends comes with the package. Rumor has it that he saw the handwriting on the wall and the three have plans for a beach house next year. I cannot help but wonder how many women's friendships have been broken by such demands. I am glad that this threesome persisted.

Kathy and Dawn

Kathy and Dawn met in art school. They were both publicly identified as lesbians. In a moment it seemed that they might even become lovers, but their timing was never right. Kathy was involved with someone else, so that ended Dawn's hopes. And Dawn eventually met a woman with whom she was deeply in love. They lived half a continent away but kept in touch by letters and phone calls. They knew each other's families and friends; they liked each other's lovers.

Kathy was asked to be on the jury of an art show in which one of Dawn's students had an entry. Not only did the student not win a prize, but Kathy went out of her way to impress the other judges with the fact that Dawn's "school of art" was passé. As often happens, one of the other judges reported this matter to Dawn. Her first concern was for her student, but as she reflected further on what had happened, she felt a deep sense of betrayal. It was not that she and Kathy had always agreed on artistic merit, but it was clear that Kathy had chosen to downgrade her as a way to curry favor with the other judges.

Kathy was new to the jury, more used to having been judged than judging. She knew that Dawn's innovative method would eventually hold sway, but for now it was simply too dangerous to affirm it if she ever expected to make it in the art establishment. When Dawn called to discuss the matter Kathy pretended that the incident had been embellished in the telling and that in fact she liked Dawn's work. She denied any intention to discredit Dawn by saying that the student was untalented. Dawn was left with the fact that Kathy had hurt her, however unintentionally. As time went on and Kathy ceased to be in touch, Dawn was confirmed in her suspicion that they were moving in different and mutually exclusive directions. They have not been in touch in more than three years. Dawn feels the loss. Kathy simply claims to be busy. I picture only a void. This happens between and among friends.

Women's Friendships Explored

In each of these cases, and in many more that could be added, women's friendships, when taken seriously on their own terms, not only have an impact on individuals, but they push the parameters of social institutions. I will mention briefly how this happens in each case and then turn my attention to the larger context in which such friendships are set, a context that does as much as possible to obscure the importance of women friends.

Deborah and Sandra reveal how static our notions of family are and how we ignore the fact that *family members can be friends.* Not only was their relationship defined by preconceived categories, but they were seemingly locked into certain assumptions about themselves and each other that prevented them from naming the nature of their own friendship accurately. Granted many such persons do not progress from the happenstance of being related to a person they both love to a friendship on its own terms. But it is possible more often than we think.

The point is that family is not often thought of as the locus of friendship. Rather, we labor under the dictum that one can choose one's friends but not one's relatives. Families are socially constructed to correspond to certain roles that begin with the heterosexual couple and flow from their usually male-dominated needs. Even under such duress friendships can flourish. But more to the point, friendship is often much deeper and richer than family ties, especially in postindustrial societies where we tend to live far away from our blood relatives.

Such a normative focus on family automatically eliminates the obvious extent to which friends beyond the blood family fulfill needs and expectations that family members may not. For example, companions at work tend to know one another better than family members in situations where we live hundreds of miles from blood relatives. This only increases with time, making the expected trip "home for the holidays" subject to serious reconsideration. If holidays are spent with loved ones, why travel so readily to be with family when friends are close at hand?

Often the so-called family of choice made up of friends is what sustains us far more than the blood ties. Why not name this for what it is without the guilt that comes from feeling as if we have "abandoned" the real family? I am not proposing that family ties are unimportant, nor that obligations, especially to elderly, very young, or needy members of the family, ought to be ignored. To the contrary, I am proposing that Deborah and Sandra's case points out the possibility of extending responsibilities that come with family ties to encompass friends. Putting friends and family on the same ethical plane, far from leading to the abandonment of family, will lead to attention to friends.

It is possible to be friends with members of the blood family, early distinctions between friends and family notwithstanding. It is not always easy to make the transition from sibling to friend, nor from parent and child to friends. In fact, more often than not socially constructed roles and complex dynamics mitigate against the relational flexibility needed to ease the shift. But if friendship instead of atomized couples were the norm I presume that more families might strive to be friends. At least we would have more role models.

Coca and Julia reveal *something new about neighbors*. The clue comes from the Spanish language, which has two words for the one English word that gives two senses of "neighbor." In Spanish the "neighbor" is either the *prójima/o*, meaning the one with whom someone lives in a relationship of accountability, as in "love your neighbor as yourself," or the *vecina/o*, meaning the one who lives nearby, the person over the back fence or in the apartment next door. Especially when women are not in the work force outside of the home, friendships between *vecinas* take on added importance. They complement family ties and provide a horizon beyond the home. Such *vecinas* often become *prójimas*.

Friendship involves both of these dimensions. Obviously the first is what we normally think of, and this would be the fullest sense in which Coca and Julia relate. But they are more than *prójimas*, even more than *compañeras* (companions, though we have no adequate English word to convey this), more like *hermanas*, sisters, in the sense of blood relatives, as well as in the feminist sense in which "sister" is a term of endearment and accountability.

They are *vecinas* as well, people who live near one another and watch out for each other. In the Aristotelian view of friendship neighbors were the most common and therefore the least important kind of friends. For Coca and Julia, and I would argue for many women, neighbors are a lifeline, a source of security and intimacy. Women do not seem to put their friends in a hierarchy as the Aristotelian model implies, with some few friends at the top and the rest arranged below in increasing numbers and decreasing importance. Still, these *vecinas* have a special tie.

The pyramid model of friendship considered from a feminist perspective looks flawed. Coca and Julia represent women finding solace and challenge with each other beginning at and near home. The male-based model is useless when applied to women's experiences. This does not imply that all women's friendships are of the same depth and intensity. Rather it suggests that friendship is an underlying stance that one takes toward the world, beginning at home and with those closest to home. Loving one's neighbor is the most logical extension of loving oneself and one's family. Friendship is political in its breadth, but personal in its depth.

Susan and Adrian spark the difficult questions of *couples as friends*. Granted they were not the average married couple, nor even the increasingly typical lesbian couple that feminism has helped out of the closet. They were not even the two nuns accused of having a "particular friendship," nor the Cagney and Lacey type team in which, though dedicated to each other, the two have clearly defined limits. No, Susan and Adrian defied most categories that we know since theirs was the kind of friendship that few talk about though many have experienced. Their love for each other was a complete surprise. They had no words for it. If anything, it put them off balance, forcing them to ask questions about themselves and each other that both might have preferred to avoid. They felt not shame but excitement, not confusion but exhilaration. They were learning a new language even though they had not signed up for the course.

They had what Holly Near sings about: "No fancy fantasy, No magic mystery, No wide-eyed wonder, Just a plain and simple love."[2] It may have felt like more than that to them, especially when the feelings they were experiencing were forbidden to be acted on for a nun and a married woman. But the fact is that women loving women is so common that it has had to be suppressed and denied in a patriarchal culture that seeks to control women. In itself it is "Just a plain and simple love," society notwithstanding.

Susan and Adrian represent love changed by death but not snuffed out. Their openness, naive as it may have been, is heartening. It reminds us of what young women untouched by patriarchal assumptions would feel. It was a vibrant love, a mature and considered serendipity if such can be.

Catherine stands as a reminder of the fact that *friendships exist in communities*, that there really is no proper singular friendship, but only *friendships*. Her own religious order was said to have been less than supportive of Catherine, especially during her struggles with the institutional church. But her wider circle of friends embraced her and held her close when the pain of being rejected was intense. Likewise she understood herself as part of a larger religious community in the fullest sense of the term. Nevertheless, her religious family was important to Catherine, and some members of it undoubtedly gave all the support they could muster. What was instructive, however, was how one, admittedly charismatic, person could inspire and sustain a range of relationships. Her friends were many and varied. I call hers a "significant multitude" in a culture that expects each of us to have a "significant other." Many of her multitude were colleagues in the various struggles for justice. Some who knew each other independent of Catherine were not surprised to find themselves in the same pews at her funeral. "Of course you would have known her," several were heard to exclaim. "She was just your kind of person."

There was a certain pathos to Catherine, a suspicion that her closest friends confirmed. It is reported that she sometimes went home from yet another meeting to confront the discouragement and loneliness that set in when change is slow and when circumstances and/or personality prevent focused intimacy. But it is an instructive pathos, teaching us that there is no one politically correct style of friendship. People who are seemingly alone are often well accompanied, and friends choose what style suits them best. Catherine wore hers well.

The threesome of Peg, Jane, and Karen points out that *love is not simply a two-way street*. It is a multi-leveled highway with many lanes that lets us speed and stop at will but not without watching in all directions. There are always more than two people involved in a friendship even though we are used to thinking of friendship in dyads. In fact, the threesome is finally quite healthy, a reminder of the many lives that are in the balance when friends attend to friends.

In one way it is hard to figure out how groups of three manage. But limiting our relational imaginations to twosomes is a remnant of heterosexism. We need to listen to people who live in this situation, hear them describe their experiences even in categories we do not understand. I am beginning to value the wisdom of three over two. Not only additional input and companionship accrue, but an equally important nod to the larger community is made as more and more people are absorbed into a circle of healthy, generative care. Few models exist, but they beg attention.

Kathy and Dawn prove that women *friends are only human.* It is dangerous to presume that women's friendships, especially because they have been obscured, are perfect. The fact is that betrayal, deception, duplicity, competition, and jealousy are all real human emotions and behaviors in which real people engage. Women friends are, sadly, no different. What does seem to be different is the degree to which women seek to keep connected. This is not always a healthy effort. There are times, as with Kathy and Dawn, when consciousness about an event or an attitude is so different that continued relating can only exacerbate the problem. One friend feels battered by the other; the other feels put upon. The result is a desire for distance. Often distance results.

Nevertheless, women friends who come from faith traditions in which forgiveness is a virtue sometimes find new depth of intimacy and certainly new respect when efforts at reconciliation take place. Letting the human condition show, forgiving and being forgiven, can revive a relationship. I repeat though that such efforts are not always healthy and should not be confused with the pathological enveloping of people into endless emotional contortions when irreconcilable differences prevail. Letting go is often the more difficult but necessary end.

These examples provide us with a shared experience base for continued reflection on friendship. Surely readers bring their own experiences as well, just as mine have shaped the way in which I reflect on these. To repeat, they do not exhaust the relational possibilities. Parallel ones could be pulled from male-male friendships as well as female-male friendships with equally useful results. The point is to have some concrete basis for looking theologically at friendship.

Context for Contemporary Friendships

It is impossible to see the power of women's friendships without taking a careful look at the context in which they are set. I have chosen for special consideration two characteristics of that context that seem to override other historical and social factors in shaping women's friendships. They are the patriarchal nature of our culture, and the rigid expectations issuing from heterosexism, that is, the normative expectation that all of us are and choose to be heterosexual in our lives and loves.

Turning first to patriarchy, it is important to clarify that this is not a political slogan so much as a theoretical construct. Four helpful sources for understanding it are found in the work of Gerda Lerner, Charlotte Bunch, Rosemary Radford Ruether, and Elisabeth Schüssler Fiorenza.[3] Gerda Lerner in *The Creation of Patriarchy* outlines the major components of patriarchy in an appendix to her useful if controversial historical volume. While some historians question the adequacy of her reading of certain esoteric sources, I find her theoretical remarks persuasive. She calls patriarchy "the manifestation and institutionalization of male dominance over women and children in the family and the extension of male dominance over women in society in general. It implies that men hold power in all important institutions of society and that women are deprived of access to such power."[4]

Professor Lerner appreciates the sinister power of patriarchy to shape a culture to exclude women. But she correctly points out that "It does *not* imply that women are either totally powerless or totally deprived of rights, influences, and resources."[5] This is especially true for white, middle-/upper-class heterosexual women. Nevertheless, the crippling impact of this power on women's friendships is what makes the transformation of a patriarchal society the lead item on my feminist agenda.

Charlotte Bunch chronicles some of the efforts to make that transformation in what she calls "feminist theory in action" in *Passionate Politics*.[6] Professor Bunch knows these efforts from the inside as one of the most prolific and persuasive of the feminist theorists from 1968 to 1986, the period she examines. Throughout her book, from a veritable Who's Who in North American (and parts of International) Feminism in the Acknowledgements, to the "Reflections on Global Feminism After Nairobi," which carry her clear political vision into the future, one feels the centrality of friends for overcoming patriarchy.

She makes this obvious when she writes: "the personal relationships of my life — both friends and lovers — have provided the sustenance and the challenges that have kept me growing. Without them, I would not have done what I have done... I have created a family of women with my friends, who have been crucial to my life and work."[7] Then she proceeds to weave these persons in the text of the history of the women's movement. They do not appear again as individuals. Yet one feels them as part of the fabric of a society that will replace patriarchy, a society that Charlotte Bunch has glimpsed close up with and through her friends.

Far from being an abstract theoretical concern or worse, a privatized analysis based on individuals, Charlotte Bunch's is a clearheaded acknowledgement of what it takes to survive patriarchy and what it is that we want to create. She notes that "the crux of teaching feminist theory is getting women to analyze and think about others' ideas as well as to develop their own."[8] Likewise, in describing international efforts she observes that "when women from different countries interact authentically, sharing our own experiences, while also recognizing that our work has cultural limits, we can learn from each other. As we listen to each others' views, we see our ethnocentric biases more clearly and can discover ways to overcome these. For while feminism draws strength from its grounding in the concept of 'the personal is political,' this also has limitations."[9] I quite agree.

This is a helpful corrective when working on friendship in a patriarchal context. It would be a mistake to dwell too much on individuals; another mistake would be to ignore them altogether as patriarchy would have it. Charlotte Bunch avoids both extremes in a text that can best be described as friendly.

Rosemary Radford Ruether takes secular notions of patriarchy and explores their religious significance. She does not belabor a definition of patriarchy as such, but lays out a "critical principle of feminist theology" that is very helpful in understanding what needs to change. She names that principle as "the promotion of the full humanity of women," and argues that

Whatever denies, diminishes, or distorts the full humanity of women, is, therefore, appraised as not redemptive. Theologically speaking, whatever diminishes or denies the full humanity of women must be presumed not to reflect the divine or an authentic relation to the divine, or to reflect the authentic nature of things, or to be the message or work of an authentic redeemer or a community of redemption.[10]

She is describing patriarchy in a nutshell, and her version of feminist theology is aimed at overcoming it.

Rosemary Ruether's constructive theological work assumes that "patriarchy is the social context for both the Old and the New Testaments, and that this social context has been incorporated into religious ideology on many levels."[11] She calls for "prophetic-liberating traditions [which] can be appropriated by feminism only as normative principles of Biblical faith which, in turn, criticize and reject patriarchal ideology."[12] She identifies patriarchy, shows its influence on the religious traditions, and proposes a way beyond it. Regardless of what one may think of her proposal, i.e., some have criticized it for being too deeply rooted in the very tradition it critiques, her astute analysis helps to illuminate the impact of patriarchy on women's friendships. In a patriarchal context there are *structural* barriers to women's bonding.

In a different but equally insightful way, Elisabeth Schüssler Fiorenza makes her theological case against patriarchy, focusing on the Bible. She insists that "a feminist critical hermeneutics of liberation, therefore, must analyze carefully the theological and structural patriarchalization of the New Testament and 'patristic' churches without too quickly resorting to biblical apologetics or to an a-historical disinterest."[13] Her understanding of Scripture as "an historic prototype" and not "a mythic archetype" helps her to evaluate the patriarchal nature of Christianity on the basis of "women's own theology and history."[14] The implications of her feminist critical hermeneutics of liberation include the need for women to develop "the Ekklēsia of Women" or what is now called "women-church." Reading of the Christian and Jewish Scriptures can be done adequately without recourse to her work now that we have seen the wisdom of her imaginative reconstruction.

Concrete alternatives to patriarchal expressions of Christianity are the practical import of her brilliant theoretical work. Elisabeth Schüssler Fiorenza's task is to expose patriarchy in its religious form in order to counter it on its own religious terms. Her skillful handling of biblical texts and her innovative approach to reconstructing the early church for our edification focuses the integrity of a feminist approach to Christianity. Her hermeneutical principles assure that all women's experiences and not patriarchy will prevail. How widely they will be used by mainline churches remains to be seen. But the history of biblical criticism, and for our purposes, the way of handling all exegetical work, has changed toward a feminist future.

These four perspectives on patriarchy make it clear why I consider it one of the major shapers of the context in which women's friendships are set. On the one hand patriarchy is a system that so imperializes men's experiences, goals, and hopes as to block the full articulation, much less the realization, of women's. On the other hand, it is an ideological construct that reduces everything to its own rubric. In both cases the results for women (and for men) are disastrous. They are limited by incorrect readings of history and they are bound by the laws of men.

In this setting women are nonbeings. So women's friendships with women are easy to ignore. If they are recognized it is with opprobrium or cynicism. The classic example is when two women dining at a restaurant are asked by a man if they are alone. Obviously they are together, but in patriarchy their relationality, their friendship, is invisible. Or, when they are noticed as friends they are taken as people to be shunned. This points to the second aspect of our context, heterosexism.

Normative assumptions about sexual preference run as deep as any patriarchal assumptions about gender roles. For women to love women, including genital sexual expression (much less in patriarchy, for men to love men with the same right), is simply unthinkable in Western Christian culture. Homophobia and heterosexism are the predictable results of such thinking. Fear of same-sex loving and costly social taboos against such behavior combine effectively to limit women's friendships. The price of love is simply too dear for many but the most exceptional and/or privileged women to pay.

To the extent that women take their friends seriously, even when physical expression is unknown or nonexistent, they are branded by the allegedly negative label "lesbian." Many a husband has accused his wife of being a lesbian when she spends "too much" time with her women friends. This has led many women to shy away from identifying their friendships with women, even those that include no explicit genital sexual expression, for fear of suffering from the stigma of homosexuality in a homophobic culture. It is a real fear grounded in the powerful apparatus of repression that must be removed.

"Lesbian" is the ultimate epithet hurled at women who do not conform to patriarchal assumptions about females, regardless of their sexual partners. Ironically, much of the work done on homosexuality in general has been done by men about men's experiences. Patriarchy may be homophobic, but it is still male dominated. It is no wonder that some of the most insightful feminist theory is being written by lesbian women who understand patriarchy through the experience of loving women.

The jury is still out as to whether lesbian experience is a subset of sexism, or whether it actually provides additional explanatory tools to describe and change a patriarchal and heterosexist society. It is my position in this book that both are true. Heterosexism/homophobia is obviously closely aligned with sexism since all lesbian women experience oppression as women. But I believe that the taboo against sexual expression with women friends is strong proof of the point that something more is experienced that sexism alone does not encompass. The reclaiming of lesbian experience as not only healthy and natural but also as morally good is part of the feminist project that will enhance all women's well-being. Simply reclaiming women's experience in general, without this specific concern, is not adequate.

The aim of the lesbian/gay movement of this century has been to work toward a new understanding of sexuality. This is based on the psychological, historical, sociological, and biological data that show that same-sex loving is healthy and natural for at least 10 percent of the population. Reasons for this are as unknown as why the majority are oriented heterosexually, but the point is that this is perfectly "normal" behavior. Data show that another substantial percentage of the human community has some kind of homoerotic experience in adulthood.

Lines between heterosexual and homosexual people, then, are not quite so rigid as was once thought. In fact, most of us are said to fall in a vast middle ground with only a small percentage of people being exclusively heterosexual or exclusively homosexual. With this information the logic of same-gender friendship as data of revelation becomes even greater. As we learn more and more about the normalcy of homoeroticism, and as homosocial and homosexual friendships become increasingly public, my insistence on a friendship norm will look increasingly obvious. Conversely, those who struggle to deny and denounce same-gender sexually expressed love will consider my proposal anathema.

Mass culture has not caught up with the new information on same-gender love. Churches are even further behind. AIDS is now providing additional fuel to the homophobic fires. AIDS is the "medicalization of homophobia" insofar as the pandemic has claimed predominantly gay men (and intravenous drug users who share needles and their sexual partners and offspring) thus far in the United States. This tragedy has been taken by some people as license to deepen their hatred and bigotry instead of as an obligation to loosen their ethical strictures.

Global projections, however, indicate that by the turn of the century the typical person with AIDS will be a heterosexual woman with dependent children in a country now known as the "two-thirds world." In short, the racism, sexism, and classism that underlie an unjust society are mirrored in the greatest public health problem of the twentieth century. This is no coincidence. Nonetheless, for now, the specter of AIDS has eroded many of the gains made by the lesbian/gay communities in the past twenty years. It has provided a homophobic society with the medical excuse necessary to do its dirty deeds to lesbian/gay people, and that same society has taken every opportunity.

It would be easy to distance lesbian experience from gay male experience in this regard since documented instances of female-female transmission of the HIV virus are rare. Patriarchy dictates that because women and men have different access to money, property, jobs, power, and even bodies, we have different ways of relating. But the fact is that even though the incidence of AIDS for lesbians is relatively small the political climate is such that irrational fear and hatred (homophobia) around AIDS includes lesbian women as well as gay men. Strategically, this is no time to part company. Would that gay men would join lesbian women's feminist struggles as readily.

Just as patriarchy is being dismantled by feminist theory and action, so too is heterosexism/homophobia being undone by lesbian and gay theories and actions. Having said that the backlash against AIDS increases the need for lesbian and gay people to work together, I must also say that as they work together it is increasingly clear that fewer and fewer claims can be made that apply to both women and men. Experiences of loving persons of the same sex may be similar insofar as both sexes are oppressed by the larger society. But there the differences end because of a patriarchally constructed society.

Respected male friends confirm that when women talk about their lives as women, just as when men talk about their lives as men, we sometimes do not have categories in which to understand each other's experiences. My sense is that trying to talk about lesbian/gay anything is like trying to speak of a Judeo-Christian culture. It simply obscures the differences and results in muddled and ultimately disrespectful discussions. It ought not to be done. Instead of making sweeping claims that do not hold up, I prefer to refer readers to the excellent work of gay historians and theologians like John Boswell and Kevin Gordon for more than friendly amendments to my work, in fact, for constructive work of their own.[15] This way I do not repeat the mistakes of false inclusion that some male writers have made when they claim to include women's experiences but in fact do not.[16] Christine Downing has shown the way in this regard in her highly nuanced and careful study of same-sex love.[17] She leaves aside none of the male material but makes clear her perspective on it.

My focus on the context that is shaped by heterosexism and homophobia, as well as my efforts to eradicate these evils from society, spring from a lesbian feminist perspective. I do not pretend to make claims for gay men, though I am ever anxious to continue talking with them so that I can learn from their different but equally valuable experiences. I am just as confident that heterosexual persons can make sustained contributions from their vantage points to the mammoth task of overcoming limited views of friendship. The fact that I do not emphasize their contribution is simply because most of it remains to be articulated. I am hopeful that my work will invite such efforts. Sources of note with regard to lesbian cultural analysis include the work of Adrienne Rich, Charlotte Bunch, and Gloria Naylor in the theoretical and literary arenas, with Carter Heyward and myself having done early work in the theological field. Other feminist theologians working in this arena include Sheila Briggs, Emily Culpepper, and Tess Tessier.[18]

Adrienne Rich's landmark essay "Compulsory Heterosexism and Lesbian Existence" launched an important conversation about homophobia/heterosexism from a feminist perspective.[19] As long as lesbian existence is denied or downgraded, all women and men are bound by the strictures of compulsory heterosexism. In addition, she argues that all women fall along a lesbian continuum insofar as women love women in a world that counsels against it. This is new data for feminist theory that has resulted in new approaches.

Other feminist scholars have disagreed with Rich's position. For example, should the word "lesbian," which carries a sexual connotation, be used to describe women whose experience does not include sexual relations with women? Or, if all women are on the so-called continuum, is "lesbian woman" a redundant term? While many scholars have critiqued Rich's work, no one denies the genius of her challenging concept, nor the extent to which it has occasioned constructive conversations. The sum of these conversations will move us toward clarity.[20]

Charlotte Bunch was one of the earliest and most highly respected lesbian feminist activists and theorists. She began by redefining "lesbian" so that people would understand it wrenched, as Mary Daly advises, from its patriarchal context. She writes that a lesbian is a woman whose sense of self and energies, including sexual energies, center around women — she is woman-identified. The woman-identified-woman commits herself to other women for political, emotional, physical and economic support. Women are important to her. She is important to herself. Our society demands that commitment from women be reserved for men.[21]

She goes on to clarify that not all lesbians are feminists, and to assert that "rejection of heterosexual sex challenges male domination in its most individual and common form."[22] She adds that "...lesbians have been the quickest to see the challenge to heterosexuality as a necessity for feminists' survival," noting that "straight feminists are not precluded from examining and fighting against heterosexuality. The problem is that few have done so."[23]

She describes heterosexual privilege as the way in which a heterosexual woman "receives some of the benefits of male privilege indirectly and is thus given a stake in continuing those privileges and maintaining their source — male supremacy."[24] I would take issue with Charlotte Bunch as to whether this accrues across the board, i.e., the rural, unemployed heterosexual woman with dependent children whose husband has left her is surely less privileged than the urban professional lesbian feminist without children. But the point that she makes, that the normative value of heterosexuality has real consequences, is germane to the context in which women's friendships exist. Two women living and working together in patriarchy find it difficult under the best of circumstances. Society ignores their relational existence and denies their family unit. Moreover, lack of access to male money makes a significant difference, especially for women at the bottom rungs of the economic ladder. Putting two female incomes together barely makes survival possible for many such women. As Adrienne Rich wrote, "Two women sleeping together have more than their sleep to defend."[25] I only caution that class, race, and national origin make a real difference as to how much any woman has to defend.

Gloria Naylor's powerful chapter "The Two" in *The Women of Brewster Place* illustrates the point more powerfully than any theory.[26] Lorraine and Theresa live together quietly in a tenement on Brewster Place. A chance slip by one of them on the stairway and a tender gesture of breaking her fall and reassuring her by the other give neighborhood gossips all the information they need to fuel the rumor mill.

It had first spread through the block like a sour odor that's only faintly perceptible and easily ignored until it starts growing in strength from the dozen mouths it had been lying in, among clammy gums and scum-coated teeth. And then it was everywhere — lining the mouths and whitening the lips of everyone as they wrinkled up their noses at its pervading smell, unable to pinpoint the source or time of its initial arrival.[27]

The obvious object of scorn is these women's love, but the description turns out to be apt for heterosexism/homophobia. In the story Lorraine is brutally gang-raped by young men who call her a dyke. They brazenly assure her that after sex with them she will not want to make love with a woman again. This unspeakable crime is a literary expression of the horrors of homophobia that many women have experienced first hand. While all lesbian identified women do not experience such violence over their choice of lovers, until all are safe to choose, none is exempt from such savagery.

Carter Heyward, feminist theologian and Episcopal priest, considered this issue theologically. She named the problem: "But it is not hard to know or imagine why homosexuality has been considered such an anathema. It is sexual. It is not in marriage (the only possible legitimating parameter for sexuality). It is for pleasure in companionship other than for the duty of procreation (sexuality's theological justification.)"[28]

For churches to baptize and confirm the homophobic insights of the society, and indeed for theology to be exposed as the root of many such notions, is the scandal that has driven many people far from the pews. More significantly, to justify the virulent attacks on lesbian/gay people by an appeal to Scripture and tradition further undercuts any reason why lesbian/gay people would relate to Christianity as anything but an adversary. Nonetheless, Carter Heyward points out that

> God needs us. Our commitment. Our hearts. Our touching and our pleasures. Our bodies, including our common sense, our intelligence, our friendships, our love. God is our liberation, the wellspring of all that we do on behalf of humankind and of the earth. And, just as surely, we ourselves are the liberation of God.[29]

Carter Heyward's later work shows how the structures of heterosexism function to control women, especially women's bodies. The threat that lesbians embody is nothing less than "a challenge to fundamental tenets of patriarchal religion."[30] The transformation of that tradition will only take place when daring scholars speak truth to power. Carter Heyward's unambiguous affirmation of women's love for women, taking its sexual expression for granted as good, is a powerful contribution.

My own early writing on this topic reflects my Catholic roots.[31] That church has distinguished itself with some of the most homophobic statements and actions on record, including the letter (October 1986) by Cardinal Joseph Ratzinger in which homosexuality is called "intrinsically morally disordered." Predictably for patriarchy, most Catholic diatribes against homosexuality are based on a condemnation of male experience.

The phenomenal growth of the Conference for Catholic Lesbians proves that Catholic lesbians' numbers are large and their influence in the church has been legendary. Our experiences are ignored and our love is denied but we are everywhere. The point of my writing has been to bring such experiences to public attention, and in so doing to contribute to the whole church's clarity. Mine in the Catholic arena, like Carter Heyward's in the Episcopal Church, has been anything but a welcome gift to those in power. Countless lesbian women from the Christian tradition have commented on the usefulness of such work for their own self-understanding, pride, and public disclosure. It often confirms their intuitions to leave their churches, but just as often it fuels their desire to make change within their denominations.

The history of Catholic women, especially women who choose homosocial religious life, i.e., members of women's canonical communities, as well as members of pious unions, third orders, or associate programs, is rich with tales of women's friendship. Nuns who came to the United States from Europe to found communities, women who went off two by two to convert the world to Christianity, teachers, nurses, and evangelizers who lived with their "particular friends," even some contemporary nuns who live and work together, are part of a priceless heritage that is only partially revealed when heterosexist/homophobic assumptions reign. These women loving each other are people to emulate. But in order to emulate we must know our ancestors.

Not all of these women who took vows were or are celibate, a fact that recent writings confirm.[32] The issue is not whether they were, nor whether current nuns are living according to the commonly held definition of the vow of celibacy, i.e., a ban on all genital sexual expression. The point is that they are subjected to male-prescribed forms of life as a condition for their bonding with women. This is simply unacceptable if friendship is the norm since all friendships include a sexual dimension however implicit it may be. The problem is far more insidious. It is the compulsory nature of celibacy for nuns and what this means especially for those who are lesbian.[33] Just as Adrienne Rich has pointed out the consequences of compulsory heterosexuality, I see parallels with compulsory celibacy in canonical communities. In each case the lack of choice and the resultant control exercised by patriarchal institutions are what is at issue. In both cases friendship is devalued, in the one case for heterosexual marriage and in the other case for so-called marriage to Jesus.

Discussion with women in canonical communities often includes mention of their dear friends, the women with whom they share their lives, the people with whom they cast their lots. With all due respect to men, it is not the prohibition on sex with men that seems to characterize their commitments, but the affirmation of other women. Yet it conjures all sorts of antimale images. Only in heterosexist patriarchy would one be seen as synonymous with the other. Affirmation of women is simply that.

Homophobia and heterosexism are rampant in most aspects of church life in virtually all denominations except the Metropolitan Community Church, which was set up in reaction to them. The contemporary ban on blessings, covenant, or marriage ceremonies for same-sex couples is simply the most obvious instance of this. The prohibition against the ordination of so-called practicing homosexuals in many denominations and the deliberately anti-lesbian/gay sermons, pastoral letters, and pronouncements leave one wondering why lesbian/gay people look to the churches for anything at all.

Like Carter Heyward, I believe that the roots of Christian homophobia/heterosexism need to be excised, and that this has to done in church circles. Rosemary Radford Ruether and Elisabeth Schüssler Fiorenza have made similar strategic decisions with regard to patriarchal sexism. This work is a logical next step. One needs to use resources that come from beyond the tradition as well as from within it in order to critique it. Thus the data of the social sciences and advances in women's as well as lesbian/gay studies are important sources for theologizing.

The challenge is how, and indeed whether, to be a part of a tradition that rejects one at a very deep level while at the same time trying to change it. I am dubious about how long it is healthy for lesbian/gay people to stay around churches that discriminate covertly as well as overtly. That is why the women-church movement, inspired by Elisabeth Schüssler Fiorenza and others, is an ecclesial safe house for so many lesbian women who come from the Christian, especially Catholic, tradition. Institutional change is key, but we are faced with the challenge of being church in the meantime. For lesbian/gay people it is a mean time indeed.[34]

What remains to be probed is whether Christianity is inherently heterosexist/homophobic, just as the question was asked with regard to sexism, or whether these are cultural accretions that can be left aside. In the absence of a definitive answer, I exercise a "hermeneutics of suspicion and hope" with the sources.[35] I locate myself well beyond the mainstream in women-church, but even there much more needs to be done for a satisfactory answer to emerge.

In all of this "feminist theology must learn to insist that liberation, like oppression, is sexual."[36] We are now finding ways to articulate the importance of women's embodied love for one another, whether genital expression, which happens with all naturalness for some, or the hugs, embraces, glances, touches, kisses, and caresses that are equally natural for others. This is part of fierce tenderness. This is why I ground my analysis in women's friendships and claim (in the next chapter) that they are a source of inspiration.

The fact that the Christian tradition, which claims that the word was made flesh, denies women's incarnation raises troubling questions. Violent reactions against Edwina Sandys's "The Christa," the powerful sculpture of a nude female figure hung on a cross, make this painfully clear. As Rosemary Radford Ruether said, "When people see a male figure hung on a cross they consider it the ultimate symbol of tragedy. When they see a female in the same way, they consider it pornographic."[37] Other artists have suggested, for example, that a female Christ should be hung on a lowered crossbar with the legs outstretched instead of the arms to reflect the nature of women's real oppression in society. In any case, revulsion at the female body by Christians is only doubled when two women are involved.

If one woman in the salvific mode is pornographic for most Christians, and if attempts to make biblical language inclusive are seen as the "castration of the Bible," then two women friends making love are beyond the pale. This is why I conclude that the whole theological project must be rethought in light of lesbian women's experiences, especially embodied love. This work grows out of feminist concern but finally adds another dimension to it. The twin elements of patriarchy and heterosexism/homophobia serve as the backdrop against which women's friendships are seen. It is remarkable in such a context that women's friendships thrive at all. I never cease to be amazed by the sincere and consuming efforts that women make to overcome such obstacles. Doris Grumbach provides a clue when she writes of a woman's discovery of same-sex love: "It was the very opposite of narcissism — it was metamorphosis."[38]

Power Reclaimed

Women's friendships point the way beyond heterosexist patriarchy. This is what makes them so dangerous in a homophobic society. They are those relationships that prove that women do not need to be understood in relation to men, and that show, without apology, that women can love women.

A common litany I have discerned of female identity, in descending order of moral acceptability, goes something like this:

> The Virgin Mary is the paragon of virtue. After her all women fall in the following descending order:
>
> > A married woman sleeps with a man.
> > A widow did until her husband died.
> > A separated woman might again.
> > A divorced woman used to sleep with a man.
> > A single woman wants to do so.
> > A prostitute does it for a man's money.
> > A lesbian does not sleep with a man.
> > A nun can't talk about it.

Even if there are cultural and generational variations to this formulation, I claim that it is the generally understood way in which all women are categorized in heterosexist patriarchy. Janice Raymond refers to this context as "hetero-reality," putting emphasis on the normative value of "the ideology that woman is for man."[39]

Differences between and among women in this model are really only differences in degree, not differences in kind. Racial, ethnic, and class differences affect the dynamics though the fundamental similarity is that all are seen in relation to men, even when men are not in the picture. This explains why women are set in opposition to one another. For example, the single woman and the wife, or the lesbian and the prostitute, are seen as polar opposites when there is no *apparent* contradiction. Only in relation to a man is there any difference. Once that way of defining women is abandoned, such women are quite natural companions. In fact, women who are prostitutes and women who are lesbian have historically made strong bonds for their common survival.[40]

My point is that each definition is flawed. Until the whole litany is thrown out, until new self-understandings are cultivated and allowed to emerge, all women are held captive in false consciousness. Naming this is a first step toward overcoming it. Friendship is the powerful experience that has helped many women to reclaim connections with one other that a male-centered model simply cannot incorporate. For example, many mothers and daughters report close ties only after their husbands/fathers are dead. Some women long to break the heterosexual couple syndrome (going out in a foursome or sixsome usually of the man's choosing) and just go out with the women. "Mixed company" in patriarchy often renders women's issues and ideas unimportant.

Moreover, women's friendships presume that women are important in their own right. The most insidious danger in denying women's friendships is threefold. First, it prevents women from loving themselves as women. If one cannot love another person who is like oneself, it is very hard to develop the kind of ego strength necessary for healthy self-love. Many women's problems with self-esteem and body image, even depression and eating disorders, are related to the failure to nurture self-love because of being taught to dislike others who are like us.

Second, heterosexist, patriarchal assumptions short circuit some love relationships, without which some women would not love at all. The fact is that for some women, notably for many lesbian identified women, but also for a surprising number of heterosexually identified women, the most important and in some cases the only deep, lasting love relationships are with women.

Love is sufficiently mysterious and capricious to defy prediction. But openness to loving women means that friendships will flower where heterosexist patriarchy would have loneliness and alienation. I heard a woman argue this persuasively with a skeptical listener. She said of her sister, a lesbian identified woman, "Would you prefer that she never love at all?" The argument ended quickly. When faced with the choice between more love in the world and accepting women's friendships on their own terms, the choice is obvious. In fact, it is so obvious that one must conclude that the power of women's friendships is simply more than a fragile status quo can bear where the obvious is rarely affirmed.

A third aspect of the denial of women's friendship in our society is its direct implication for women's friendships with men. While this is not my primary concern, it is crucial to point out that the whole human community is affected by denials or affirmations of love in any of its sectors. The prohibition on women's friendship has skewed the relational configuration of our society. The message that, in order to love, a woman must love a man and a man must love a woman has not only prevented same-sex love, but also put extreme pressure on female-male relationships. The high divorce rate (roughly one out of three marriages in the United States) is but one barometer of this phenomenon. Others include the deep alienation of women and men in the work place (where women are usually in the service sector while men are usually in the managerial sector).

Another indicator is the high incidence of lesbian/gay people who marry (heterosexually) before coming out. Some comment that they thought they might change their orientation by marrying, but studies show that this is simply not the case. Others say it never occurred to them that they might love someone of the same sex, or in fact that they might not find themselves in a committed one-to-one relationship at all. They simply imagined no options under the pressure of society.

Heterosexual marriage is not inevitable, like growing old. It is but one among many relational options. Treating it as the only legitimate way has caused personal and social damage. But surely some could be avoided with less restrictive expectations. Certainly women and men could make freer decisions about their intimate friends if they were not cast into the heterosexist mold. No one knows what might result, but some experimenting is in order, if only for the children's sake. Such experimenting is well under way. The need now is to look at it from a supportive theo-ethical perspective.

I am cautious about projecting women's friendships as a panacea. Still, I am amazed when people break out of the mold and begin to make choices, albeit counter-cultural ones, that reflect their deepest longings. The very fact of having to go against an entire social structure in order to love well has its own price. Some women's friendships reflect the internalized oppression and horizontal violence that characterize other oppressed groups.[41] Others become "neurotic minuets," as John Frye called clingy, conflictual relationships. I do not blame what may be individual problems on a social system. At the very least I can say that the system does not help. This is not an excuse so much as an observation of where change is necessary.

It is important to note that jealousy and other lesser human emotions are no more female than male in their expression. Attempts to characterize women's friendships as bitchy and competitive need to be looked at in light of the foregoing analysis of how society treats women in order to be evaluated fairly. Indeed it is a wonder that any women love women in the face of such odds.

These problems notwithstanding, the sheer delight that many women take in women friends is contagious and powerful. My friends know that my favorite weekend of the year is Sisterfire, a two-day outdoor music and cultural festival that is so civilized as to be accessible by public transportation! It is over in time for a refreshing shower before dinner! Friends come from far and wide to bask in the glory of women's talent, in fact to bask in each other's presence. The food and drink, perhaps even the entertainment, are all incidental to the community gathered. By the end of the weekend I feel refreshed for another year. I feel empowered by women's love, the love of my friends and of the friends I see around me.

Being with women has this effect on many people. Anna Quindlen, a *New York Times* columnist, described her experience:

> I have recently returned from a week of female bonding.... A friend and I flew south with our children. During the week we spent together I took off my shoes, let down my hair, took apart my psyche, cleaned the pieces and put them together again in much improved condition. I feel like a car that's just had a tuneup. Only another woman could have acted as the mechanic.[42]

I have felt equally energized after a week at the beach with four women friends, several of whom were twice my age. The comfort of our care and the depth, sometimes unspoken, of friendship gave me new energy.

The Threat Factor

The intuition that women's friendships are so powerful as to be dangerous to the status quo is right on target. One hears it articulated, usually by men, in the sneers and jokes that accompany women-only events or when serious conversations between women are written off as gossip or "girl talk." Sometimes this is the only way for people (women have been known to sneer, too) who are threatened to cope with what they correctly perceive as shifts in the relational power equation.

Women are susceptible to this same rejection of women's power that we associate with men. I once invited an audience to listen to the awesome words and music of Bernice Johnson Reagon's "Every Woman" and rise to their feet and call out her name if they had ever loved a woman. In my mind it was an invitation to express the commonality of our experience as women, a way to affirm our love publicly for all women, and of course a way of saying that when all women love women no women will be stigmatized as lesbians. To my delight, the majority of the women stood proudly. I was especially impressed by one friend who, despite the fact that certain enemies would brand her a lesbian as well as a powerful exponent of women's right to choose, made the connection between issues and stood solidly.

Years later it was reported to me that at least one, and I suspect others, in the audience had felt manipulated. It was as if somehow admitting to loving women, any women, was something shameful. This is a very dear price to pay for stigmatizing the ways in which some women love one another. Imagine not wanting to stand in honor of one's mother or one's daughter, one's sister or one's lover. At least one such love should have been enough to mitigate the fear of being identified as a lesbian. One such love should have been enough to prove that loving a woman is simple, natural, common, that lesbian women are someone's "mother, daughter, sister, lover." But pressures are strong. Woman-hatred is rampant for women who have been taught that loving women is a sin, that women are unlovable.

I was struck by what I have seen over and over in heterosexist patriarchy, namely, women's internalized homophobia and self-hatred. There was also precious little understanding of the hard and costly intellectual and political work it takes to move our society beyond these barriers. Help over the top is what friends are for. I urge the repetition of this exercise until every woman can stand proudly.

· 3 ·

Friendship as Inspiration: A Study in Theo-politics

Still — in a way — nobody sees a flower — really — it is so small — we haven't time — and to see takes time, like to have a friend takes time.

—Georgia O'Keeffe

Friendship Quilts

The theo-politics of friendship comes quite naturally in my neighborhood, just a block beyond the Washington, D.C., border. Washington, as Meg Greenfield wrote, is "the only place in the world where 'friend' is a bad word." She went on to say that here "friendship is thought of as something that can compromise you, make you less trustworthy, blind you to your larger institutional interests. And so finally it is seen as something that can ruin your otherwise promising career... sort of like being a kleptomaniac or a drunk."[1] This was especially true in the Reagan and Bush years when corruption among friends was the order of the day.

It might seem odd, then, that I would link theology and politics, much less friendship and politics, when I want to claim that friendship is a source of inspiration. But to do so I have chosen a lovely metaphor, the friendship quilt, that I hope will illustrate both the necessity and the content of such connections. The quilt provides an image for holding these together in a rich variety of ways.

57

Friendship quilts were a form of folk art that peaked in the 1840s–1850s.[2] They were a popular way to combine craft with sentiment, design with communication. Thousands of such quilts were made in New England. Many were given to pioneers as they headed west. Unlike common folk quilts that were used as covers, friendship quilts were often considered too precious to be used every day. So they were preserved in chests and on walls as decorations. This accounts for the number of them that are still in very good condition, preserving for us this imaginative and, I will argue, revelatory testimony to friendship. Typically a friendship quilt was made of pieces that were all of the same shape sewn together in a pattern. The most popular designs were the "Chimney Sweep" and "Album Patch." Some quilts were quite elaborate, others quite plain. They could have one maker or be the product of several women's work. What distinguished them was the fact that friends personalized them by signing their names, sometimes adding their address as well, thus immortalizing their friendships, especially when loved ones moved west.

Autograph books preceded friendship quilts as a way women recorded their affection for one another. Letters, of course, were popular, with the quilts sometimes functioning as a kind of address book, keeping friends in touch at a distance by having their data at hand. Information was put on the quilt — signature, date, place, and usually relationship to the person who was to own the quilt. Many times a message or a bit of advice, even a poem, was added. All was written in indelible ink or cross-stitched for longevity. Women were practical as well as artistic in these endeavors.

Friendship quilts were not simply given to women as wedding or going-away gifts, although that was a popular custom. They were exchanged by friends. Sometimes they were given by sisters to one another. They were passed down through the family as part of the inheritance because, like later family photo albums and now video tapes, they contained a record of women's lives that could not be duplicated.

Two curious features of friendship quilts make them an apt metaphor for the theo-politics of women's friendship. First, "with so many choices available for making friendship quilts, it is remarkable that the results were so similar.... It is true that, with time, certain standard patterns for the friendship quilt emerged."[3] Friendships themselves emerge from a variety of starting points, but the ones that endure and become prototypes for other such experiences share common characteristics such as generativity and an orientation toward community. Second, friendship quilts are among the only remaining evidence of the existence of some women. Before 1850 "only the names of 'heads of families' were listed on government census records.... A woman's name was listed on the census only if she herself were the head of the household, generally due to the death of her husband."[4] Women's lives were recorded in the family Bible and on the gravestone, but the former was often lost in successive generations, and natural forces like storms and erosion often did away with the latter. This is part of why women are invisible historically.

Incredibly, it was on friendship quilts that women wrote themselves into history. As Linda Otto Lipsett notes:

> It was not woman's desire, however, to be forgotten. And in one simple, unpretentious way, she created a medium that would outlive even many of her husband's houses, barns and fences: she signed her name in friendship onto cloth and, in her own way, cried out, "Remember me."[5]

My observation is that it is not by coincidence that women wrote themselves into history. They were literally forced to by their circumstances. Nor is it a coincidence that they used friendship quilts to do the job. These were concrete symbols of their most trustworthy relationships. They knew that the owners of such quilts would guard them carefully, look at them periodically to be reminded of their friends, and treasure them long after their friends had died. Even more than family, friends were enduring. The quilts, and the practice of making and preserving them, are a source of inspiration.

Theo-politics Explored

The friendship quilt stands as a metaphor for what women need in the theological world. Women have been systematically excluded from participating in theological reflection, kept from places where that reflection is chronicled and preserved as part of the legacy of a faith tradition. Women's experiences, hopes, and dreams, commitments, doubts, and religiously motivated work for justice have been absent, until very recently, from the theological mainstream. This has diminished men's work as well.

My choice of women's friendship as the experiential starting point for a study of feminist theology is linked to the friendship quilts. While each woman is unique, as was each quilt, there is enough overlap in women's experiences to see some similar patterns and to make some, albeit very limited, shared claims. Further, no one will preserve women's history and the integrity of women's experiences if women do not do it themselves. Women have to lift to public expression their own faith, name what is ultimately meaningful and valuable for us. The result, like a friendship quilt, is both useful and artistic. It will last as part of history. Otherwise, women's stamp on creation will be superficial at best. Women from many different racial and class backgrounds made quilts, a clue to preserve and display equally diverse theological claims.

Women do that best in community, or in groups of friends, what I call unlikely coalitions of justice-seeking friends. Like the women who made the friendship quilts, it is necessary to express, chronicle, save, and share information about women's lives and loves and to probe their meaning. This is what feminist theologizing does. Like stitching names on a patch for a quilt, different women's experiences are stitched into the fabric of theology through conscious and often costly efforts. For example, nineteenth-century women's theological writings are preserved now in the history of feminist theology only because later women befriended the materials. Through little help from the theological establishment, which to date still pays them scant attention, the work of earlier women is known. It is a legacy that has been preserved by women. Still I shudder to think how much has been lost, the tattered quilts of our collective history turned into dust rags. It cannot happen again.

Theo-politics signifies the fact that theology does not exist in a vacuum. It is part of a larger context, i.e., heterosexist patriarchy and much, much more. Similarly, theo-politics is not an objective science that stands on its own. It reflects some of the most deeply held values, including religious values, of a culture. The theo-political reason why women's friendships have not been taken seriously as data of revelation, as a source of inspiration, hinges on the word "power." This understanding of theo-politics comes from the liberation schools in the past twenty years. While African American, feminist, womanist, Latin American, Asian, and the other liberation theologies all have different characteristics based on their various starting points, they have in common the fact that they challenge the prevailing power dynamics in theology. They critique those as being imperialist and exclusive. They strive to replace existing power dynamics with a more participatory and egalitarian approach.

The theological establishment is still made up of those who hold sway in denominational seminaries and university-based theological schools. Affirmative action gains notwithstanding, they are still overwhelmingly white, male professors who believe that theology can only be done according to strict methodological rules that "happen" to correspond with theirs. While there is nothing inherently wrong with their approach as one among many ways of doing theology, the problem arises when it is seen as *the only* way. Openness to the liberation schools in the late 1970s and early 1980s is reported to be almost over. A rise in neoconservative theo-politics is making itself felt in many theological schools. Regrettably, future generations of students seem to be experiencing backlash, a return to the so-called classical, traditional, institutional approach to theology. Again, there is nothing inherently wrong with such theological projects, though I claim that they represent class, race, and gender agenda; they simply are not all there is. Challenges from liberationists have been opposed vigorously. In some cases the establishment has simply denied the validity of the work. In other cases teaching appointments, tenure, publication, or even critical discussion are denied to those who work out of a different framework. Deconstruction of the prevailing theological method has been the common project of liberationists, and to a certain extent, their success. I consider myself in this number as a feminist and hope that I am incorrect in my pessimistic view of contemporary theo-politics.[6]

Still there is a long way to go before the particular insights of the various liberation schools are incorporated by the other liberationists, much less by the mainstream. The trajectory is clear, that changing the persons who are part of the theologizing community will have an impact on the product. But much work remains if we are to claim interstructured approaches. For example, Hispanic women point out the need for culturally specific feminist analyses; likewise, liberation theologians in Latin America are learning to integrate feminist concerns.[7] While there is much to be done in this regard, I caution against losing the primary and common agenda, which is to challenge the hegemony of one particular style of theologizing. At base we are all engaged in shifting the power equation.

Theologizing, as understood by liberationists, is the organic and communal process of sharing insights, stories, and reflections on questions of ultimate meaning and value. The answers that a community gives to such questions are then evaluated in light of the tradition, weighed with respect to the culture in which they are set, and pondered in relation to the ineffable mystery we call the divine. Only then can tentative and always changeable, faithful, and serious answers be shared. Such a method has been disparaged as "untheological" so that certain value-laden presuppositions will always emerge as normative.

The negative reaction of the theological establishment to most liberation theologies has been aimed at keeping certain kinds of people from engaging in this process. This highlights the political dimension of theology, the extent to which factors other than those that are seemingly logical and reasonable are at play. Masked as academic excellence or scholarly rigor, such efforts still have status-quo-preserving results.

Examples abound. In some theological schools Spanish is not considered a "theological language" even though major work is being done in Spanish (and Portuguese). This discourages students from doing dissertations on liberation theology, a subtle and effective way of keeping it from the mainstream. Another example is the firing of the respected feminist ethicist Elizabeth Bettenhausen from Boston University School of Theology for alleged "insufficient scholarship." While it is true that Elizabeth Bettenhausen has not published an opus in the form that the theological establishment recognizes as definitive, she is a highly regarded scholar who has contributed far more than some whose works gather dust. Her helpful work has given denominations, women's groups, her own students, and the theological world at large some important insights. Yet she is kept from the mainstream.[8]

Theo-politics is not the unique discovery of liberationists. It has been a well-known, if unnamed, phenomenon in the theological world for centuries. It has been at play when, for example, women's experiences were written out of history, when women were excluded from theological schools, and when ethical reflection did not include women's experiences as moral agents. Only when women and others who have been marginalized began to claim their rightful place in the center was theo-politics named as such.

Now that we all understand the rules of the game we can play fairly, although obviously race, class, and gender are automatically determinants of advantages and disadvantages. Claims made from the partial, limited, and contextual framework that surrounds the theological establishment will be evaluated as simply that. They are not to be discarded simply because of their privileged social location. But neither are they to be taken with any more seriousness because they are part of the establishment. This is what it means to shift the power dynamics. Accordingly, I name my starting point as feminist with the responsibility to define it and to limit my claims on the basis of its boundaries. I do so gladly, asking only that all theological exercises include the same step. Otherwise liberationists are even more disadvantaged if they limit claims while others continue with their blanket statements and their sense of entitlement.

Feminist Theology

Feminist theology in the United States takes many forms as women from various religious traditions, principally Jewish, Christian, Neo-Pagan, and Goddess, ask questions of ultimate meaning and value. Note that I am confining my sweep to the United States both because it is my context and because it is premature to evaluate feminist theology in a global sense. It is important to note, however, that feminist theology is far from a U.S. phenomenon. Excellent work is being done in Europe, especially in Holland and Germany, as well as by women in Latin America, Asia, and Africa.[9] I look forward to similar theological assessments that will reflect women's experiences of friendship in those contexts.

Few feminist theologians have taken friendship as a guiding category. Nevertheless, let me review a bit of the history of feminist theology, highlighting some of the immediately relevant sources for friendship, in order to locate my reflections in this theological tradition. Four distinct periods provide a useful outline: preparation, criticism, construction, backlash.

A period of *preparation* began in the late nineteenth century when Matilda Joslyn Gage wrote what many scholars consider to be the first scholarly work in contemporary feminist theology.[10] The work of Elizabeth Cady Stanton and her Revising Committee on *The Woman's Bible* proved that women were perfectly capable of exegetical work, albeit in their time without modern tools of biblical criticism.[11] Although neither of them made friendship a predominant theme, Stanton's celebrated friendship with Susan B. Anthony played a formative role in her own life and work. Stanton's collaborative work style, her belief in the power of women to make social change through the study of Scripture, and her faithful friendship with one of the leaders of the women's suffrage movement make her a convincing prototype of a woman-oriented scholar.

Stanton's regard for women was obvious: "If Miriam had helped to plan the journey to Canaan, it would no doubt have been accomplished in forty days instead of forty years."[12] And her sense that the Bible needed critical attention only becomes more urgent with time:

Verily we need an expurgated edition of the Old and New Testaments before they are fit to be placed in the hands of our youth to be read in the public schools and in theological seminaries, especially if we wish to inspire our children with proper love and respect for the Mothers of the Race.[13]

The *critical* period, when all theological thinking had to be reconceived on the basis of feminist insights, began well into the twentieth century. Protestant women were ordained in many denominations, giving them a new form of religious leadership and of theological respectability. Catholic women, especially nuns, were busy founding schools and hospitals to carry out the social mandate of their faith even though they were not allowed into theological circles. Circuit riding preachers were spreading their news; some black women were founding their own pentecostal churches. It was not until the second wave of the women's movement was launched in the early 1960s and feminist claims were being heard in many professional arenas that critical feminist theology came forth.

The theological mainstream kept such "problems" at bay until 1960 when Valerie Saiving wrote the first article of what we now consider consciously feminist theology.[14] She lifted up the fact that women's and men's ways of being in the world are sufficiently different that human experience cannot be known on the basis of a male model. Since her writing, theology cannot be done as if male experience were normative. This foundational methodological insight changed the course of theology. While Valerie Saiving did not use varying experiences of friendship as a case study, she did contribute invaluable insights that can be applied to friendship. She stated her position clearly:

> It is my contention that there are significant differences between masculine and feminine experience, and that feminine experience reveals in a more emphatic fashion certain aspects of the human situation which are present but less obvious in the experience of men. Contemporary theological doctrines of love have, I believe, been constructed primarily upon the basis of masculine experience and thus view the human condition from the male standpoint. Consequently, these doctrines do not provide an adequate interpretation of the situation of women — nor, for that matter, of men, especially in view of certain fundamental changes now taking place in our own society.[15]

Contemporary feminist theology has so thoroughly incorporated Saiving's insight as to render it rather unremarkable today. My effort is to apply it to the particular experience of friendship since this is one of the areas around which fundamental gender-based conditioning is radically different. Thus the theological and ethical claims that arise from such friendships will also vary widely.

Mary Daly's work is probably the best known feminist theology. It is safe to say that she opened up the second period by the publication of *The Church and the Second Sex*, and later *Beyond God the Father*, the latter being the watershed volume in the field.[16] Mary Daly's impact was threefold. First, she gave women the experience that they could go beyond patriarchal religion and still survive. Religion is a voluntary activity, but for many the deeply ingrained teachings of a faith tradition produce a kind of spiritual paralysis when the foundation is shaken. Mary Daly cured all of that, or at least provided the strong medicine capable of effecting the cure, painful side effects notwithstanding.

Her courageous move to the boundary and beyond, while not followed by everyone, showed the way. She literally cleared the psychic space for others to move beyond the parameters of patriarchal religions. Having been freed in this way, women are quite ready to surrender other long-held patriarchal notions as well. In fact, it is easier to jettison old thinking on something concrete like friendship when the work has been done on something seemingly more foundational and more abstract like views of the divine. Mary Daly has given practice in living and thinking anew. Women can abandon old notions of friendship, leave aside degrading definitions, and thrive with confidence while creating a postpatriarchal world as friends. Women can theologize on women's own terms and need not worry about rejection from people and places that should be discounted. Most of all, women can shape and model new ethical awarenesses without fear. As religious agents women are responsible to act on what we know. That is Mary Daly's legacy.

Second, Mary Daly couched her vision in an exodus community with "Sisterhood as Cosmic Covenant."[17] Sisterhood is not an exact synonym for women's friendship, but it does describe a close theological antecedent to my concerns in this book. She went on to name Crones and Hags, later Websters and Women-Touching Women, always redefining the patriarchally tainted words to reflect their proper etymology and woman-friendly usage.[18] While her usages border on the neoromantic at times, her creativity and courage to name things in a new way is exemplary.

In calling for sisterhood, Daly was onto the fact that massive social and intellectual changes do not come quickly nor in private. They must be intuited, articulated, expressed and lived out in community. In fact, it is only in a communal setting that shared vocabulary starts to change, normative assumptions shift, and people begin to live differently. To do so alone is to run the real risk of being considered crazy. To do so in a community of sisters, or better, I would argue, in a community of friends, is to give and receive the necessary reinforcement to change habits and to sustain hope while others follow suit, albeit more slowly. I prefer "friends" to "sisters" because I want to underscore the voluntary nature of friendship, and because I want to distinguish it from any blood tie. However, given my conviction that family members can learn to be friends, there is reason to use the terms interchangeably. At least sisterhood is a close cousin, a name that many women use when talking about close friends: "We are as close as sisters." "She is just like a sister to me."

Some readers have trouble applying Daly's work to the practical order. But this, in my judgment, is a failure to incorporate her powerful model for change that includes, Be-Longing: The Lust for Happiness; Be-Friending: The Lust to Share Happiness; and Be-Witching: The Lust for Metamorphosis.[19] What Mary Daly means is that happiness shared by women friends is indeed transformative. It changes individuals and communities in ways hitherto unknown under patriarchy. Ironically, this concept of Mary Daly's is far more practical than people give her credit for, simply because they do not make the explicit connection between friendship and politics.

Mary Daly is eminently practical when she makes clear that not all women can be friends. Material constraints on time and energy as well as differences in personality limit the possibilities. More so, class, race, age, social location, and sexual preference play a large part. Still, the energy of women's friendship when we "be-friend" and are "be-friended" has been vastly underrated.

However, "the work of Be-Friending can be shared by all, and all can benefit from this Metamorphospheric activity."[20] She defines "Be-Friending" as "Weaving a context in which women can realize our Self-transforming, metapatterning in Being. Therefore it implies the creation of an atmosphere in which women are enabled to be friends."[21] While the language may strike some as cumbersome, the issues are clear. She avoids the greeting card approach to friendship by moving immediately to a global example. She focuses on the publication of Simone de Beauvoir's *The Second Sex* as an instance of women being Be-Friended. Writing is a generative activity, one of the hallmarks of friendship. The book provided women with a concrete referent to which to direct conversation, channel ideas and energy. Most of all, it was a touchstone by which to find other women who were thinking the same thoughts. Simply having read *The Second Sex* meant, in the early years after its publication, that the reader was thinking about previously unthinkable topics. Mary Daly allows that while Simone de Beauvoir was not personally involved with the thousands of women who read her book, "It can be said that she has been part of the movement of Be-Friending and that she has been a catalyst for the friendships of many women."[22] An author can hope for little more.

Third, Mary Daly developed a whole new context in which to set her vision of sisterhood. It is a world in which "Virgins" are "Marriage Resisters" and "Soothsayers" are "Courageous Truth-sayers."[23] She has taken the next step with her vision and begun to gear up the powerful intellectual forces necessary to make it normative. She leaves herself open to the charges of neoromanticism or even elitism. Does a word really mean what I want it to? But her method is consistent and her contribution vital to living the new now. I suggest that any less favorable reading is finally anti-intellectual. She has proved prophetic once again. Without an entirely new context there is little point to theologizing about women's experience including friendship. It will only be lost or co-opted in heterosexist patriarchy. If allowed at all, it will be taken as a grand and glorious exception, something for the literary set but not for all women. Mary Daly's change of context results, ironically, more forcefully than tinkering with taboos, in space for women on their own terms. Altering basic assumptions by redefining words turns out to be a more efficient way of making change than some have given her credit for. Regardless of whether one credits Mary Daly or not, it is amazing to see the ongoing power of her concepts.

The drawback, of course, is that one talks meaningfully only to the converted for a while until the rest catch up. But assuming that conversations are replicated at least among friends, there is good reason to hope that change can take place in this way. It is remarkable to hear people use phrases like "beyond God the father" or even "Crones and Hags" as if they had always been a part of polite conversation. This is Mary Daly's legacy, to give us whole new ways of thinking and being so that social change can happen. Without new words we would have no way to articulate new concepts. While I favor a more politically explicit agenda, I remain in her debt for the conceptual work that perhaps precedes, and surely at least goes along with, social change.

Changing the context must happen if friendship is to replace such a deeply rooted assumption as the marriage norm. Women need to give content courageously and without equivocation to the meaning of friendship. I like to think that I have been doing that since I told my mother about Susy, i.e., even children can do it if we listen to them. Being an astute scholar and an excellent pedagogue, Mary Daly knows just what she is doing. While I do not agree with her full philosophical program, I am persuaded that these three factors, inspiring women to imagine a way beyond patriarchy, providing a concrete conceptual alternative in "Sisterhood as Cosmic Covenant," and especially by redefining words, Mary Daly helped to set the stage for and provide an example of constructive feminist theological discourse on friendship.

The beginning of the *constructive* phase of feminist theology in the early 1980s did not signal the end of critical work. Far from it. But it did signal that new ideas and insights are flowering on their own terms, not simply in response to other work. Rosemary Radford Ruether and Elisabeth Schüssler Fiorenza are widely regarded as having made some of the most substantial constructive contributions. Even though they do not employ friendship as a guiding metaphor, I suspect that they might describe relationships with the divine, "Holy Wisdom" in Rosemary Ruether's formulation and "Sophia" in Elisabeth Schüssler Fiorenza's formulation, as friendly. Carter Heyward's work, mentioned earlier, is also part of this constructive moment. I suggest that exploring the desired relationship with the divine in each of these, we find a generative quality, as well as a concern for difference but not distinction, that is analogous to our best experiences of friendship.

The most explicit hints in constructive theological and ethical work on friendship are provided by Beverly Wildung Harrison in her insightful ethical writing.[24] It is not friendship as such that she lifts up, but a feminist Christian ethical framework in which we can view friendship on women's terms: "My basic thesis [is] that a Christian moral theology must be answerable to what women have learned by struggling to lay hold of the gift of life, to receive it, to live deeply into it, to pass it on...."[25]

She goes on to affirm that

> we must learn what we are to know of love from immersion in the struggle for justice...[because] women have always been immersed in the struggle to create a flesh and blood community of love and justice and...we know much more of the radical work of love than does the dominant, otherworldly spirituality of Christianity.[26]

Beverly Harrison's insight into women's experiences of struggle for justice corresponds to my own claims about justice-seeking friends. She uncovers the "reified masculinist idolatry" of the Christian theological tradition that would downgrade mutuality for some mythic higher relationship with the divine.[27] A feminist vision, on the contrary, finds within human mutuality all of the richness that others ascribe to the divine. Beverly Harrison's is a tough but gentle love that issues in "a spirituality of sensuality."[28] This is a context in which women's friendships flourish.

Turning her ethical acumen to the connections between misogyny and homophobia, Beverly Harrison argues that to understand these one must "examine this problematic tendency of Christian theological tradition to neglect, ignore, or denigrate the body."[29] The identification of the body with lower things and the mind with higher things immediately sets up a dualistic framework in which sexual expression, even in marriage, is always of a lower order. For friends, especially friends of the same gender, to touch one another rather than to be together in a kind of disembodied, intellectual way, is simply unacceptable in this bifurcated worldview. The implications of Beverly Harrison's analysis, especially that patriarchal homophobia is "a pathological source of human sexual disorder," are helpful.[30] Given that homophobia is part of our social fabric, Harrison, coupling it with a patriarchal worldview, argues that we suffer from "learning security in intimate patterns of inequity."[31] Work to overcome such conditioning is difficult especially for women, but it can be done. Friendship is a relational mode in which security can be felt in intimate equality.

Such work, in my judgment, is best done by women in friendships with other women. Far from lacking the "otherness" that Freudians have foisted on us for too long, women loving women who are conscious of the dynamics of homophobic patriarchy have at least a chance to experience equality in relationship. Of course this has to be distinguished from any blurring of personal boundaries and identities that sometimes plagues women. Lesbian women are said to have particular trouble keeping boundaries clear since sexual intimacy involves a certain melding. But to experience security in equality is a new and welcome experience for most women. Once having had it, we know the difference. Sometimes even without having it we long for it. One day men, too, may experience such equality on a routine basis. For now we are paving the way for what is not only "sensual pleasure, but sensual trust."[32]

Mary Daly hinted at this when she described the patriarchal reversal that happens when one is said to need a partner of the opposite sex in order to experience the fullness of "otherness." She pointed out that, ironically, women find more authentic "otherness" in other women. Our sameness as women provides a shared experience that allows the *particularity* of each one, the real "otherness" unmediated by patriarchal baggage, to emerge. How obvious yet how obscured this insight has been in a patriarchal heterosexist society. Beverly Harrison's work is helpful for thinking about justice-seeking friendship. Friendship is one of the ways in which women "making the connections" are transforming an unjust world.[33] Harrison's wisdom on the issue begins the constructive work from well within the boundaries of the academic discipline of moral theology and from well beyond those boundaries in her own praxis.

In another style, Sallie McFague writes about friendship with special attention to friendship with the divine. Her work, however helpful, is disappointing in that she does not differentiate women's friendships in any way. She neglects to use many sources that express women's experiences of friendship. Instead she falls into the trap of establishment theology. She notes "Aristotle, Kant, Hegel, Bonhoeffer" among those who have written on the topic, and cites C. S. Lewis over and over without ever mentioning the reason why women's writings on friendship and women's friendships themselves have been passed over by Christian theologians.[34] At least she is dealing with friendship as a theological category, but much more needs to be said.

While each of the well-respected male scholars that Sallie McFague lists had something important to say about friendship, it is by no means clear that their insights were equally applicable to women's experiences. That is, after all, the achievement of feminist theology, to glean from women's as well as men's experiences and to let theology be shaped differently by each. Nor is it any longer academically respectable, i.e., after Valerie Saiving et al., to take male scholars' however brilliant insights at face value as if they were applicable to all humans. For example, the fact that C. S. Lewis could say that friendship is "the least *natural* of loves; the least instinctive, organic, biological, gregarious and necessary" is preposterous from a feminist perspective no matter how nuanced the statement may be.[35] Why even entertain it? This, coupled with his assumption that there is a wide gap between friends who are normally "side by side, absorbed in some common interest," and lovers who are normally "face to face, absorbed in each other" shows how far Professor McFague is from a feminist understanding of friends.[36] While this is ultimately an inadequate effort when evaluated from a feminist perspective, at least she lifts up friendship in relation to the divine, providing future scholars with a valuable stimulus.

A recent collection that is relevant to the constructive phase of feminist theology in this regard is *Embodied Love: Sensuality and Relationships as Feminist Values*, edited by Paula M. Cooey, Sharon A. Farmer, and Mary Ellen Ross.[37] The essays, though uneven, are stimulating. They come from a variety of perspectives and represent a wide spectrum of theological concerns. However, it is striking that little if any attention is paid to friendship as a constructive category in these essays. Many people's primary experience of embodied love, that is, the focal experience for many people of sensuality and relationship, is friendship. There is the real danger, even for feminists, of falling into abstraction when discussing difficult theoretical issues. Nonetheless, the volume provides a useful display of current debates between and among feminist theological constructionists. For example, Sheila Davaney raises an interesting question by asserting that Mary Daly, Rosemary Ruether, and Elisabeth Schüssler Fiorenza have more in common than they and others think they do. Differences notwithstanding, all three, Professor Davaney claims, assume a "correspondence between feminist visions and ontological reality and the at least implicitly made claim that feminist-conceived symbols refer to such a reality."[38] This type of debate is helpful in clarifying the theoretical frameworks in which future work will be set. But the volume leaves unanswered what models of relationality are emerging from feminist experience. I respectfully suggest that friendship is one model that the book leaves largely unexamined and therefore that the collection limps as a vehicle for really exploring the fullness of embodiment.

A few male ethicists are beginning to take up the issue of friendship during the constructive phase of feminist theology. James B. Nelson's work stands out. He has begun to incorporate feminist insights into his writing.[39] Focusing on men's lives, Nelson observes that men

> seem to handle our lives with an activity-achievement style, we handle others with a style of dominance and submission, and we handle our psyches with a style that prizes logical and cool level-headedness. None of these characteristics is particularly conducive to nurturing the capacities for intimacy and friendship.[40]

Nelson mentions that friendship is almost entirely absent from the contemporary theological scene. This is due primarily to the fact that "males have dominated the theological tradition, and men have had problems with friendship — particularly friendship with other men."[41] He wisely confines most of his work to men's relationships with each other. This is a prudent approach at a time when the catch-up work that men need can only be done by other men. Later on women and men can find common bonds. This method is eschewed by those who wish to keep everyone together even at the expense of the tough work that transitional separatism signals. White people had to learn this lesson during the civil rights struggles; North Americans are learning it now from Central and South Americans who need to name their own future. Professor Nelson is evidence of the fact that some men have heard most women's wishes in this regard.

James Nelson's major contribution to contemporary male views of friendship is his insistence on the extent to which deeply internalized homophobia prevents men from becoming friends. This is a common assumption in Men's Studies materials on friendship. But his treatment of it marks the first time that it has been brought into the Christian ethical mainstream. He asserts in his chapter on friendship with God that "to love God in the very midst of loving another human being is sheer gift — and revelation."[42] Although I recoil at the use of the word "gift" (it seems to be a favorite of those who refuse to grapple seriously with the seemingly inexplicable), I quite agree with him on revelation. Perhaps the fact that he does not spell out the implications of this statement accounts for why this book is classified under Psychology instead of Religion. Nonetheless, we concur that what has been obscured is only now coming into focus, that is, being revealed.

Some readers may wonder why I include James Nelson's work with constructive feminist theology. On the one hand, I include it parenthetically since it does not bear *directly* on women's friendship. It is not feminist theology per se. On the other hand, I include it without qualification or apology as a gesture of hope that such work, when taken in conjunction with volumes like this and others that feminist women and men are writing, will move us toward renewed female-male relationships. Meanwhile, I do my work confident that James Nelson is doing his, and that the synthesis is ahead of us. Read together, such work provides a sound basis for such a hope.

A new resource for feminist theological construction is the companion volume to *Womanspirit Rising*, the second collection of editors Judith Plaskow and Carol P. Christ, *Weaving the Visions*.[43] It is clear now that many perspectives inform feminist theology, that womanist theology is important on its own terms, and that "transforming the world" is the immodest but important goal of the entire enterprise. Of special relevance to ethical study are the essays in the section "Self in Relation" that echo many of the constructive themes contained in this work.[44]

The fourth phase of feminist theology is that which has developed in reaction to the constructive work, namely, *backlash*. As we enter the 1990s this can be found in some ultraconservative Christian women's groups that have co-opted women's issues. It is also found in antichoice efforts by Catholic bishops who claim to join women in an undifferentiated concern for fetal versus maternal lives. And it is most violent in right-wing diatribes against lesbian/gay people that are coming from conservative churches and political groups.

A more subtle and insidious form of backlash is found among backsliding liberals who are realizing that changes in the theological power equation have a greater impact on them than they had imagined. It is expressed when, for example, feminist theologians are compared, so that "softer" feminists are pitted against "harder" feminists. Competition for jobs, especially in church and seminary bureaucracies that are filling their small quotas, makes this polarizing obvious. Lesbian women are especially hard hit when set over against heterosexual women. Asian, African American, and Hispanic women, while seemingly on everyone's short list for jobs, continue to experience discrimination as they are played off against white feminists. Once hired, many of them report being so overwhelmed by work that they are too worn out to be creative, a subtle but sure way of limiting their contributions.

It is important to note that backlash does not signal the end of construction. To the contrary, it is usually a measure of the progress that has been made which some feel must be turned back. As such, backlash is a useful measure, perversely, a sign of progress made, but one that most of us would just as soon do without.

My feminist theological work on friendship, as history would have it, is set in the nexus of construction and backlash. I am indebted to the theologians whose work in the periods of preparation and criticism set the stage. I join the constructionists in a concerted effort to stem the tide of backlash. While we cannot ignore it, neither can we afford to let backlash dictate our constructive efforts.

It is not accidental that one of the first themes chosen by the Consultation on Lesbian Feminist Issues in Religion of the American Academy of Religion was friendship. It is a key to survival. The constructive work continues apace even in the face of serious and sustained backlash. It is not work for lesbian women only, but in fact for all who wish to bring to the light of theological day the data of women's experiences, the stuff of theological reflection.

Some Historical Examples of Women's Friendships

A complete history of women's friendship is beyond the scope of this book. In fact, Janice Raymond has laid out a genealogy of female friendships so thoroughly that it is more than enough to refer the reader to her work.[45] She focuses on the Beguines, Catholic nuns, and Chinese Marriage Resisters as three categories of women who put women first. Their friendships are a legacy for us. I admire this approach and I also agree with Janice Raymond on the importance of naming the friendships between famous women of our time such as "Helen Keller and Annie Sullivan, Margaret Mead and Ruth Benedict, and Eleanor Roosevelt and Lorena Hickok" so that we will have recognizable examples of what we are discussing.[46] Such role models are important for our own self-understanding. Homophobia and the trivializing of women are the only conceivable reasons not to make these friendships explicit.

I could add countless names of church women, many of whom would lose jobs and/or privilege if the full extent of their friendships were revealed. This threat is reason enough to bring a theological light to the subject. If the world would be shocked and punitive about the depth to which they love one another and the choices they make about the physical and emotional expression of that love, then we are missing more than I can ignore. The task of feminist theology is to prevent such a loss in future generations.

The powerful example of Ruth and Naomi, who promised each other that they would maintain their bonds even in the absence of financial security and social acceptance, graces the Hebrew Scriptures. In the text, especially Ruth 1:16–17, we find a clear expression of friendship between two women. I never cease to be amused when I hear this formula used for heterosexual wedding vows, providing the first pastoral clue that women's friendships are a good model for human relationships in general. It does not seem to follow that heterosexual marriages are a very good model for women's friendships. Some interpreters have tried mightily to play down the friendship factor in a stream of exegeses about the familial patterns that made such a promise so extraordinary. It was, they conclude, just a special kind of family bond. This leaves aside the detail that there was no blood relationship between them. Although kinship requirements gave their bond a dimension we do not experience today with in-laws, why not simply call their friendship by its name? That would elevate friendship over family, something that patriarchal societies fear.

In the New Testament another friendship constellation is sighted in the relationship between Mary and Elizabeth. Commentators have tried hard to describe them as cousins, missing the obvious friendly relationship that prevailed between these family members. Again the reader is puzzled as to why such an obvious link is passed over, until one admits that in a patriarchal context it is assumed that relations between women are mediated by a third party, usually if not always a man. Family meant male-centered, property-conscious family. Stressing that tie, at the expense of passing over the affective one, is considered routine exegesis. Paying attention to friendship reveals something more in the text and inspires something beyond it.

The more interesting cases, as Elisabeth Schüssler Fiorenza's innovative methodology would have it, involve the relationships between Mary and Martha, or the woman at the well and her friends, women whose lives and friends can only be reconstructed imaginatively.[47] I await more of this scholarly work in the belief that friendship is one of the most helpful exploratory and explanatory frameworks that will aid in the reconstruction effort. Then we will have not only a fuller picture of our tradition, but one that reflects women on their own terms. Renita Weems in her biblical studies moves in this direction and provides useful questions for others to take it the next step.[48]

Monastic groups were a logical homosocial environment in which women's friendships could flourish. We are only now discovering the depth and expression of some of those friendships. As Janice Raymond noted, "the power of female friendship in convents derived from the fact that friendship is by nature a spiritual communion, but that women are not and never will be pure spirits. With nuns, as with all women, friendship is mediated through and only becomes Gyn/affection in the material world."[49] We lack a definitive study of the women's experience of the period, one that would match Adele M. Fiske's comprehensive treatment of male *Friends and Friendship in the Monastic Tradition*.[50] But we can and must imagine if our history is to be complete.

That study, while detailed and philosophically rigorous, is based on men's experience in previous centuries, e.g. Augustine, Boniface, Anselm, Bernard of Clairvaux, Aelred of Rievaulx. Professor Fiske's command of the original sources and her thoroughness in chronicling the period using friendship as a guiding metaphor make one wish that she had trained her sights on monastic women instead of or as well as men in monasteries. Still, I would be loathe simply to lift the insights from male experience and foist them onto medieval women, even nuns. The work remains to be done with a feminist hermeneutic of friendship as a guide.

While I agree with Augustine that "life without friends would be too hard to endure for a day," I am not sure that women were content with the spiritual kiss that Aelred thought included both friends and Christ. Dr. Fiske, writing prior to the "feministization" of theology, must be credited with a nascent feminist insight that friendship itself is a key category for interpreting human life, even if her work only told part of the story. Moreover, Adele Fiske was astute enough to limit her claims: "Each generation can understand fully only its own questions and answers."[51] This makes the fact that she did not turn her considerable research skills and insights to women's experience all the more regrettable as the dual data would have provided us with some rich material on the period as well as perhaps an early start on gender difference and the difference it makes. Of course it must be noted that part of the reason why scholars wrote as they did was because data simply were not available about women.

She concluded her study by positing that "the understanding of friendship is an index of the level of a civilization."[52] As women's experiences are taken seriously on women's own terms, the way of understanding women's friendships will indeed judge our society. Until now ignoring them seems to be a form of scorn.

Examples abound of women's friendship in the contemporary period. What is fascinating, however, is how details sometimes fade away. They are often erased, only to be restored in friendlier times. For example, the original name of the Sisters of Loretto was "The Little Society of the Friends of Mary under the Cross of Jesus."[53] The official title now is "Sisters of Loretto at the Foot of the Cross." As feminist consciousness grows, the group is returning to its roots that include this powerful relational component. Thinking about the original title, Marian McAvoy, former president of the group, wrote: "Perhaps because they were thinking of Mary as standing at the foot of the Cross, they knew that the need at such a time for Mary was for companions, friends."[54] She went on to encourage members to "grow in the ability to be friend — certainly friend to one another in community and to others whose welfare we seek in ministry; more than that, to try to relate to all so that no one is servant."[55] This is friendly advice that corresponds faithfully to the roots of the Loretto Community.

Realizing the importance of women's relationships with one another is crucial for the formation and development of any sort of community. Friendship takes the power away from an external authority and relies on committed bonds to prevail. Such a move to friendship bodes well for a canonically affiliated group that may eventually choose to sever ties with male authority and continue its woman-centered work in the world. Then women will finally be religious agents, able to name their own experiences, make decisions on the basis of them, and live accountably on the basis of these choices without male interference. Such agency is a rare but important goal that ought to be normative.

Another powerful example of women bonding is found among poor, *pobladora* women in Santiago, Chile. The Casa Sofía is a women's center that I visit regularly when I participate in "Women Crossing Worlds," a project of international sharing through WATER, the Women's Alliance for Theology, Ethics and Ritual. The project is our way of embodying the gospel imperative to go and make friends in all nations. And indeed it is because of our friends that we visit and share resources. Support groups flourish at the Casa. Women provide one another with literacy training, mental health care, and other practical assistance. The hidden yet most important aspect of that center is the bond women form in a society that would keep all of them powerless:

> Beyond a doubt, the overwhelming discovery in these groups is friendship. For many women, this fire comes alive for the first time in their lives, it then grows and expands and provides the strength to confront their often monumental difficulties.... The obstacles of repression, cynicism, and scoffing by those who would keep women at home or in church are at times overwhelming.... We no doubt need visionary, accompanying, passionate, stirring and remarkable friendship.[56]

To visit this center is to experience the warmth of women who know that their survival is contingent on their bonding. Theirs are not friendships of convenience but of necessity, born of the need to survive together against crushing odds. This insight into the need for friendship in order to survive inspires others of us to act accordingly. It parallels the early work of Charlotte Bunch, who insisted that necessity and not ideology grounds and sustains efforts at social change. While in no way denying the very real love these women feel for one another, it is made all the more powerful by the horrendous situation of political, economic, and social (especially macho) oppression in which they live.

Some might wonder why an overview of theological materials leaves out the contribution of male scholars in the history of women's friendship. The answer is simply that very few if any sources exist. In fact, the best bibliography I could unearth on the topic, which covered Western sources from Plato to Saint-Exupery, cited virtually nothing on women's friendships and few works by women.[57] This can only improve.

The same problem accrues when one tries to search, à la Sallie McFague, through the sources of male theology. While the insights are helpful in a general sense, the new material that will shape the tradition in innovative ways is what women's friendships reveal. Engaging male sources that do not take account of women's experiences seems to me to be counterproductive. It reinforces the false generic of human experience based on males, and it distracts from the task at hand, namely, focusing on women's lives. Those who would do so in the name of "the tradition" forget that the very tradition has been shaped without concern for women's well-being. While Martin Buber and others may have begun to move in the direction that feminist theology is now pursuing, they too lack specific attention to women. This does not mean that men's friendships or even female-male friendships are not important. It simply means that when scholars seek to discover what has yet to be considered it is women's friendships that appear. Women's friendships reveal something new and inspire something powerful.

Women's Friendship as Inspiration

Inspiration is a technical theological term that can also be used more informally. Women have traditionally shied away from such words due to something I label "theology anxiety." It is like "math anxiety," a peculiarly (though not exclusively) female problem, which has been outlined in feminist theory. Two strong parallels exist.

First, as with the teaching of mathematics, women were not given proper instruction in theology. At least with mathematics they could take the courses. The prohibitions were more subtle, such as the teacher calling on boys more than girls, or helping out the boys more than the girls with problems. In the theological world women were not admitted to many degree programs until quite recently. There are still theological faculties in this country, and many places around the world, where women are not permitted to study or to take advanced degrees in theology. Those are reserved for the clergy who are male. This lack of knowledge produces an understandable anxiety about the unknown. It results in control by those who can manipulate the jargon and concepts of the discipline to keep women as permanent outsiders.

It will take several generations to overcome theology anxiety, but we are well on the way.

The second reason for theology anxiety, again like math anxiety, is that many women are not convinced that everything they have been taught is the way things *really* are. For example, in mathematics, many women are not convinced that two plus two must really equal four. Many intuit that numbers are "only" a linguistic and mathematical convention that has been used to make certain social interactions and scientific explanations easier. In this sense they are not ultimate but convenient. Many women do not impute unchangeable truth to numbers. Such women are not recalcitrant. They just refuse to give the discipline of mathematics too much power. With the odds stacked in favor of the discipline, this can cause anxiety even though it is a defensible position.

Likewise, many feminist theologians have gained deeper and deeper suspicions about the language and concepts that have been given in the name of a faith tradition. Women are now quite sure that God the Father, Jesus his only Son (no daughters), and a male-dominated church are not adequate to pass on to children. Theology anxiety is correctly placed even though it creates serious problems for women who want to "make it" in a patriarchal church. Still it is well grounded in our exclusion and in our doubt. A healthy response to such anxiety is to theologize from women's own starting points. Of course no such work begins in a vacuum. Witness: the periods of preparation, criticism, and now construction/backlash. Women come to the notion of revelation with little of the usual baggage. So rather than enter into a technical comparison of various theories of revelation, most of which revolve around who decides what is revealed (and eventually who decides who decides, all of which is finally claimed to be revealed by someone to someone else, illustrating the *reductio ad absurdum* that has given theology a bad name), I prefer to begin with friendship, lifting up the dimensions of human experience that are made obvious and then note what it is that inspires imitation. This is a plausible way to develop a theory of how inspiration works, i.e., by observation rather than fiat. Of course more needs to be said, but this is a reasonable beginning approach, given the historical exclusion of women's experience from the data of revelation.

Several presuppositions come first. I begin with the assumption that revelation is ongoing or not at all. As a working definition I assume that revelation is that which continually reinforces, albeit always differently and usually to our great surprise, the fundamental goodness of creation and the simultaneous need for divine-human cooperation that keeps creation in process. Inspiration, far from being secrets blown into the minds of those who chronicle history, is simply the way in which generations glean insights from one another. I refer not to inspiration in the technical sense in which it is used for Scripture (though I think there are parallels here) but to the common passage of meaning and value through time.

Friendship, at least as women's friendships prove, reveals a good deal about ourselves, one another, the natural community in the world, and our relationship with the divine. It inspires those same dynamics in future generations. In each category we find, by way of women's experiences, something that we did not know before, something that women sense is connected to the fundamental way things are. This is why friendship can be said to function in a revelatory way, making obvious what has previously been obscured when women's friendships were not recognized or were consciously kept from view. This is how friendship inspires change.

Such language implies an ontological claim. Friendship is a real experience that cannot be negated. But it is at the same time a perspectival claim insofar as that which is revealed is contextualized in time and place. Still, certain claims must be made if women's experience is to move from the margin to the center. This move does not mean negating the claims made by those who already find the light of revelation shining on them, i.e., what comes from male experiences. Rather, it means extending and expanding the rays to encompass ever more diverse and even diffuse experiences. Put another way, it means looking at the heretofore dim as well as at the shining examples.

There is a deliberate move here away from what is revealed by the divine and passed on (i.e., inspired) to a more expansive, ultimately more trusting sense that much remains to be seen. Inspiration is what we can see without special apparatus if only we are encouraged to look. In this sense women's friendships can be said to inspire a good deal:

1. *Women's friendships reveal something about women themselves.* The most insidious problem created by the refusal to acknowledge women's friendships as existent, much less meaningful, is that without them women are kept from understanding themselves as loving human beings. If such love does not count, or if it must be seen as secondary, less important than the real thing that will come later if at all with a man, then women do not have a true picture of themselves.

Failure to acknowledge friendships with women as embodied love functions as one more barrier to women's self-love. Being prevented from loving those like ourselves casts into doubt the possibility of loving ourselves. In a patriarchal society this is quite convenient. But as women come into our own as moral agents we discover that such self-love, far from being solipsistic, is necessary for our healthy integration.

Likewise, because in friendships people express their worst capacities as well as their best, we all learn something about limitations. We see how capable we are of evil, of hurting and being hurt, of forgiving and being forgiven. Most of all we learn that without challenge and limits we will not necessarily do what is best for all involved. Friends are some insurance against our worst selves.

Friendship is an honest mirror, but it must be allowed to reflect or its power is lost. This may seem pedestrian, but it strikes at the heart of a patriarchal society's means of control, namely, alienation. Insofar as women need men in order to be a part of what is defined as the way things are, then it will be necessary to keep the lid on women's love for one another and for ourselves, indeed to keep the mirror hidden. Otherwise we risk massive social upheaval. Obviously I favor such upheaval. Women's friendships inspire it. But I acknowledge the deep dangers it portends for those who favor the status quo and whom the status quo favors.

When the mirror is used, friends find that they are part of the goodness of the created order. Not only are people empowered in the personal sense; there is no excuse for ignoring the brokenness of the human community. Accountability is increased since women are obliged to name clearly, unequivocally, and without fear even when it means exposing the limits of full humanity. Rather than romanticize women, we see how our authentic experiences, both positive and negative, serve to inspire future friends. Friendship implies a new way to think about our responsibility to participate in the divine-human matrix. Ours is not an outsized responsibility. It is a consequence of personal mortality. As Rosemary Ruether described this eschatology:

> We do not know what this means. It is beyond our power and our imagination. It is not then our direct responsibility. We can do nothing about the "immortal" dimension of our lives. It is not our calling to be concerned about the eternal meaning of our lives, and religion should not make this the focus of its message. Our responsibility is to use our temporal life span to create a just and good community for our generation and for our children. It is in the hands of Holy Wisdom to forge out of our finite struggle truth and being for everlasting life.[58]

Friendship is, finally, in the hands of Holy Wisdom, but we would be remiss if we did not name what we know and whom we love. That naming inspires new naming, beginning with ourselves.

2. *Women's friendships reveal something about one another.* We learn something about ourselves as loving and loveable persons through friendship, but we learn similar things about one another. In friendship we are forced to confront the sometimes ugly reality of human perversity, the devastating fact that humans, including some of our friends, are capable of the most horrendous torture and deception. This is not a pretty picture, but it is part of the picture that cannot be negated lest inspiration be misconstrued as always positive.

Being with friends is the clearest way to understand embodiment. How else could we be except in the finitude of our physical selves? This is why touch and communication are so crucial. We say things without words to friends. Gestures, glances, silence, smiles take on shared meaning with intimates. Sexual relations are usually most satisfying when carried out between close friends. A meal, sports, prayer, work, theater are all heightened in the company of friends.

Anna Quindlen captures some of the spirit of this when she writes about conversation between women friends:

> Most of the time we talked and talked, not in a linear way, but as though we were digging for buried treasure. Why did you feel that way? And what did you say then? What are you going to do about that? How long did it go on? It was an extended version of the ladies' lunches in which we bring our psyches out from inside our purses, lay them on the table and fold them up again after coffee.... [59]

This is what it means to take embodiment seriously, to acknowledge that women's experiences are radically contingent but can be and ought to be shared. It does not make them better or worse than men's, simply different and worthy of attention. But it does signal why so-called "girl talk" is so much maligned in a patriarchal society.

The putdown of women's conversations is a defensive, trivializing reaction against what it is imagined women must be saying to one another. It is "efficient" to dismiss such conversation as something unimportant rather than acknowledge that different embodied experiences will inevitably result in lacunae in communication between women and men. Most men's notion of "girl-talk" is most women's idea of "buried treasure." So much for universal experiences! This underscores the need for women's friendships to be explored on their own terms if anything meaningful is to be said of friendship as a whole. Men too will learn the seemingly unlearnable about women only when women speak on their own terms.

3. *Women's friendships reveal something about the natural order.* We are taught to think of friends as people with whom we can relate. But I am increasingly struck by women's experiences of nature that reveal deep connections with the nonhuman realm that many people have written off as unimportant. While I admit certain biases in favor of human beings, I have long been persuaded that animals, plants, and other living things have much to teach us. I am of course wary of a romanticized view of nature that links women to it as if there were some inextricable relationship, once again repeating the "biology is destiny" mistake. Likewise I have my doubts about approaches to animal rights that privilege the needs of animals over the material needs of people who are poor. But somewhere there is a middle ground, one that women stand on to be able to hold together what many men see as competing claims.[60] I suggest that our experiences of balancing friendships, i.e., the woman who balances friendship requirements for herself and her fetus when making a decision about reproduction, give us practice in upholding the importance of the natural order alongside of the human order.

It is often said that "man's best friend is his dog," something all too believable given how many men treat some of their human friends. While I have rarely heard it said that women's best friends are their cats, it is interesting to imagine what it would mean. For example, May Sarton has written about "the fur person." I know many cat lovers who are as devastated by the loss of their pets as they are by the loss of a parent or a spouse. But the point is that friendships with animals, and a friendly posture toward the rest of the created order that women have long championed, reveal something about the oneness of the cosmos. The gradual blurring of lines between human and animal life means increasing friendliness to both.

Our nonhuman friends teach us the necessity of developing distinctions that are not categorical. These distinctions take account of the nuances of differences between and among us rather than, as patriarchy would have it, the hierarchical prioritizing of humans over animals as God is over humans. We are compelled by our friendship with animals to the kind of animal liberation activities that denounce medical and pharmaceutical experiments on defenseless animals, that urge eating lower on the food chain, and that seek to evaluate animals' rights to life and limb alongside of humans'. These are basically friendly postures that are transforming the way in which we live.

Likewise, ecology is the act of befriending the earth and its inhabitants, guaranteeing for future generations access to the natural world that we have enjoyed. In some parts of this country it is considered a fad that will fade; in some parts of the world it is seen as First World guilt for having caused environmental damage to begin with. In any case, ecology is a way of embodying the friendship that the earth deserves.

What is revealed in this expression of friendship is the essential harmony of the natural order. Periodic disturbances, like hurricanes, tornados, and the like are equally natural albeit unfriendly. Our interaction with the earth and its inhabitants, both human and nonhuman, is a part of this harmony. When the harmony is broken, as it so often is, we know the unfriendly results. But when things are in harmony, as in a walk through the woods with a beloved pet or when a summer storm has just passed, there are glimpses of this friendship we call ecology.

4. *Friendships reveal something about the divine.* Irrational reactions to inclusive language about God/ess are a clue to what is being revealed about our friendship with the divine. When She is our Mother instead of our Father, common assumptions about the nature, relationship, and function of the divine are called into question. When He is Father and never Mother we sense the imbalance. Feminist theologians have been quick to point out that the deity has no gender. Linguistic conventions for referring to "it" are simply that. But the violent reaction that accrues when religious language is changed, e.g., those who proclaim that the Bible is being castrated when the text is rendered in inclusive language, reveals that some deep chord has been struck. Friendship with the divine, whether he, she, or it, is inspired by human friendship, and vice versa. This does not trivialize the divine nor elevate the human. It simply names friendship as the most adequate relational referent. As women begin to value friendships with women, the referent for divine-human friendship is given new content. It is, perhaps, too early to say how it is changing. But in a preliminary way it inspires new depths of friendship in both arenas.

This is more realistic than claiming that the divine is a many-breasted goddess whose goodness fairly oozes forth. Rather, as in all women's friendships, the potential for nurture and nastiness, comfort and challenge resides in all divine-human relationships. So, too, the divine friend surprises with Her revelations at times, inspiring humans to the same serendipity.

What then of inspiration? Women's friendships reveal something about ourselves, one another, the natural order and the divine that inspires anew. But what makes this inspiration and not simply some insight that could be disproved just as quickly? The simple answer is nothing, admitting that inspiration does not need to be something special that relies on belief or capitulation of will in order to be true. Rather, in the sense in which I am using the term, inspiration is obvious when it unveils some previously hidden data that will further humanize the world. This is what I claim women's friendships do.

These themes need to be probed as women's friendships are increasingly taken for granted. But the most telling characteristic, revealed simply in the act of taking women's friendships seriously, is justice. It is only *just* to lift up, name, and celebrate the bonds between and among women. It is only *just* to acknowledge love where it comes to rest. It is only *just* to recognize women's equality not only in the job market but among friends. It is only *just* to rectify the depravity and suffering that women experience at the hands of patriarchy. It is only *just* to acknowledge erotic love where it is. Justice, as I will stress later, is a hallmark of women's friendship. Glimpses of justice inspire action to assure more justice.

· 4 ·

Fierce Tenderness:
A Model for "Right Relation"

I was darning your socks
when waves of tenderness
took my arms.

Last night when you retold
the Sears and Roebuck joke
a storm of joy plowed up
your most trite phrases,
engraved and illuminated.

I burned your dinner
and it turned into incense.
Your name crashes
against my most fragile china.

I find myself
listening to your footsteps
after all these years.

—Patricia Ryan
"Vulnerable"

Model Making in Feminist Theology

The absence of substantive theological reflection on women's friendship is an invitation to develop some. Once we discover newly revealed insights, the usual theological reaction is to put them into a larger context, to seek some way to understand them in light of the larger faith tradition. My theological generation makes this contribution on the question of friendship. It is a way of taking seriously the feminist work that has been done. Instead of simply criticizing it in order to replace it with our own, as the male theological tradition developed, feminist theologians acknowledge debt and of course differences with other women and move on, constructing anew.

User-friendly theology is necessary if the medium is to reflect the message in this case. Fortunately, a theological approach to friendship with the patriarchal linear, historical, convoluted treatments simply does not measure up on women's terms. One is forced to look anew, confident that the sources can be evaluated just as critically and used just as carefully without falling into the old patterns.

Moreover, it would be counterproductive to try to ferret out of the theological literature sources for a linear exposition when in fact we are, as Anna Quindlen wrote, "digging for buried treasure." The temptation to insert women's experience into already existing models, however limited they may be, is a natural one. It would be easier, but it would lack the integrity that taking women's experiences on their own terms produces. In short, women's friendships, because they have not been considered rigorously before, allow a fresh approach to theologizing.

One promising approach that I propose is to listen creatively to women's experiences of friendship, then try to develop a model that will facilitate talking about and evaluating those experiences, and then use the model to do just that. This is constructive theology, literally building ways of thinking and acting. It will result in new social and personal norms approximating the intent of a faith community to live in "right relation" while maintaining traditional ties.[1] The norms, tried and tested over time, produce new experiences of friendship that challenge and reshape the model. This is a hermeneutic spiral approach, not simply a circle that repeats endlessly, but a spiral that encompasses more and more as it goes.[2]

This spiraling process produces dynamic, community-centered theologizing because it involves people in reflecting on their own lives using a referent that attracts them. It does not skimp on social scientific data nor on theological sources. It allows experiences, on their own terms, to be woven into the process of developing new norms. This process is not for the intellectually faint-hearted, nor for those who think that experiences alone should dictate. Rather, it is for communities that are open to experimenting without being awed into accepting novelty for its own sake. And above all it is for persons who find that the prevailing norms do not reflect their experiences. In this sense it fits women very well.

Model building is a crucial step in the process of changing norms because ethical inertia, or the path of least resistance, is the greatest single barrier to the development of new mores. People tend to teach and learn the easiest, most taken for granted norms, allowing exceptions to them rather than reconstructing the whole. Model building leaves people open to wholesale change.

It allows placing ethical decisions in a new light, replacing the ethical hooks that already exist with newly arranged ones. It allows persons and communities to move from well established but outmoded ethical assumptions to renewed ones. It alleviates the problem that arises when old norms are discarded without a mechanism for new ones to emerge. Clarity and inclusion, not chaos and discrimination, result.

For example, as lesbian/gay relationships are increasingly visible and accepted, a major issue is what ethical norms will guide such relationships. This is an appropriate question, one that lesbian/gay people ask. It is not enough to say that all is now permissible where nothing used to be allowed. Nor must indiscretions be emphasized as the transition takes place from heterosexism to relational justice. There are simply plenty of new ethical questions to ask and plenty of new people asking them. This is what it means to be involved in a spiral process where one answer leads to new questions and questioners.

What about age differences, multiple partners, casual sexual encounters? Old models that condemn homosexuality out of hand are not helpful here. But neither is it fair to leave a large segment of the population without moral anchors, indeed to leave everyone with the impression that there are no lesbian/gay sexual ethical parameters. That there are, and that they may differ from and influence the existing ones based on heterosexual relationships, is something that will come about only by trying on or experimenting with various approaches. The proposed method is intended to facilitate that process.

Theology must be clear and accessible if it is to be useful. Much of patriarchal theology relies on terse arguments to persuade or cajole, sometimes even to bore the audience into agreement with a particular position. This repels many people who have theological concerns, but who are put off by the esoteric ways in which questions are handled. They feel that they are marginalized by those who control ethical reflection through privatized language, by those who revert to degrees or position (e.g. minister, professor, etc.), by those who generate fear. So much for a participatory process. Theology was not meant to be inclusive, we are told, and certainly not of people who will raise substantive questions.

Feminist work in theology proves on the other hand that there are a variety of ways to reflect the values and meaning systems of a community. These ways are inclusive of persons, especially persons who are not theological professionals, encouraging them to ask and answer questions of ultimate meaning and value. Thus the resulting insights and syntheses are faithful to a larger group's experience and not simply to the demands of an ever more erudite guild.

This is why I am proposing a model that emerges from various women's experiences. Readers can refine, reshape, even reject the model if necessary. It is also why I limit my claims to what emerges from my white, middle-class, U.S.-based context since I do not pretend to encompass all experiences nor do I assume rampant consistency between/among women. Such a modest starting point, far from weakening the finished product prematurely, reflects the fact that theology is intended to be an interactive art, a participatory science, indeed a communal undertaking. As such no formulation is perfect, but of course some are more adequate than others. The point is to keep, as it were, friendly relations that result in many conversations, only the sum of which will approximate any usable generalizations.

The many sources necessary for feminist theological discourse include letters, journals, songs, Scripture, poems, novels, paintings, sculpture, even dreams, in addition to the traditional philosophical, psychological, sociological, economic, theological, and historical sources understood from a critical feminist perspective. Liturgy and ritual carry the message of what is ultimately meaningful and valuable for a faith group. The lack of them in the case of friendship is a deeply felt loss that I address in the next chapter.

The "digging" that characterizes women's friendships needs a framework, a starting point, and some limits within which the looking takes place. It needs a model. Model making is an important form of feminist theological discourse. It is a way of presenting a schema or an outline that is a heuristic device, something that helps in the learning process. It is not a magic formula for making things so. Nor is it a way to confine or limit experiences. It simply helps out in the search for ways to live in right relation by clarifying and pulling together various elements.

The model itself is up for discussion. Its function is to get such sharing started and to guide it along. I caution against rejecting the model prematurely before the substance of what it has to offer is explored. Still I encourage refinement and development if/when the model is inadequate to the experiences in question.

Models are difficult because they can convey the impression that anything that does not fit into them is somehow odd or unusual. While this may be so, I insist that the model itself emerge from a set of experiences of friendship and that it be used to discuss and evaluate some others. The resultant refinements can be incorporated into a new model. Such a dynamic process should not be used as an excuse to say that the model itself is so pliable as to be without merit. On the contrary, the very flexibility of the model is what guarantees that it is actually being shaped by as well as shaping the experiences at hand. We are not used to such elasticity, which is rare in a patriarchal context. Only use of this model will prove its resilience. Such a flexible way of thinking is refreshing in itself.

Background of the Model

Where does a model come from and what assurance do we have that it represents women's friendships adequately? Obviously it is the fruit of a variety of sources, but it begins with the insight of feminist ethicist Eleanor Hume Haney about the centrality of friendships for women:

> To make friendship central is both to transform the power relations that most often hold between individuals, groups and people and the earth, and to be a participant in that transformation.[3]

Marriage and childbirth, often touted as the peak experiences for women, are not necessarily the organizing aspects of women's affective lives. My contention is that friendships, especially friendships with women, more often function as the central relational experience for women. Of course some women's friendships are with men, especially with husbands or male lovers. But ever so often one hears a woman say, "I'm married to Dave, but my best friend is Donna," or, "I would never dream of telling Bob, but Pamela and I were talking about...." Letty Cottin Pogrebin notes:

> True friendship is rare between women and men because sex separatism is so rigorously ingrained during childhood. Most parents rear male

and female children as though preparing them to live in two different worlds.... Before they reach school age girls and boys have become strangers to one another, with incompatible play habits, different ideas of fun and few grounds for friendship.[4]

She goes on to describe the long-term impact of this conditioning:

Gender hierarchies are not conducive to friendship. Sex can flourish between unequals, and love can thrive between them, but friendship requires equality. Unlike love, it cannot be unilateral or unrequited. Unlike sex it cannot be imposed. Friendship must be mutual.[5]

The implications of this insight for women are quite different than for men. In heterosexual patriarchy male bonding reigns supreme. But male bonding is not what I mean by friendship. In the same context many women's friendships are denied, ignored, or thwarted. Economic, political, psychological, and other differences between the genders result in the fact that women find it difficult to be friends with men and vice versa. This is not new. But in order to change it new models of mutuality are needed, modes that I suggest are now more readily found between women friends. Only by highlighting and examining them will we learn what we need to know to improve the quality of female-male friendships and male-male ones.

Inequality is a function of what Lois Kirkwood calls "structural enemyhood."[6] This same dynamic is at play between and among persons of different classes, races, sexual preferences, ages, and nationalities. Friendship is not a panacea, a cure-all for social ills. But it is an important step in that process for two reasons. First, it has the potential to link persons who are, for practical purposes, structural enemies. For example, women of different racial/ethnic groups do form friendships despite barriers. Second, friendship provides the motivation for friends to change social structures because of their commitments to each other. These same women, for example, rely on their bonds to keep struggling for racial equality and to deal honestly with each other in the meantime.

By contrast, the patriarchal model is based on Aristotle's view, although he argued as if such barriers did not play an important role.[7] His treatment is considered definitive by many who have written theology and philosophy on the topic. He considered friendship something that decreased in quality as it increased in quantity; the more intense the friendship, the fewer people with whom it was possible to enjoy it. Aristotle's approach makes a certain logical sense, given patriarchal time and energy constraints. But there is more to the theory than meets the eye. He envisioned three kinds of friendship, the first two of which were based on usefulness and pleasure, the third on goodness. We could call them acquaintances, companions, and intimates respectively for purposes of discussion although our modern terms do not translate exactly. Nonetheless, the dynamics of Aristotle's position is clear.

We have many acquaintances with whom we work, shop, and do business, according to this view. They are a necessary part of our relational landscapes. They provide what is useful to the common good. Utility, then, and not love, mark acquaintances according to Aristotle. A second kind of friends is what Aristotle would call companions, those few and far between persons who know us well and with whom we share a certain intimacy. Aristotle indicated that having many of these is not likely, having a few is usual. Pleasure or mutual attraction is the prime link for companions. A third kind of friendship, the highest according to Aristotle's relational hierarchy, is intimates. One or two persons in a lifetime come along who are "most completely friends, since each loves the other for what the other is in himself [sic] and not for something he has about him which he need not have."[8] These friendships are based on mutual goodness and the desire to respond in kind to that goodness.

In Aristotle's day only men could be the intimate friends of one another. Marriage, that is, romantic marriage as we now understand it, was a relationship of a much later period. But Aristotle claimed that "the friendship of father for son is not the same as that of son for father, nor that of husband for wife the same as that of wife for husband."[9] These are relationships of unequal persons in his scheme.

Commentators are divided on the point, but I conclude from the text that women's experiences were not intended to be taken into account when describing friendships. Rather than simply writing this off as a sign of the times and then adding women's experience to the Aristotelian model as if they should have been there in the first place, I propose that this is precisely why a new model is necessary. To evaluate women's friendship, women's experiences must be factored into the development of the very categories in use. This is precisely what is lacking in current efforts to think about friendship that rely fundamentally on Aristotle. Given that virtually all Christian ethical reflection on friendship is predicated on the insights of Aristotle, there is no choice but to begin anew if women's experiences are to be part of what shapes the hermeneutic.

Aristotle's hierarchical model of friendship was not only a product of male experiences, but worse, limited to men in its scope. I am not suggesting that this invalidates it completely. Rather, I am suggesting that because it is the prime philosophical referent for most theological treatments of friendship it is inadequate to evaluate women's experiences. A new model is needed.

Only when the insights generated by this new model have been integrated can we begin to explore human experience. However, I counsel against premature enthusiasm for such a project until the dynamics of women's friendships have been absorbed thoroughly in society.

A similar point will be made later in exploring *ekklēsia*, the Greek word that is translated "church." It was based on a civil model that involved free, male citizens who gathered to vote for all in the polis.[10] Women-church is a way to discuss a "discipleship of equals" from a feminist perspective because only by adding women to the concept of church is there the potential for equality.[11] It is simply too early to imagine what a fully human church might look like. Ironically, "women-church" includes men since their experiences are reflected in what it means to say "church," whereas "church" excludes women since their experiences are not a part of the mix. I hope my model of fierce tenderness will be useful for men as well as women since it emerges from a context in which male experiences are normative. Aristotle's model was so partial as to exclude women's experiences; my model is sufficiently broad to encompass men's.

Aristotle's position is based on and results in an ideological ignoring or passing over of women's experiences. Admittedly it is based on an anthropology different from what is currently accepted. But it makes a new model of theologizing necessary, a model based on the renewed sense of how women and men function in our society if the philosophical and theological referents for friendship are taken into account.

Female and male experiences are not *totally* different. Women often experience the phenomenon of "best friends." For example, Barbara Ehrenreich writes in favor of "the revival of a fine old institution."[12] But even she has a different twist on the topic:

> When I was thinking through this column — out loud of course, with a very good friend on the phone — she sniffed, "So what exactly do you want — formal, legalized friendships, with best-friend licenses and showers and property settlements in case you get in a fight over the sweaters you've been borrowing from each other for the past ten years?"

No, of course not, because the beauty of best friendship, as opposed to, say, marriage, is that it's a totally grass-roots creative effort that requires no help at all from the powers-that-be.[13]

Her view lacks a sensitivity to the experience of women whose best friends are women, i.e., lesbian women who are interested in legal changes to reflect the family relationship that committed lesbian couples experience. Property and inheritance laws discriminate blatantly against same-sex friends as opposed to cross-gender friends who have the right to marry and all that it entails. Hospital visitation rights for lovers and decision-making over the life/death of a same-gender companion must be handled by business-like arrangements (e.g., durable power of attorney, power of attorney for health care, etc.) rather than by the social recognition of an intentional relationship, i.e., friendship. Nonetheless, Ehrenreich's position reflects the fact that women's experiences in heterosexist patriarchy are sufficiently different from men's that simply trying to fit them into an Aristotelian model is futile.

Even best friends for women are different from what Aristotle had in mind as revealed in his texts. They are confidants as well as critics, companions as well as challengers. Whether friends are good, better, or best is not the issue. The point is that women friends, lots of them, are necessary for women's survival in an often unfriendly environment.

Survival of women and their dependent children is the foundation of a "womanist" approach to ethics and theology. Delores S. Williams points out that the survival needs of women and dependent children are primary in an unjust society that she refers to as "demonarchy."[14] Demonarchy is "the demonic governance of black women's lives by white male and white female ruled systems using racism, violence, violation, retardation, and death as instruments of social control."[15] It is "a traditional and collective expression of white government in relation to black women. It belongs to the realm of normalcy."[16]

In such a setting Aristotle's prioritizing of friends is futile if not counterproductive. Survival is contingent on joining forces of all kinds of justice-seeking friends. Williams's view is far more realistic, intuitive, and politically useful than Aristotle's for most women. It is a view that informs my proposed model.

Of course there are those friends who are more intimate than others. But the point is that survival needs demand a horizontal reaching out to those who will help. Only ruling-class men whose survival is not in question have the dubious luxury of looking up and down at their friends, companions, and acquaintances. Most women simply do not. Nor do women consider it a desirable approach since far more is lost than gained. Living in "right relation" does not permit hierarchy.

The Aristotelian model is the major inherited philosophical source in the Western Christian tradition for dealing with friendship, in fact for making sense of most relationships. Thus, ethical decisions about, for example, sexuality are made on a quantitative basis following Aristotle: how much, how far, how many. Family ties are counted in this way — degrees of consanguinity, number of spouses, seemingly endless opportunities to have children, how many grandchildren. A feminist model of friendship, deeply influenced by the womanist perspective of Williams and others, suggests something quite different. It is a qualitative approach for which a bit more background will be helpful before exploring the model. What is striking is that women do not seem preoccupied by the number, duration, and level of their friends as Aristotle would have it. Women's concerns focus on the quality of *each* relationship and its place in the whole picture. Two examples help to make this clear.

First, political commentator Mary McGrory departed from her usually objective style in an article to describe a person who "was to friendship what Jane Austen was to the novel and Leonardo da Vinci to painting."[17] This is not faint praise from McGrory, whose usual tough, no-nonsense approach gave way to a moving tribute to her dear friend Nance MacDonald: "Her genius was for friendship, 'those relations one chooses for oneself.'"[18] Note in the definition that she places no limit on the number of such friendships nor on their duration. She implies no hierarchy and insists on no formula. Still she provides a credible definition, one that captures the essence of this voluntary association that is fierce tenderness.

In McGrory's brief essay the fierce tenderness of her friendship with Nance is revealed. Love between them, and indeed with their third, "our other inseparable friend," is palpable in the piece. Friendships come in plural, McGrory implies, the more the merrier. She goes on to describe how power between/among those friends ebbed and flowed as Nance's illness slowly brought her life to a halt. Still her dignity was intact; she never gave up her poise, prizing her physical appearance and control to the end. Her friends made sure of it. One even wrote about it to preserve it, like a friendship quilt, forever. Embodiment is obvious as the friends travel, picnic, shop, and deal with the inevitable, death. Mary McGrory insists that even while her friend was ill, she never came empty-handed: "her basket overflowed with goodies like fresh-baked lemon squares," reminding us that the physical manifestations of friendship are what signal attention.[19] This is what I mean by the spiritual dimension of friendship.

Spirituality takes a little detective work, as the term is so often reserved for the religious realm. But it is fair to say that Mary McGrory is making a statement about it when she recalls the final conversation with her friend Nance. When she was ill Nance did not want to receive someone who came to care for her because she felt that she was not up to entertaining! Mary McGrory asked in wonder, "Nannie, what are friends for?" She concluded that "no one knew better than Nance MacDonald."[20] This is what it means to make claims about the quality of life from the perspective of fierce tenderness, to affirm the choices friends make and to appreciate their attention.

A second example that outlines the method I propose is found in a letter by a teacher, Dorothy Haecker, to her student Elizabeth.[21] This complicated relationship, which symbolizes so many others (therapist-client, minister-parishioner, lawyer-client, doctor-patient), is fraught with the problems of unequal power and vulnerable love. Dorothy Haecker handles both with aplomb by reminding her student that "I've looked at you, and you've looked back: the ever changing, ever possible mirroring that women of all ages and stations and experiences can do with each other."[22] Would that all mentors handled their friends with such style.

She admits that the classroom is an atmosphere where much change takes place:

> How can we not come to identify with each other in all of this? In you, I walk over ground I have travelled well, but this time with your eyes, heart, and mind as company...I think you walk over new ground with me as company. I think you depend on my sense of your possibilities....[23]

Her grasp on the fine line that runs between love and power, her careful nurture of her student *and of herself* shows how these treacherous but treasured relationships can be made into the stuff of deep friendship without violating the integrity of the persons involved. It takes maturity and consideration, but most of all attention. Unfortunately these qualities are not always present in sufficient measure to keep professional lines clear. Too often the boundaries are crossed with disastrous results, for example the sexual abuse by clergypeople of their parishioners that Rev. Marie Marshall Fortune decries.[24]

Dorothy Haecker deals with embodiment in the same vein by acknowledging her student's dream about her ever so gracefully: "You are utterly special to me. I am graced by your courageous dreams, and have, as you see, dreamed up a reply."[25] It is a subtle affirmation of the attention she receives without overstepping necessary boundaries for professional work. Both teacher and student are affirmed. Neither is violated nor indulged.

She handles the choices about the quality of life, what I call spirituality, by inviting her student to release her from the pedestal and let each of them "come back to our selves."[26] Only then can the learning and teaching that go on for each of them be released. It is fierce and tender. They are women friends, modeling for others how such complicated dynamics can work justly.

Broken down in this way the letter sounds almost trite. But the impact of reading the whole "Letter to a Friend" is powerful. What is remarkable is how gracefully Dorothy Haecker is able to weave a friendship of integrity in so challenging a relationship as that of teacher and student. Hers is a model for many who have failed in their attempts, a beacon for those who are just beginning to make sense of such highly charged opportunities. She proves that it can be done with style. Elizabeth's reply, that the reader can only imagine, would, I suspect, confirm this. Of course, the student's approach and issues would differ due to her circumstances, but in time their positions may be reversed. This is how friendship works.

These two examples make clear the kind of material I draw upon to propose a model of "right relation." The reader will note that my proposed model is not hierarchical, nor does it differentiate by gradation or degree the importance of various friendships. Some may see this as a flaw, which I deal with subsequently under "Shortcomings of the Model." But I contend that it reflects women's experiences of variety and diversification in friendships. It is an affirmation that the same dynamics and necessities attend friendships with family members as with employees even though there are obvious differences in longevity and intention.

Introducing the Model

The model I propose is made up of four elements: love, power, embodiment, and spirituality. Each of these four elements is present in women's friendships, albeit to differing degrees depending on the persons and circumstances. Other elements are present as well, some of which might fruitfully be added to this model. But these four elements provide at least a bare outline of a friendship. It is around these four that we can cluster other components as they emerge. It is on the basis of these that we understand the relational dynamics and that we name a particular relationship a friendship and another one something else. The working definition of friendship is refined by these four elements, inviting us to see the commonalities of relational experience and the differences in degrees of actualizing the various components.

When the four elements are present in harmony we see a friendship that works well. It is something like listening to a singer with a well-tuned piano played skillfully by her long-time accompanist in an acoustically advanced hall. This kind of friendship, like such a musical event, is as much a matter of luck as of planning. It is as much a gratuitous event as something that can be staged. But when it happens, and a friendship works, everyone seems to know it. It generates something new for both persons and for the larger community of which they are a part. *Generativity is the hallmark of friendship.*

When a friendship does not work, when there is stress, tension, discord, even the threat of breaking off the relationship, it is because these same four elements are present but out of balance. This results in destruction of the persons involved. There is a loss of energy for the community. Everyone knows that, too.

The model looks like this:

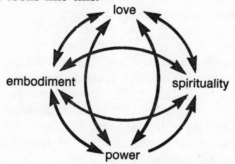

The primary danger of such a model is the temptation to reduce everything to fit it, to reduce complex components into easily reconcilable elements. No such reduction is intended here as the explanation of the elements that follows will illustrate. I choose to run that risk however by even presenting a model since its usefulness far outweighs the danger.

Another problem inherent in this model for friendship is the temptation to mechanize what is finally a mysterious experience. Why Susy loves Deb and not Joan, why Martina is Anne's friend is something that no model can ever reveal. Still, the usefulness of the model outweighs even this concern because it allows friends to see their relationships not under a microscope that distorts but in the light of what women's friendships reveal.

Working Definitions of the Components

These four components have emerged from a variety of women's friendships made known through first-person accounts, literature and films, letters, counselling, and more, all filtered through my experiences. I make no claim for their universality, especially insofar as particular dimensions like race, sex, class, age, nationality, sexual preference make a difference. But I offer them as a way to stimulate conversation on the topic, as a way to streamline and systematize data in order to ask and answer questions of ultimate meaning and value, i.e., to theologize about friendship from a feminist perspective.

Love

No one has come up with a satisfactory definition of love. Or if anyone claims to I would worry that it is the ethical equivalent of buying medicine water off the back of a wagon. But there must be some working definition for a model of this sort.

I venture to say that for women friends *love is an orientation toward the world as if my friend and I were more united than separated, more at one among the many than separate and alone.* Love is the intention to recognize this drive toward unity and to make it increasingly so over time. Love is the commitment to deepen in unity without losing the uniqueness of the individuals at hand. It is the force of attraction that generates something new out of a unity that is somehow separate from and beyond the two. Even in trying to describe it words are limited.

For example, having a child, whether through heterosexual intercourse, adoption, or self-insemination is a common expression of love. However, it is by no means the only nor necessarily the best expression. Friends can form a business, throw a party, build a house, collaborate on a project, take part in a social movement, and experience a similar generative energy found in bringing forth children. I do not mean to downgrade the importance of having children, nor to equate human life with anything trivial. But I do mean to expand the notion of generativity to include the many things that come forth from this same experience of unity in diversity.

Power

The word "power" scares some people who have experienced only the abuse of power. But power is present in every friendship whether we recognize it or not. *Power is the ability to make choices for ourselves, for our dependent children, and with our community.* Power is usually considered to be the privilege of a few. But it is increasingly clear that many who deny the existence of power are only denying participation in dynamics of relationship that exist regardless of the name we give to them.

Power dynamics are complex because they are found at the intersection of social/structural power and personal/individual power. For example, we say that racism, classism, ageism, sexism, and heterosexism are part of the power equation in our society. We talk about individuals who have power or are powerful, people who are charismatic, with strong personalities. What is difficult about assessing power in relationships is that both of these sets of factors are at play simultaneously.

The first, social/structural power, takes careful study. To understand how abuses of power, what I call injustice, mutilate human community it is necessary to see the world through the eyes of those who struggle to survive. This is what the Latin American Catholic bishops so aptly named "a preferential option for the struggling poor." Justice-seeking friends attempt to transform structural powers. Most of us live in the midst of such dynamics. It is on the basis of these structures that choices about taking power and relinquishing, giving up or sharing power are made.[27] Empowerment is called for. But it would be a mistake, "cheap grace," to move too quickly to empowerment without recognizing power for what it is, namely, the enviable and achievable ability to choose for oneself and within one's community of accountability. We are a long way from such a goal either personally or politically, but it is useful to have a positive definition of empowerment to move toward.

The second sort of power is personal/individual. This power is an equally complex interplay of psychological, sociological, economic, and unaccounted for factors. Even after years of psychological analysis it is not clear that we will ever know exactly how early childhood, much less prenatal experiences, have influenced what is called personality. Some things are obvious, of course, like the impact of an alcoholic parent or the presence of a nurturing adult. Experiences that inhibit or build self-confidence become clear quite early. But all of the analysis imaginable will not finally deduce the recipe for personal power or for the lack of it.

Still, personal power is a significant factor in friendships and one that, as the examples will make clear, is often the most difficult to fathom. Personal power, when set in a social structure, results in the complex factors I am labelling simply "power."

Friendship is that relationship in which empowerment and relinquishment are most likely to take place. It is the setting in which the exchange of power and the transformation of power dynamics will be stimulated. Equally, friendships often come to an abrupt halt when power differences go unrecognized, unchallenged, and finally unchanged.

Embodiment

Early discussions of these dynamics found me using the word "sexuality" or "sex" for what I now call "embodiment." But the confused, awkward, and sometimes overly interested response I got to this one element cued me to a problem. Sometimes interest in the sexual dimension was so high that the other dynamics were passed over. This convinced me that it is central and that a less loaded term like "embodiment" would do the same job while avoiding some of the pitfalls.[28] However, let there be no mistake about what I mean. Sex between friends needs serious and sustained discussion.

This physical dynamic of women's friendship refers to the fact that *virtually everything we do and who we are is mediated by our bodies.* Whether we touch, mime, eat, cuddle, exercise, talk, play, make love, comfort, imbibe, relax, watch movies, massage, pray, sleep, or celebrate, virtually every relational act is a physical event, something that is influenced directly by our bodies. To call humans embodied beings borders on the redundant, but it must be stressed in feminist theology to make up for the centuries of disembodied writings that have shaped the Christian ethical tradition.

This is a necessary step toward changing our ethical norm from heterosexual marriage to friendship, from an exclusive focus on bodies that are married to an inclusive understanding of the deeply significant extent to which all friends relate in an embodied way. Giles Milhaven makes a similar point, emphasizing the physical but refusing to be limited to genital sexual expression in his description of falling asleep with another person.[29]

This is made clear when persons who are physically disabled remind those of us who are temporarily able-bodied (as they refer to us so wisely since it is a thin line of chance that separates us) that our bodies are not to be taken for granted. Civil society must be transformed to assure equal access (for example, closed captioning on television news for the hearing impaired, explanations at the theater for the visually impaired, public transportation made accessible for those who have mobility impairments). It is embodied beings who are friends.

Embodiment reflects access to the goods of the earth. For example, proper nutrition is still, regrettably, a privilege, not a right. The same applies to health care, leisure time for exercise, rest, vacations, and sports facilities. Inhumane physical work that can result in a series of environmentally caused illnesses and even death (e.g., black lung disease, certain cancers, high blood pressure caused by stress) is a reminder of embodiment. It is an inescapable aspect of being human and one that friends cannot avoid.

All of these factors influence friendship. They make it the case that some people will live longer than others because of the circumstances of their embodiment, e.g., in Western culture most women live longer than men, white people longer than African Americans. Choices about how we will share our bodies in friendship reflect a concern for the entire human family. For example, the choice to have a child influences a wide circle of friends. The choice to take up a sport or to travel or to move all have concrete implications for friends. This is part of responsible friendship. This is what it means to say that friendship is a political commitment.

It is equally the case that at times we simply hurl caution to the wind and relate to one another in fully embodied abandon. This is best exemplified by the physical passion of sexual expression. Much has been written, especially with the AIDS pandemic, about safer sex practices and the need for caution in the exchange of bodily fluids. Young people are given stern warnings about sex causing death. While this is all true and necessary, more needs to be said about the positive aspects of safer sex even in the face of AIDS. One cannot overemphasize the goodness of physically expressed love at a time when reactionary forces deny it.

Pleasure for its own sake needs to be understood in a culture that has made people feel guilty about any kind of enjoyment. Of course this must be done within the parameters of responsible relating. But in the face of negative media on sex, it is the job of moral theology to stress the goodness and creativity of pleasure. This is after all the essence of embodiment, enjoying the *choice* to love and be loved in the fullness of physical selves.

I am the first to insist on safer sex practices and on sex education programs, especially for young people. I am equally insistent on the virtue of pleasure. Further, I consider sexual expression a human right for everyone, not a privilege reserved for those who will bear children in heterosexual marriage. Thus, sex between friends, if/when both are consenting, careful, and committed to the well-being of themselves and one another, has everything to recommend it.

The proposed model helps to sort out the many ways in which embodiment is at play in friendship. But most of all it encourages the frank and honest acceptance of embodiment, indeed the celebration of human beings as incarnate beings who make choices. Women friends teach this to one another. Women touch, cuddle, embrace, kiss, comfort, massage, make love, pat, prod, and otherwise show feelings in a physical way without the degree of homophobic embarrassment that limits most men to distance or athletic, buddy-like behavior. This is worth teaching children of both sexes.

Women are learning to reject the media hypes about body images that have led so many to feelings of inadequacy or worse. No one is tall, thin, light, young, pretty enough to conform to the pale, nearly anorexic cult of youth and slenderness that dominates fashion magazines. This is exaggerated male fantasy to which some women quite literally succumb. We need other women's help to reject it as the unhealthy trap that it is. Friends reinforce a sense of what is possible and desirable given the great variety that heredity, environment and individual makeups combine to produce as human beings. Friends love each other just as we are embodied. Friends encourage one another to love themselves, to achieve healthy, integrated embodiment.

A friend of mine once observed, "All women are beautiful." She captured in a phrase what so many feminist writers on the subject of body image and feelings have attempted to convey.[30] Getting women to believe this is another task. But the reaction to my friend's remark by some women who had previously believed the media myths and found themselves wanting was one of gratitude. It is a stark reminder to take ourselves more seriously than we take the media, not an easy task when media messages prevail.[31]

One does not check one's body at the door when one enters into friendship. And what are friends for if not to delight and be delights for the senses? Attention to embodiment in woman-centered terms is a challenge to a society that is both misogynist and homophobic.

Spirituality

I include "spirituality" as a component of the model even though I am wary of it. It has come to mean everything and therefore to mean nothing. Usages that border on "the spirituality of popcorn" or the "spirituality of gardening" make me nervous. I appreciate the sentiment but reject the imprecision. Let me clarify what I mean by "spirituality," lest anyone derive a less than rigorous definition from my usage.

Spirituality in my model means *making choices about the quality of life for oneself and for one's community.* Admittedly this is not the definition some would think of first. But it is one that reflects my conviction that the religious impulse toward meaning and value is expressed in very concrete ways. It is attention to the many options that exist to influence the way in which we live regardless of how long we live. It is attention to quality, not quantity.

Spirituality, privatized and sanitized by contemporary expressions that aim at easy slogans and sound like a religious version of psycho-babble, are what I oppose. Of course it is easy to imagine that extending the vaunted word "spirituality" to something as mundane as friendship will strike some as an exercise in futility. I contend that this definition of spirituality as a concern for quality corresponds with the best of the Western Christian tradition. Fasting, for example, is a choice about how to use one's body. A vegetarian diet is a way to attend to the animal world. Meditation is a way to focus on a limited sphere in order to move beyond it. In this sense, spirituality is used legitimately to describe some of the New Age efforts to return to the attentiveness of the past.

Spirituality is part of an intentional, accountable process of making choices that affects the whole community. I do not mean trivial choices like among various colors for a dress or the flavor of ice cream one prefers. Rather, I mean attending to the way in which people recall their faith history, bury their dead, and make religiously based social change. I mean attention to films, music, and theater, knowing that our support makes some and not others possible. Spirituality is expressed in the encouragement a society provides for the arts and for political change groups, all of which affect the quality of life individually and in community. While it may seem that spirituality in this sense is hopelessly broad, just like what I have critiqued, I mean to underscore its scope and importance. Before moving to concrete examples from which the model flows and for which it is useful, let me suggest some preliminary insights that emerge from the model itself, regardless of the particular ways in which it illuminates individual examples.

Preliminary Insights from the Model

The model reveals and reflects certain givens about friendship. One is that *friendship is available to everyone*, from the tiny baby to the oldest, sickest member of the human community. Nothing about the model demands that friends be of the same sex or of the same race, of the same age or of the same class or ethnic background.

Nothing in the model assumes that there is one guiding relationship, nor any special formula for a relationship that has priority over all others. For example, the family relationship and heterosexual marriage are usually taken as normative with everything else being seen as a kind of relational also-ran. But nothing in the model indicates that this must be so. To the contrary, the model is sufficiently flexible to include a variety of relationships that obtain between friends.

The model does not limit the possibility of one friendship far outdistancing the rest in importance. Neither does it call for the prioritization of one kind of friendship over all others. Put another way, it allows for best friends but does not make them the essence of the experience. Of course in practice we find that certain friends take on greater centrality, at least for a time. But there is nothing inherent in this model of friendship that determines *a priori* that one form of relationship must be valued above all others.

My approach suggests that a friendly attitude toward all of creation is possible. Particular friends are instances of greater intensity of the four elements rather than some special category available in a certain measure. This is why some people choose or find themselves in a one-to-one residential relationship with another person. Others, for reasons as varied as the persons involved, find that their relational needs are met by various people without living with any one of them. Still others find value in living with a group while focusing attention on one or two friends.

This model does not presume that heterosexual marriage, or even homosexual coupling that seems to have everything except the legal and religious approval of society, is the pinnacle of human relating. Nor does it assume that a celibate commitment lived out in a community of friends is only for emotionally immature persons. Rather, it gives a framework in which to understand the dynamics of these many experiences in order to understand them on their own terms through many women's eyes. Men will find parallels in their own experience as well as deep differences. Priority is given to those who are most directly affected so that judgments will not be made from an outside, disinterested stance. In fact, judgments should be few and far between, letting experiences speak for themselves.

The model cannot be said to encourage promiscuity. Neither does it automatically demean sexual variety as the stuff of fickleness. I have learned too much from the usually condemned relationships of those who are not in monogamous commitments to write these off without examination. Likewise, young people, those who have lost a close friend or spouse, all who are not coupled as heterosexist, patriarchal society and church would have it, do not deserve to be condemned out of hand because their friendships are expressed sexually. Nor do they need to be told that a monogamous committed relationship is the essence of human interaction for which they should strive. They deserve to be respected and learned from all the same.

I propose with this model that the shoe ought really to be moved to the other foot. The most adequate and meaningful relational possibility, namely, friendship and not marriage, is available to all of us. Once we make that shift from the limited option of marriage to the unlimited possibilities of friendship we will have a common frame of reference within which to locate the many ways in which people find relational fulfillment without insisting on one certain form for everyone.

The proposed model simply reflects the components of friendship and assumes that they are present albeit in different configurations in all friendships in one way or another. It lets the friendships themselves tell the rest of the story to those who have ears to hear. There is no need to name a new relational norm as such. There is no lack of role models. Friendships that endure, excite, and edify are available even if they have previously been obscured. This is what Janice Raymond points out about genealogies of female friendship. There is plenty of data if it is recognized as such.

The model also highlights the fact that *friendships are ambiguous and fluid*. There is no place on the model where a friendship can be pinned down finally. It does not reside in the center where the lines cross nor in that little interstice that is the overlap of all of the various elements. Rather, friendship is found in the dynamic process that is pictured. Friendships have all of the complications and messiness that the diagram depicts, as well as all of the simplicity.

Without one of the partners, friendship does not exist. But simply having both people blithely assuming such a relationship is not enough either. There must be some intentionality, some orienting of feeling and action toward the other, some attentiveness. There must also be a context in which friendships can flourish. These dynamics can often differ so widely between the two as to cause irreparable splits or prevent bonding altogether. But that is the luck of the draw as much as something that can be programmed. Ethical behavior must take this capriciousness into account.

Friendships change, but the experience is just as real when it is over or when it has receded into memory as it was in its full flower. For example, people talk about friends whom they liked when they were in grade school. One says, "Colleen was my best friend" without implying that she is no longer important simply because the intensity of friendship has waned. What is meant is that she is an important part of a friendship history, someone with whom one "practiced" friendship even though not a close friend today.

What I experience now as friendship incorporates that childhood reality. Rather than obliterating the youthful experience as if it were not the fullness of friendship, "the real thing," it is integrated. Of course it was at a different moment in life when different capacities for love, power, embodiment, and spirituality were brought to bear. Friendships happen and are expressed differently at various life stages and cannot be separated from them. People can teach and learn friendship, and every friendship is in some measure practice for the next one. It is a reason why friendship is never really a singular experience, but one that always incorporates past friendships and prepares the way for friends to come. Not all of the experiences are happy; we bring those dimensions with us as well. But all have an impact.

This model also shows that *friendships are qualitative experiences, not quantitative ones.* Criteria for relational excellence shifts. But quantitative measures like longevity, heterosexuality (recall that Kinsey's widely used scale is a measure of sexual preference on a quantitative basis from how heterosexual to how homosexual), and monogamy will be replaced by qualitative measures. Qualitative criteria are more difficult to assess. Factors such as compatibility, fidelity, and generativity can be applied to a variety of relationships with far more just results, though measuring them requires creativity. Friendship will speak for itself as in a powerful observation made by one of the guests at the commitment ceremony of a lesbian couple: "Annie, you are the reason for a smile of uncommon radiance on Lynnae's face." The model does not measure anything. It simply brings to attention what exists, and by so doing helps to encourage friends to intensify the experience within the limits of their possibilities.

For example, longevity, while desirable for friendship, is by no means the definitive measure of its success. Legion are the number of marriages (friends can be married!) that endure and endure and endure long after the quality has become so thin as to render it nothing more than an emotional distance race. Staying together "for the children's sake" has often modeled a very negative example of friendship for the children. While such breakups of families are never easy, and while the divorce rate shows that they are frequent occurrences, they do provide children with a realistic perspective on friendship insofar as every friendship does not last forever. Loss and new starts are a part of life, although a painful, uncertain, and difficult part.

Women friends experience the same dynamic, albeit minus society's structure of divorce. Careful attention should be paid to the way such female friendships break up and often emerge in new forms. For example, the effort by lovers to become friends is frequently noted in lesbian circles, something that men and women who break up their partnerships/marriages might learn from and imitate. On the other hand, such splits are often so painful as to need distance between the former friends, something that divorce usually signals.

Similarly, there are fleeting experiences of friendship. People who meet travelling and share some significant part of the world together will often refer to each other as friends. After the experience is over there may not be conditions for an ongoing relationship. For example, distance may intervene. But that does not mean that there was no friendship at one time. Likewise, there may be an attempt to deepen the initial bond, never losing sight of the original overture. The Western tendency is to measure friendship by time, and inevitably find a brief encounter wanting. The satisfaction of endless shared experiences is not there. Shared memories are missing, something that the eminent Christian ethicist John C. Bennett once noted are such a delightful part of long-term commitment. He offered this useful reflection in response to those who were praising the virtues of "free love" in the 1970s. They may love many people, he said, but there is something important about looking back together with the same person.

None of these quantitative measures in and of themselves finally issue in the qualitative experience that is friendship. Friendship is enhanced when given time to grow and ripen. For example, friends love to share their histories — looking at old photo albums and scrapbooks is something to which one subjects only friends. I have even seen friends take pictures of each other looking at pictures of themselves when they were younger to be looked at when they are older! The point is that time is not all that is at play. Such an exercise can be pure nostalgia or duty if the friendship is not still alive on its own terms, if it is simply rehashed for the occasion. Friends know the difference.

These three insights, that friendship is potentially available to everyone, that it is ambiguous and fluid by nature, and that it is a qualitative and not a quantitative experience, are data revealed clearly by looking at women's friendships. The model reflects this. Any renewed ethical approach will incorporate these elements in a search for usable norms for future friends.

The Model in Action

In order to show how the model works I return to the examples in chapter 2 of women friends. I look at each set of friends using the model as a guide. In evaluating these I also find ways in which the model is lacking.

Deborah and Sandra

These friends provide an excellent example of a friendship that seems to be working well. The unity that *love* signifies is deepened by their insight about being friends and not simply in-laws. They have chosen to spend time together, *embodying* their relationship through the shared experience of travel and social change work.

Choices or *power* are shared as they go. The reason for their trip south is to be a part of the transformation of social conditions for women throughout the world, part of a *spirituality* for creative survival. Of course they probably have their difficult moments, but the model helps to illustrate what is so attractive about their friendship both to them and to others. It is a friendship that seems to work, at least for now. It is enjoyable to be around them. They generate community.

Coca and Julia

These women are equally well matched. Their *love* is tangible in their constant accompanying of each other at home and in public. They engage in concrete tasks that *embody* their solidarity, helping each other to raise a family, make a living, make political change in their neighborhood, and enjoy life in the process. Countless times they have drunk *mate* together, a common herbal drink in Argentina that is consumed with subtle ceremony. The *mate* is served by one person, but everyone drinks from the same straw, passing the container back to the server after each turn. It is a communal drink that symbolizes their communally attentive friendship.

Their *power* is more than doubled by being together. They are marginalized by society. By uniting with each other and with others in their neighborhood they can achieve tangible goals that will improve their living condition. They function with a *spirituality* that emerges from a deep conviction that they deserve to be a part of decision-making. No model is equal to the power of their presence, but this model helps us to see how they exemplify the fierce tenderness that one feels being around them.

Susan and Adrian

These friends provide another angle on the model by highlighting what is absent as much as what is present. Together they experienced a push toward unity, *love*, that surprised and delighted them. They *embodied* it in every possible way — sports, conversation, travel together. They were flustered when they discovered that each one was entertaining the possibility of a sexual dimension to their friendship. To their amazement even that seemed natural.

Then came death. The *power* to make choices about their collective future was gone. The absence of the one left the survivor with little desire to attend to the quality of her own life, her *spirituality*. This is why Susan's effort to communicate with Adrian was so important. It was a move, however tentative, toward taking responsibility for her future without Adrian, a future that would be better for their having been friends. Nothing will substitute for this loss, but at least Susan can understand the dynamics of her often confusing grief.

Catherine and Her Significant Multitude

We do not have much experience thinking of friendships in such plurality. The model can be helpful here. *Love* is almost an understatement in Catherine's case. Many people experienced her solidarity and companionship. No one doubted that the primary motivation of her work for justice was an enormous commitment to the unity of the human family. The myriad ways of *embodying* that in struggle and protest, in globe-hopping accompaniment of marginalized, downtrodden people who needed her, bear hugs and endless, exhausting meetings marked Catherine as a fully embodied friend.

Every other word from her seemed to be *power*. It was in order to change the "fundamental power equation" that she tried so hard to empower people. Who sat at the table, who made decisions, who was visible were concerns that made her commitment to restructuring power so obvious. The *spirituality* or attention to the quality of life that Catherine shared with her justice-seeking friends was a far cry from what one might have expected from a person with her religious formation. While she maintained some of the basics of her Catholic tradition, she cast aside any romantic version of the word "spirituality" and let the fiesta, the conversation, even the choice to love a little animal express her sense of values. All of this was done with many people. The model is sufficient to encompass even the human overflow that was Catherine's relational legacy.

Peg, Jane, and Karen

The model presented offers us a variety of useful insights into this situation. *Love* is obvious among the three women, but it is also the case that Peg is very much in love with her soon-to-be husband. She should not have to make a choice among the competing claims that they make on her, but in fact conflict and complexity are inevitable when striving for unity with many people. The model implicitly affirms that it is possible, and provides a framework in which to see and determine how this dynamic works.

Embodiment is equally clear. No one has figured out how to be two places at once, but Jane and Karen expect that their friendship deserves some of Peg's time. They cannot be with her in the abstract; their week is sacrosanct in their schedules and friendship demands that she will honor that commitment. Likewise, her fiancé is being asked to share his experience of embodiment with other people, something that prior property laws on which marriage was based would render impossible.

Power dynamics are infinitely complicated with three people. Apart from the vacation issue, the three friends have long worked on how they live and love together. Jane has a tendency to lead the pack, to expect a certain deference, while Karen has tended to be taken care of by the group in her moments (and they have been many) of need. Peg has always gone her own way, a reason why the marriage and possible breakup of the threesome was not a total surprise. But among them, the fact that they came from similar economic, racial, and ethnic backgrounds helped to make their power differences less determinative of their friendships.

It is not clear that any of them have given much thought to *spir-*

ituality in their relationship. Peg always insists that they buy fresh flowers for their vacation haunts and Jane is perennially in charge of the wine selection for their long dinners. Karen attends to the agenda, ever vigilant that they include enough time to think ahead to their next adventure. Though none of them would use the word "spirituality" to describe these actions, it is certain that without attention this threesome would have parted long ago.

The model is most helpful when used in three dimensions in this case, placing one set of dynamics (e.g., between Peg and Jane) over another (e.g., between Jane and Karen), over another (between Peg and Karen) over another (between Peg and her fiancé). This calls for a certain ethical adroitness. But it produces an intricate pattern of accountability that is fierce tenderness.

Kathy and Dawn

The breakdown of friendships, which I will focus on in the next chapter, is explicable using the model to understand these two friends. Theirs is a case of *love*, or the drive toward unity, lost. Distance increased over time for them. Attempts at shoring up what unity there had been were unsuccessful. Their *embodiment* lessened. Time together, letters, phone calls all decreased until finally there was a memory of friendship but little else.

Power dynamics became one-sided. Choices were made by one for both of them, i.e., Kathy simply pulled out without any mutual decision-making. *Spirituality* or quality of life was a nonissue. There was nothing to share really, no attention to one another. Negative feelings developed on Dawn's part. This is not what she wanted, and efforts to change it were met with resistance or ignored. There is, finally, no friendship here, model or no model.

These examples illustrate how a model does not make things so, but helps to explain and clarify them. The model has its shortcomings. But for discussing friendship it provides shared vocabulary. For looking at future friendships we have some hints.

Shortcomings of the Model

As helpful as the model may be, it has some obvious limitations. I will name three as I begin to critique it, inviting others to evaluate it just as critically in a communal effort to think anew about friendship.

Reflecting on what the model does not do, I am struck first by the fact that it does not account for the mysterious, grace-filled, serendip-itous dimensions of friendship. No model can do this, of course, and the very act of using a model can be seen as an attempt to move away from the whimsical, gratuitous aspects of any relationship. Using this model to evaluate Kathy and Dawn, for example, leaves one with a sense of finality. In fact they could restore their friendship through work and luck. Does the model encourage this?

Second, the model emerges from women's experience. Can it be applied to female-male relationships, or male-male ones? Is it so completely enmeshed in women's experiences that it has little or no transfer value? More to the point, is it so class-, race-, culture-, country-specific as to be useful, if at all, for a very limited segment of the population? Will it inhibit some women from developing their own ways of looking at the ultimate meaning and value of their friend-ships? Will it be helpful in seeing their relationships with their children or in a mixed-gender marriage? In short, is it limited by its own starting point?

Third, the model is allegedly one that spirals from the insights gained in naming and evaluating one relationship to the formation of new ways of being in future relationships. I claim that friendships take practice, but how does the model facilitate this process? Will simply processing friendships using this model lead to new experiences? Will friendships survive the scrutiny?

These questions, far from invalidating the model itself, begin what I hope will be the process of its critical refinement. It will only be by using it that its strengths and weaknesses will become obvious. I encourage readers to use it.

· 5 ·

The Limits of Friendship in Loss and Celebration

As closed hands open to each other
Closed lives open to strange tenderness.
We are learning the hard way how to mother.
Who says it is easy? But we have the power.
I watch the faces deepen all around me.
It is the time of change, the saving hour.
The word is not fear, the word we live,
But an old word suddenly made new,
As we learn it again, as we bring it alive:

Love. Love. Love. Love.

—May Sarton
"AIDS"

Friendship is clarified in limit experiences, those that reveal the edges of possibilities, like loss and celebration. Most of the time we simply live with friends as a natural part of our relational landscape, neither awed by their presence nor noticing their occasional absence until something or someone calls our attention to them. This attention, what I have called spirituality, is essential to a feminist theology of friendship.

Children hate to move because moving often means the loss of their friends. They do not usually have the wherewithal to keep in touch when distance intervenes so they intuit that this friendship is over. Children recognize loss when they experience it. The death of a young friend is traumatic, remembered long after other friends of that era are forgotten.

Adults often recall a childhood playmate who moved away, wondering in later years what ever happened to her or him, recalling her/him as an early friend. Most people have known loss from early on and come to expect it in friendship, though each time it happens people are traumatized anew. Even if one lives in the same place all of one's life the loss of friends is a common human experience.

Few children can give a cogent definition of a friend, but somewhere along the way they were taught that "friend" is the category used to describe playmates, neighbors, little ones whom they like. Unfortunately they are taught to distinguish between family and friends, a gap that as adults many people spend years trying to close. But friendship is different from family, especially from the ideology of the nuclear family, which has so limited the imagination that society has not created viable, friendly support systems. Part of the reason for all of this is that celebrations, holidays, fiestas in Western patriarchy are too often confined to the immediate family. Even death is held close, with "immediate survivors" different from friends and colleagues, often the real loved ones.

AIDS is taking its toll among my friends. Children with AIDS raise the specter of meaningless death. Gay men are dying in large numbers. Each funeral is a wrenching reminder that not even friendship staves off death. Estrangement over sexual preference is still commonplace, necessitating the formation of "families of choice" for many gay/lesbian people with close friends. While the mixed metaphor makes me nervous (why choose the relational constellation, the nuclear family, that one has been rejecting?),[1] attending to loss is brutal enough to excuse it. Women with AIDS are dying in larger numbers than most seem to care about, infected by their so-called friends and sometimes passing the disease on to their children. It is a strange world when one tries to make sense and give meaning to this pandemic. So we grope for celebrations, ways to lift to public expression the lives of the deceased while at the same time infusing life into the community of survivors.

Sacramentalizing Friendship

I suggest that we sacramentalize friendship by lifting to public expression the everyday love experiences that are friendships. Throughout this study I have been assuming that not all relationships are friendly, but that friendships are good. Friendship is a relational experience that can be achieved in a variety of ways with a variety of people, never simply one to one. Friendships sometimes fade; some never materialize in the first place. But all friendships need some kind of public expression to give them reality and stimulus beyond the minds of the friends, indeed to make them part of what will transform an unjust society into a friendly one.

Friendships need reverence, candor, space, and specificity. Most of all they require some sort of periodic celebration to renew and refresh the bonds in a community of friends. This is what it means to say that we sacramentalize friendship. The language of sacrament has usually been reserved for heterosexual friendships that result in marriage in the Catholic tradition (including Anglicans and Lutherans). But I urge that feminist theology reclaim the words "sacrament" and "sacramentalize" because the concept is too rich to be consigned to the religious institutions of late twentieth-century Christianity.

To sacramentalize is to pay attention. It is what a community does when it names and claims ordinary human experiences as holy, connecting them with history and propelling them into the future. There are no magic tricks nor impossible dreams. It is simply taking time to attend to the people around us, to see in real lives (not in novels nor in Scripture) the stuff of human existence: birth, pain, growth, bonding, breakup, loss, friendship, and to recognize it as such. This is what sacraments are for. They are concrete experiences with food and touch, dance and drink, prayer and silence, affirmation and music. Think of a good dinner party. What could be holier? How one-dimensional much of what passes for sacraments in churches is by comparison.

By sacramentalizing friendships, friends and their communities become aware and accountable. They take them seriously; they vest them with transcendent significance, meaning that goes beyond the immediate situation and says something about values shared. This is not an exercise in making friendship an object, nor elevating friends beyond reach. It is a communal way of recognizing something good, naming relationships that embody the highest relational ideals, and thereby making them ever more accessible since people now have examples.

People recognize something about their experience when a similar one is brought to attention. For example, I recently attended a festive dinner party in celebration of the tenth anniversary of the couple who were hostessing. In a brief comment between courses they explained the significance of the day for them and thanked their friends for being a part of their life together. It was sacramental. It gave me some ideas about my own life. The community gathered made something very special happen. Society has great control over sacraments. Although the word is starkly religious, I contend that sacraments, paying attention to the ordinary in a way that makes something extraordinary happen, are really secular experiences.

Lesbian and gay people often experience emotional dissonance at heterosexual weddings. Even in the most progressive settings where the woman and man express their love in public for communal affirmation (as opposed to the more traditional ceremonies where the minister pronounces them "man and wife") some are made to feel as if such love is unattainable. All rational thoughts about one in three such marriages ending in divorce evaporate in the smell of flowers and the general good will that surround such events. Tears at weddings are not always joyful. Even the most secular of heterosexual weddings has this sacramental flavor that people recognize from the outside and want to share. Sacraments are a human right.

It was not until I went to a wedding for two women that I realized that public expression of love and commitment, what I call sacramentalizing, is a secular as well as religious right, not a privilege. The ceremony and reception were lovely. The couple was obviously committed in a mature and thoughtful way. Friends were pleased to honor them by presence and to affirm with them the goodness of their love and the love of a community. It is their right to celebrate in this way. There is of course lingering pain when family members, so used to society's strictures on such sacraments, choose not to attend or cannot be invited because of their limited abilities to comprehend this simple point.

This event and others like it help to break the hegemony of heterosexual marriage and to usher in the relational norm of friendship. It may take two to tango, but no one ever said it had to be two persons of opposite genders. Same-gender marriages or equivalent covenant or commitment ceremonies are a step in the right direction. I caution against wholesale importing of the heterosexual marriage ritual for same-gender couples. It is simply too limited to convey the fullness of community-based friendship. I urge a pushing of horizons, new ways of naming and living out friendships that will give heterosexual couples new ideas. Music, art, clothing, and customs originating in the lesbian/gay communities have eventually filtered out and become normative, and I am confident imitation will follow shortly in the relational realm as well.

Friends Replace a Friend

Another step remains, however, and that is the celebration of friendships in their plurality and not simply as one-to-one commitments. If the relational norm of heterosexual marriage is to be replaced, then we must get used to naming what most of us know, namely, that friendships always come in plural. Celebrations that heighten the one-to-one nature of *a particular friendship* between two people are finally quite misleading. The point is not to make the world safe for dyads, but to shift the focus from "the two" to "the many." Granted this is a challenge in a culture that still argues about "the one and the many," but reinforcing unhelpful patterns will only delay progress. For friendships to move from a secondary position to the center of relational consideration will take more than same-gender marriages that are modeled on the heterosexual pattern.

Friendship in the plural and celebrations that reflect it are as important as the one-to-one commitments. Commitment to one person is challenge enough, but commitment to several is in fact what most of us experience. We may have a live-in friend, a sibling who has become a friend, a pet that we love, friends abroad who come to visit and the world stops for them, colleagues in the work place who make legitimate demands on our social time, and of course the hardest friend of all to name and celebrate, perhaps the easiest to lose, oneself. A goal in this period of ethical transformation is to find communal models of friendship and to celebrate them in order to reinforce their value. Groups have all but replaced the nuclear family and its heterosexual foundations as society's norm for loving well.

An early critique of my theological model of friendship was that it was overly optimistic and somewhat idealized. I did not take into account the other side of what can be a powerful experience of bonding, namely, loss. Nor did I stress the importance of rituals or liturgies that would lift to public expression the everyday love of friends. What follows is an effort to deepen these introductory insights and to invite further reflection from readers as new models emerge. Any model that attempts to illuminate friendship needs to take account of limit experiences like loss and celebration, points at which the strength and usefulness of the model is forged and tested.

Understanding Friendship Histories

It is useful to reflect on our friendship histories, asking ourselves what patterns emerge over time. To do so I suggest that readers divide their lives into convenient sections: early childhood, high school, college or early work years, job change, retirement. Then look back on the friends who were important. Were they girls or boys, women or men? What racial/ethnic groups were they from, what economic classes? What languages did they speak? What kinds of activities did you enjoy together? Questions of this sort help to orient us in terms of what our friends reveal about us. Then we can theologize.

For example, the fact that most of my friends were white when I was a child reveals something about the racist culture in which I grew up. I broke that pattern quite consciously in later years, something that is reflected by my friends. Similarly, I can see a change in my friends when I lived in Argentina. Most of my friends during those years spoke Spanish and so did I, enlarging and enriching my relational horizons in another language. They remain close to me today. I love in different languages; I learn languages in order to be able to communicate with my friends on their terms.

Similar patterns emerge when looking at the fact that most of my significant, life-changing relationships have been with women. This is a big clue to my sexual preference. There are of course some men whose names appear in my friendship history as important for my self-understanding and growth. But the overwhelmingly consistent pattern is with women. What is your pattern? Likewise, some interesting patterns of friends of various ages emerge. I have frequently had older friends as well as those of my own age. These show me something about the value of cross-generational friendships. Now I begin to have younger friends as well as friends within my decade. I like the variety. What about your patterns?

Exercises of this sort are very helpful in understanding the way in which friendships shape us. Any feminist theology of friendship must include this kind of reflection and some discussion of it if the process is to be organic and communal. We see where we have departed from our usual patterns and with whom we have had life-shaping experiences. We note that some people disappear from our relational histories, a disconcerting but real observation.

We can pinpoint certain parameters of our relational lives by noting the loss of friends. Death is obvious, but there are also people who simply slip beyond our ken; correspondence stops or the holiday we used to celebrate passes unnoticed. Likewise, recalling when we celebrated a friendship such as marriage, a commitment to a religious community (presumably, of friends), or simply sending a birthday card are all useful reminders of the state of the friendship.

This kind of consideration helps us to see loss and celebration emerge as dual poles of friendship with what happens in between them being "ordinary time."[2] We live in ordinary time most of the time, fortunately, so the losses and the celebrations stand out when they happen.

Looking at Loss

Friends are sometimes not appreciated until they are gone. Then we realize how one person has shaped us in new ways, called forth a dimension of who we are that would have otherwise remained dormant. I recall a friend from Europe who pushed the horizons of my Yankee consciousness. I can never forget how deeply affected I am by being a U.S. citizen after her careful tutelage in the ways of international power. She taught me a lesson in social location long before the current literary preoccupation with "place" came into vogue.

It was only when she had returned home, and more so when I visited her, that I began to see the world from her vantage point and to realize how very different it looked. I realized that the insight into privilege and the lessons about sharing resources that she had imparted did not go with her. I had internalized them thanks to our friendship. She had had an impact on me; I would never be the same again. It was more than a cliché. It was a life-changing insight.

This has happened to me several times since, not only with international friends, but with people in my own country whose experience of it is vastly different from mine due to race, class, gender. Friendship forces us to see the world through other eyes. Cultural myopia can be treated by friends, especially friends who insist on the fierce tenderness of truth-telling. Friends mean a loss of innocence and a loss of innocence can mean a loss of friends. Loss of friends takes many forms. Illness and death are the most common, though distance and personal change account for a measure of loss as well. As illness takes its toll, the question is what relationship persists when a person is so enervated that she is, as we say, "not herself anymore"? Or, when death comes and the usual way of relating is gone, how do friends handle the loss?

This is where the model is helpful in sorting through issues. When embodiment changes drastically, all of the other components shift as well. Friendship usually persists albeit in a different form. Sometimes it does not and there is no necessary explanation any more than there is any necessary cure.

While it would be nice to think that friends stand by one another through change, it simply isn't always the case. In fact, illness is a common reason why friendships break up. People drift apart when they can no longer do what they used to do as friends. A friendship nurtured while playing cards, making love, or going to a concert will suffer from the lack of those activities. There is a tendency to lose touch more than to break off, but the net result is the same. Embodiment is a key to relating. Some find it hard to be friends in the new ways demanded by a disabling illness, for example. Nothing is as lonely as being in the hospital without friends. One by one friends excuse themselves under the pretense of "not disturbing the patient." But hospital chaplains, nurses, doctors, and other health care professionals attest to the fact that lack of friendly support during illness in what is usually an unfriendly, clinical surrounding is a major medical problem. It can lead to serious depression and almost certainly has an adverse impact on the patient's prognosis.

Conversely, support from friends has proven to be a source of healing. Many friends shift their activities to accommodate illness or incapacity. They work around particular problems, inventing new ways of being together. Mental illness makes this especially difficult when the emotional and psychic interaction that characterized a friendship is no longer possible. But friends find infinitely clever ways to reorient the embodied character of their friendships.

Examples abound. Barb and Samantha had lived together until Barb started medical school in another city. About the same time Samantha was diagnosed with a form of cancer that required months of living virtually without human touch as her immune system was rehabilitated. What had been a friendship involving physical as well as emotional expression was transformed into one in which sound, pictures, and even visualization had to suffice. These friends weathered the storm through creative and constant schemes to be together. The hospital officials did not always approve of their antics — their favorite music blared through the halls, phone calls came and went during odd hours — but they pushed the legal limits in order to preserve and even to deepen their bonds. It worked. Upon Samantha's release from the hospital they resumed their life together with an even deeper appreciation for the goodness of their friendship. They later reflected that if they had not gone to such extraordinary lengths to keep some special bonds they might well have drifted apart as so many others do.

May Sarton writes frequently of the effects of aging on her characters. In *As We Are Now* the protagonist begins by saying, "I'm not mad, I'm just old."[3] Ageist stereotypes be damned, Sarton seems to be saying; people can think, decide, and act for themselves long after most in our throw-away society think it impossible. It is illness and not ageing itself that causes problems. New wisdom and integration achieved in later years are shared by older friends.[4]

Experts have revised their thinking on sexual activity for senior citizens. It isn't over until it is over. Many seniors report boredom in retirement communities that do not permit children and younger adults. They crave the friendship of people in different parts of the life cycle. However, in some cases illness interferes with growth in friendship. But this is not to be confused with aging itself. I delighted to watch my father discover the brother he never had in a new friend he made in retirement on the golf course. They could enjoy the game and a leisurely lifestyle like young chums. The spark of new friendship evident in their phone conversations and even their body language made it clear that they were fully alive.

By contrast, my mother, known for her vivaciousness and vast array of friends, suffered a stroke. She recovered without physical loss, but her short-term memory was impaired. She had trouble for several years following conversations on new topics. Reminiscing with friends and family was done easily but making new friends was a chore. Many friends were patient but over time it became apparent that making friends depends heavily on common activities. The cumulative effect of a stroke, heavy medication, and the resulting lack of self-confidence simply put people with illnesses of this sort at a disadvantage.

If physical luster returns, so too, I suspect, will her former ability to interact and make friends. Making friends is learned behavior. Like riding a bicycle, it does not go away; it simply requires a little readjusting, perhaps not going as fast nor covering so much terrain as before, but the ability is there. Such is the serendipity of friendship, the factor for which there is no accounting, what I simply call luck.

Many find that the richness of friendship persists well into the final years of life, sometimes even after death itself. I met such a remarkable woman when I was training as a chaplain in a women's prison. She was nearly ninety, mentally sharp and spiritually generous. Her "debt to society" long since paid, she stayed in prison to have "a room of her own" that no nursing home could guarantee. For several years after I left the job she sent me bulging envelopes of articles she had clipped from the three newspapers she read every day. She knew that women and religion was a special interest of mine so she clipped a vast array of materials which were a real aid to my research. This unlikely friend made clear that age and circumstance are not barriers to friendship. I only hope I was as generous to her in my youth as she was to me in her later years.

As elder friends die I realize that even though their deaths are expected, the loss is just as real. They take with them experiences that I do not know: life before television or the automobile, what it was like to live through a depression and world wars, what women did when they stayed home with their children. I mourn the loss of these memories as much as of these people. In short, whether young or old, every friend who dies or moves on represents a loss and leaves a memory of friendship. This becomes a part of our friendship history.

Little is written about friendship in the theological literature, but virtually nothing is said about the loss of friends. Loss of parents, children, siblings, even pets, captures attention and receives pastoral concern. There is scant insight in theology about what betrayal, death, distance, or attrition mean among friends. Yet theology purports to be about *ultimate meaning and value*, about making sense and giving purpose to communities, generation after generation. If it is all marked in blood ties with callous disregard for where most people find deepest love and affection, namely with friends, then theology will continue to have little to offer to a world that seems increasingly less interested in its musings.

My look at loss and celebration together is an effort to think theologically, that is, to think in ways that no other writers nor helping professionals claim to think, to think about ultimate meaning and value, with regard to friends. Of course others who look at these issues from a psychological or sociological perspective have valuable insights to convey. But the point is that theology has abandoned its calling in this arena, as in so many, by circumscribing its concern for the most immediate and predictable people. Feminists doing theology do not want to repeat that mistake.

Most people simply do not like to talk about experiences of loss because they are too painful to relive. People have not internalized the fact that friendship takes practice, and that loss is an inevitable part of the equation. The tendency is to shrink from intimacy for fear of loss. But as the Hungarian gambler observed in *Desert Hearts*, "If you don't play, you can't win."[5] Being friends means losing friends. That is why I link loss with celebration, to underscore the fact that just as many dread loss so, too, do many people keep our distance from celebration. It is perceived by some as slightly embarrassing to tell people how much they mean to us. By others it is taken as bad luck, a way to tempt the fates; maybe after we celebrate it will be over. Holding these together, the reality of loss and the value of celebration (whether joyful as in the anniversary of good friends or sorrowful as in a divorce or death), is part of fierce tenderness.

The death of friends is painful. It is a reminder of one's own ageing to bury friends. Children expect to bury parents, but if they have become friends it is even more difficult. The trauma of parents burying their children is profound. This unexpected turning of the tables often signals a friendship that never bloomed, especially if the children are very young. Burying any friend is a time to reflect, a time to note the passing of an era in one's life, a time to signal the end of shared memories, a time of growing up. No one welcomes it but there is little choice. A funeral can be an occasion when friends experience a new maturity, indeed when new friendships form out of loss and shared grief.

The death of a lover or a friend is perhaps the most painful loss, made worse by a culture that recognizes marriages and blood ties yet all but ignores friendship. It is only a very recent occurrence that major newspapers like the *New York Times* are finally acknowledging longtime companions of deceased persons as survivors in addition to family members and spouses. People eventually drove home the point that accurate reporting is not fulfilled when a lover and/or companion of longstanding is ignored just because a blood or legal tie does not exist. That many newspapers still ignore this is proof of the blindness that heterosexism causes when the survivors of the deceased must be related in so narrowly prescribed a way.

For example, Jan and Pat were longtime companions, known to their friends as a committed couple. But to Jan's family they were "just friends." Her sudden heart attack and instant death left her and Pat with no time to set the record straight, as it were, nor to inform their families that their powers of attorney, wills, and insurance policies all reflected the true nature of their commitment. The funeral was tough enough for Pat, but it was compounded by the family's ill will upon learning that she, and not they, was the beneficiary of Jan's considerable fortune. Ironically, Jan had left her estate to Pat with instructions to share a portion of it with several social justice groups. Jan assumed that her siblings' children were well provided for by their parents. She knew that these groups of justice-seeking friends would make good use of her resources, continuing her spirit in their work for social change. They were her friends, closer to her than her blood relatives. Her family learned a painful lesson that society should be teaching in gentler ways. The same can happen with unmarried heterosexual couples with the same devastating results.

Illness and death are inevitable aspects of life. But breakups of friendships, the loss of friends over differences of opinion or expectation, the gradual moving apart due to indifference or lack of nurture in a relationship, are always painful. Sometimes they are for the best though, since constant conflict in a friendship is not proof of commitment but of incompatibility.

What dynamics contribute to this frequent occurrence? The model proposed earlier provides us with some clues. *Differences in power are the most prevalent reason for the breakup of friendships.* According to the model it looks like this:

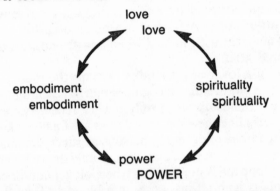

Differences in power dynamics lead to a complete breakdown in communication, eventually a loss of trust, and inevitably a parting of the ways. Reasons are invariably complicated. Power dynamics, both personal and systemic, continue to make this a very complex situation. Nonetheless, the model helps us to determine where the problem is in order to solve it. The model does not, repeat, does not solve problems of this sort. But the clarity that it provides helps people isolate and work on those aspects of a friendship that need attention.

Therapists and clergy are challenged to understand more clearly how power dynamics work in order to provide counsel and solace to those whose relational worlds fall apart. That is why a deeper understanding of friendship cannot be ignored in favor of full concentration on family systems, marital dynamics, and the like. Friends are often an ignored factor in the efforts by helping professionals to achieve relational equanimity. This is done at the peril of those involved.

Loss of a friend can be as dramatic as a divorce. Often divorce is another way to name the same thing. But at least with a divorce there is the cultural, religious, and legal framework in which to interpret and resolve the situation. People at least know to whom to say they are sorry; why someone who is divorced is upset or depressed is obvious and in a certain way socially acceptable. But with the unexpected breakup of a friendship (or the dissolution of a lover relationship) no such social supports exist, minimal as they may be. Often there is not even a vocabulary for naming what was and what is no longer. Pain in invisible. All of this is a consequence of trivializing friendship.

Other friends, family, and work colleagues are at a loss to explain changes in behavior or new relational constellations that emerge even when they sense that something is different. This lack of vocabulary is more than a linguistic problem, it is a theological concern. It robs people of ways to articulate what is ultimately meaningful and valuable. Friendships participate in a transcendent realm, much as family and marriage do. That is why there is finally no good explanation for them. But without the acknowledgement and the reflection on the meaning and value of friendship, that is, without sacrament, there is no way to bring that richness to the whole community. More to the point, individuals are robbed of the chance to live out their friendships in a supportive context.

Another significant reason for the loss of friends is important differences over *embodiment*. The most common experience of this is obviously sexual, though few people think about this immediately in the case of women friends. By "sexual" I mean first the most ordinary way in which women friends make choices about intimacy just as mixed-gender friends do. It is less common to hear "She wanted sex but I didn't" as we hear between women and men, but this happens, too, between women and women and men and men, and needs to be worked out.

In many instances the conflict in embodied choices is somewhat different. One friend may wish more time with the other. She may say: let's go to the movies, take a vacation, talk on the phone every day, work together. All of these possibilities are subject to different needs, interpretations, indeed different whims. How one feels about some ways of being together, how long, how often, and other quantitative measures, can have an impact on the qualitative experiences of friendship. When the differences are simply more than the friendship can stand, the friendship falls apart. If one feels too much or too little pressure, feels too constrained or not enough attention, lack of breathing room or a loss of self, hard decisions about distance usually portend the disintegration of the relationship.

The model looks like this:

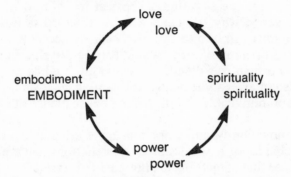

The differences in embodiment are real and need to be taken seriously. Failing to do this results from a common blind spot in a heterosexist society.

Loss of *love* is no less common. I have heard friends say, "She loved me and I don't know why she doesn't love me any more." There is usually some other manifestation of a problem. Still, this happens, often for reasons that are equally mysterious to the lover as to the beloved. Lots of it is now being explained by some of the studies that focus on problems of intimacy, especially the literature related to Adult Children of Alcoholics.[6] There is great validity and usefulness to these studies. They have helped many people make sense of seemingly inexplicable dynamics. But even these do not tell the whole story and reductionism is to be avoided.

Friendships can break up because one of the friends is incapable of sustaining the degree of intimacy wanted by the other in order to push the friendship to new depths. Still there is also a degree of the unknown here — almost a mystery — as to why a certain friendship will not work.

I do not mean to pass over the excellent therapeutic work done by contemporary mental health professionals, nor to write off a whole body of literature with a mention. Rather, I want to affirm all of this and still insist that there is at least a dimension of friendship that even the best therapists cannot succeed at unearthing. This is where psychology and religion intersect, in the struggle to understand aspects of human experience that defy easy categorization. Anti-religious biases have pervaded contemporary psychology, often with good reason given the guilt-producing content of some major traditions. Still, it is unwise for a counselor to pass over the spiritual content of a client's being just because some spiritual bases are flawed.

For example, Ellen and Iris were colleagues at work. They became acquainted through the parents' club of the school their children attend. At first they were simply attracted to each other as single mothers who understood the problems inherent in raising today's teens. Then they drew closer through the club, working on projects, going on vacation together with their children, spending holidays at each others' homes. It was a mutual friendship of support, discussion, and enjoyment. Gradually, for no explicable reason, Iris seemed to distance herself from Ellen. She found excuses not to be available. Nothing specific happened. It was just that over time her feelings changed, almost imperceptibly at first. She no longer felt the pull to be together. In fact, she felt a need to be with other people. Eventually she came to resent Ellen's repeated phone calls. Ellen wasn't getting the message so Iris eventually had to speak definitively. Ellen felt the loss; Iris felt relief.

Therapists rightfully spend time figuring out these dynamics. Motivation is complex and often hidden, always worthy of such efforts for all parties involved. But my point is simply that friendships reveal that there are occasions, events, even relationships that are simply inexplicable. Why love was but is no longer present, why the urge to be more united than divided passes away is something that cannot always be explained. Friendship defies reduction. It is to be enjoyed. At times it is to be mourned when it is over.

In this sense, friendship and not pleasure is the opposite of suffering. One has only to participate in a long hospital vigil or watch a paralyzed person with little hope of recovery to be convinced that suffering is somehow beyond explanation. On the face of it, suffering calls into question the wisdom, power, and justice of any Life Force that permits it. On closer reflection the only dimension worth discussing is how others, that is, not the one who is suffering, acquit themselves. And even then meaning is thin, veiled, and unconvincing except in the struggle to love well along the way. Friendship has these moments.

At other times, of course, the change in love is totally explicable. Perhaps Ellen's children drove Iris mad by their boisterous ways. Or maybe Iris was moving into another relationship and simply did not have time for it all. Perhaps Ellen was otherwise engaged and Iris intuited it. The point is that there really are times when none of these is the case. In fact sometimes no one knows why the loss of love takes place. It just happens.

In this case, the model appears as follows:

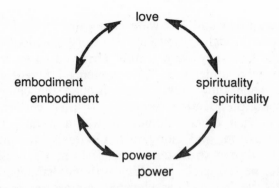

We have a hard time accepting this, especially in circles where therapy, whether individual or couple, is thought to be the cure-all for any sinking relationship. By contrast, a theological explanation is not simply to toss one's hands in the air with resignation. It is to use the best resources of the social sciences, but at the same time to be open to the fact that people do not finally control the universe, neither the natural order nor the created order. We cooperate in it. We play an active role. This model presumes that other factors are at work as well. This is what it means to say that friendship is transcendent.

Regardless of the reason, loss is always accompanied by the equally and sometimes more difficult challenge of letting go. Whether it be letting go of a friend who has been debilitated by illness or accepting that death means the loss of someone who will not easily be replaced, the letting go aspect of friendship means finally giving up the embodiment, love, power as they have been known. Letting go in this sense is a kind of loss that I can only label the spirituality dimension of friendship. The quality of collective and communal life is altered. Choices are no longer mutual but predetermined. Minus this dimension it is hard to imagine what a friendship would look like.

In the case of lovers who come to a parting of the ways, or family members who determine that for everyone's best health it is better to make a break, the pain of letting go can be excruciating. It means admitting that quality of life choices will not be made together ever again. It means acknowledging that love is altered, and usually coping with the fact that power dynamics have changed radically and are not to be repaired. Of course there is always a slight chance that things will turn around, but apart from certain disputable returns from the dead and some isolated examples of reunification after devastating breakups, the chances are slim.

I do not mean to treat this in a cavalier fashion nor to downgrade the vital importance of therapeutic help when necessary. But just as it is sometimes why people become friends — we call it chemistry in shorthand — it must be acknowledged that friendship is not simply rote learning. It is a highly differentiated set of experiences that cannot be duplicated nor fully understood. It does have a certain mysterious dimension that is expressed in loss as well as in celebration. People need to interpret and internalize so as to make sense of experiences. This is the challenge to feminist theology.

What Does Loss Mean?

All forms of loss can be given meaning, some more accessible and easily acceptable than others. Humans cope as best they can. To be human is to find ways to give meaning and value in order to be able to carry on with life. This so-called grief work over the loss of friends makes it easier to move on to new friendships or to deepen existing ones.

The simple point is that loss happens to everyone. Prevailing Christian theological views that stress an omnipresent God provide little room for impermanence, transitory experiences, momentary pleasure, or relationships of short duration. If there is room for them, they are considered secondary in the scheme of things, somehow imperfect and therefore subordinate, unimportant in the eternal realm. But friendship, allegedly a good experience, can end, a clue that perhaps this model of the divine as omnipresent is inadequate.

The first contemporary crack in this theological door came with the "death of God" movement in the 1960s.[7] It was a response to the rigors of theological liberalism and neo-orthodoxy, a religious attempt to grapple with the insights of Marx, Freud, and Darwin. The "death of God" movement was, ironically, short-lived. Political theology, and later the many liberation theologies (feminist, Latin American, black, Asian, and others), replaced it with varied models of the divine, most of which persist in the same basic understanding. I suggest that friendships, especially acknowledging the reality of loss and the need for celebration, teach something about the relational nature of the divine.

Loss of friends is, in the first place, a careful and painful reminder that finally, as communally oriented as people may be, each person is radically alone. This is why befriending ourselves — loving our bodies, enjoying our work, finding ways to relax and reflect alone — is so very important. Then we can see the loss of friends for what it is — a severe and disconcerting experience but one that we will survive. We can persist with this model of friendship, confident that we are friends, if only with ourselves. While this approach smacks of a certain schizophrenia, for many people it really is a missing piece in a complicated struggle to live faithfully. The affirmation that we are radically alone can be overwhelming. But the realization that in our individuality we are always and of necessity related, if only to the many components of ourselves, is a comforting discovery.

It is an empowering experience to know that we can survive loss. We discover our friendly selves; we are surprised by the many people who befriend us along the way. And we come to a deeper appreciation for the friendship we have with the divine nexus of all creation, *that through which all that is is connected.*

The experience of suffering begs a feminist theological treatment although it is beyond the scope of this book. Clues about its importance emerge, as do clues about the importance of friendship, from two sources. First, suffering is a universal experience. Obviously everyone is afflicted in different ways, but there is virtually no adult (and very few children) who has not had some suffering: illness, death of a loved one, loss of a friend, disappointment in work or career, crisis of meaning or identity. Second, suffering generates a visceral reaction so that it is unmistakable. We are coming to understand the physical impact of depression, for example, or the connection between emotional problems and physical diseases. In short, a feminist theology of suffering, a kind of doing theology with tears in our eyes, remains to be articulated. The absence of the divine, like the absence of a friend, is instructive.

Theologically a divinity that overarches all that is, remains static even as people change, is unnecessary. To the contrary, loss of friends teaches that being alone is inevitable, that even the divine abandons people, or so it seems. Befriending ourselves and making new friends teach that being alone, while real, is temporary in an interconnected universe. Who wants a divinity that does not measure up to reality? Loss shows that being radically alone, even without a divine friend, is an experience one can survive. A God who is absent is a venerable yet vulnerable part of the Christian tradition.

Secondly, the loss of friends teaches that nothing is permanent, not life as we know it, not love as we would like it to be. While this, too, can be disconcerting, it is finally a comfort to know that one cannot step into the same relational river twice. No two friendships are alike. No two relational mistakes are the same.

It is one more proof of the fact that friendships take practice, that each relationship is a rehearsal for the next one. Perhaps death is the final friendship, the relationship for all eternity in which love and power, embodiment and spirituality are perfectly balanced. It is an attractive concept at least, something we deserve after endless, ever tentative tries to achieve this during life.

Because nothing is permanent, persons cannot be prized as private property. I am not suggesting license for promiscuity, nor am I assuming that there are no monogamous committed relationships. Rather, I am suggesting that promiscuity is not the only alternative to long-range fidelity. Changes happen naturally. Even the happiest monogamous committed relationships benefit from many more people being integrated into their relational web. Whether children or friends, growth and change in the relational constellation are healthy and necessary. It is good practice for what is to follow.

This dimension of friendship provides a hint about the divine, that God is not changeless, the still point of an ever dynamic universe. Rather, the divine is mutable, affected by us as we by the divine. Our losses count in the scope of things. Feminist process theologians have been helpful in underscoring this point even though they have not used friendship as an example.[8]

Finally, loss underscores the extent to which friendship is infused with a certain measure of luck. While you cannot win if you don't play, it seems that some people simply are unlucky in love, others enormously fortunate. This is not the stuff of astrology charts. But it is equally inexplicable and probably just as serendipitous as astrology. No one knows why one person finds another and becomes friends, why some are at the right place at the right time to meet people and others miss the chance. I like to think that this is what the Christian tradition has meant by the presence of the Spirit — a force for unity, a movement toward wholeness. The seeming absence of this force is just as evident when some people go for years at a time without a new significant relationship. That I can only acknowledge and bemoan. I cannot explain it finally, but I rejoice when it turns around.

This measure of luck, perhaps what theologically is called "grace," is another clue to the nature of the divine. The sustaining power of the Spirit in the Christian tradition is as a guarantor of continuity and goodness. But it is unmanageable, unpredictable, finally uncontrollable, still real.

Some examples of loss will illustrate these three points. The fact of radical aloneness coupled with constant opportunities for some kind of friendship is illustrated by an elderly couple. Monica and Michelle lived together for fifty years. Though both were well into their eighties, they were inseparable companions, lovers who still found pleasure and meaning in intimacy. Monica's death left Michelle bereft of the

support that she had counted on during their long and rich life together. She did not want to outlive her friend, and in fact, as is so
typical of mixed-gender friends (usually spouses), she died within a
year. During that year she confided in her young housekeeper that she
felt very much alone, yet strong in herself and thankful for the time
that she and Monica had had together. Her desire to live into this
insight was surpassed only by her eagerness to share it with Monica.
Finally perhaps, only the housekeeper benefited from the last generative drop of their love, and it was enough to sustain her for years
to come.

Another example of loss illustrates the lack of permanence.
Brenda, Chris, and Holly had a tradition of spending the winter holidays with Karen, Eve, and their children. For ten years they had all
gathered at one house with pets and friends, spouses and in-laws. One
year Chris decided to go on retreat for the week, a choice to avoid
the exaggerated activity and emotions of the season and to take advantage of the respite at work to collect her thoughts and start the
New Year off in a centered way. The experience was so peaceful and
pleasant that she decided against making the "family of choice" scene
again. The group missed her. Some members resented her seeming in-
dependence, not realizing fully her need to be alone. Their tradition
had been broken. Resentment grew. But Chris felt stronger and freer
having found a new niche that fit. On other special occasions she
would be with the group, even tolerating their questions and hopes
that she would return for what they considered the most festive time
of the year. What they all eventually understood was that no tradition, however freely constructed, is sacrosanct. No one can be taken
for granted. No expectations can go unquestioned. Indeed, they all
had to admit that nothing is permanent. The group eventually grew
to understand Chris's need for privacy and to enjoy her company
when she did come. One year she even spent the winter holidays
with them, her own needs having shifted. So much for permanence.

A third example of luck or the lack of it can be seen in Cary's
chance meeting with a group of women who belong to a religious
community. She was thinking through the next steps in her career,
feeling the effects of a recently broken friendship, and generally not
in top emotional form. A workshop on health care planning took
her to an urban training center where she met the group. During the
workshop she came to know one of the members. Afterward they kept
in touch, and when her spring vacation gave her a few free days she
visited the group again. There seemed to be a certain "fit," an inexplicable but very real resonance between her ideals and theirs, her values

and their willingness to explore them with her. She liked the fact that the group lived simply but well, without ties to any particular institutional church. She felt at home with their deep reverence for the earth and its people. What luck, she mused, what pure and unadulterated good fortune. And it was. Her broken friendship paled before the richness of the group, and there was even a special person whom she was in the process of knowing more intimately. Such is luck.

Critical feminist theologizing does not incorporate such analysis with much more ease than the traditional forms do. But confidence is necessary to admit that no one knows why such things happen without feeling as if the pursuit of knowledge has been abandoned. All knowledge in this realm is not available through carefully constructed models nor through well reasoned arguments. Much of it is intuitive, more process than product, demanding a kind of rigorous openness coupled with critical distance.

These examples, while finally inadequate to convey the full meaning of loss, give a flavor for how some people experience it. They can be summed up in an insight that one finds in many feminist experiences, namely that where women's friendships are concerned very little is ever lost. As one theologian put it, "nothing is wasted among us."[9] Experiences are recycled into new experiences. Friendships past become part of friendship history upon which are built new and deeper forms of intimacy. This does not mean that loss will cease eventually. Rather, it means that people make more and more sense of it. Friendship is ecological that way.

Still, loss hurts. The shudder of a friend I hold in my arms as she cries for a love that is no more is all the reminder I need not to make a virtue of necessity. Perhaps my being there conveys the reverse side of loss, the ongoing possibility for friendship.

Celebrating Friendships

The celebration of friendship is an important component of the whole picture. It is not done often enough. In fact there are few actual celebrations of friendship woven into our social fabric. I do not mean a perfunctory birthday party at the office or an annual reunion or inevitable holiday that everyone endures. I mean ways in which we take seriously the commitment that friendship entails and say as much to each other whether in private or in public. These celebrations need not be fancy nor frequent. They simply need to happen if meaning and value, the stuff of theology, are to be nurtured and expressed. Cultures have always used rituals to give order to chaos, to bring meaning alive and to pass on truths from one generation to the next. Many of the rituals have been religious, infused with the beliefs and practices of a faith community. These are reason enough to develop celebrations of friendship, especially at a time when religious institutions are woefully inadequate to the task. For feminist theology there is a strategic imperative: changing the ways in which relationships are celebrated will reinforce the changes in their perceived value. Celebrating friendship and not only marriage is part of the process of changing mores. Neglecting to celebrate means abdicating a rich layer of symbols and experiences to those who would maintain the ethical status quo.

There are even fewer public ways to acknowledge the loss of a friend. Whether through divorce, a parting of the ways, or death, we simply do not have socially shared and sanctioned ways of bringing closure to friendship. Wakes and funerals are seen primarily as family times. Loss by death is often more profound for friends than for some far-flung relatives who may not even know the deceased anymore.

Divorce rituals, while increasingly common, are still a rarity. Seldom do we reflect in any communal way on what we have learned from a relationship, how we could use that learning to avoid the mistake in the future. Almost never do we give thanks together for what has been good. This is a function of the privatizing effect of therapy, the extent to which it focuses on individuals and at most on families. Why not develop rituals that will allow this kind of reflection to take place as part of the common wisdom, not simply focused on one loss but on the extent to which this is a common human experience?

Therapists, ministers, and others who accompany people in loss have yet to turn their attention to celebration. How we befriend and are befriended, especially how we find meaning and value in friendship, whether in loss or in development, is best expressed in ritual and by symbols. These convey what words at best can only hint at.

Few if any such rituals exist in Western Christian culture either to celebrate loss or to facilitate friendship. Resistance to planning and conducting these is a logical extension of the hesitation to deal with the pain of loss. But if my preceding effort to give loss meaning and to affirm the value of what loss teaches is successful, then it ought to be able to be ritualized.

Wakes and funerals are among the few culturally acceptable forms for dealing with loss. Many feminists' alienation from mainstream religious practices leaves few resources for "feminist farewells." For example, how is it appropriate to bury one another when the usual patriarchal religious rituals do not fit the wishes of the deceased nor, more important, the needs of surviving friends? Fortunately some women are turning their attention to this problem and coming up with very creative results.[10] Feminist groups are creating their own celebrations, complete with music, pictures, shared memories and internment rituals for deceased friends. Others are holding the feminist equivalent of an Irish wake complete with music and dancing, where friends share food and fellowship to strengthen them as they reshape their community in the face of loss. More resources are needed as groups handle this difficult task.

Loss takes many forms other than death. The most common, as noted above, is a breakup of friendship whether through a physical move, change in interest, or the myriad ways in which the love-power-embodiment-spirituality equation shifts. Knowing what to celebrate in the midst of these more subtle but equally devastating losses is a challenge that invites our creativity. This is equally true for male-male relationships as for female-male ones. Any hints are helpful.

Sometimes a letter is enough to name the loss and make the break. No one likes to receive a "Dear Jane," but finally it is more honest than silence. At other times protracted discussion is needed to complete the process of breakup. Even a meal together, or a last movie or evening out is the kind of farewell that helps to bring closure in this public and symbolic sense that is so necessary, however painful.

On a less permanent note, this is the intent behind bon voyage parties, retirement dinners, and other rituals of *despedida*, or departure. In each case, the important thing is that some acknowledgement is made that change has happened or is about to happen. Some effort is made to name what has been good, to give thanks, and to move on. These are a natural part of a civilized society. It is only when they do not happen, for example, when a long-time employee gets her last pay check and not even a thank you and good luck, that people notice. The same principle holds true for friends. If things just taper off without fanfare it is sometimes easier but rarely as satisfying in the long run.

Celebration is needed not only in the moments of change or loss but in the normal course of relationships to mark their stages and to encourage their deepening. This is missing both in church and society. Sacramentalizing friendship, as Catholics would express the matter, is simply not done. This reflects the low-priority status of friendship, the extent to which it is considered an also-ran to marriage or even commitment to a religious community, for which sacramental or quasi-sacramental ceremonies exist.

In the Catholic view (and I think there are good secular reasons to claim this as well), sacramentalizing makes something so. Lifting to public expression an everyday reality like friendship invests it with meaning. The very act of doing so functions as a way of making it happen. For example, gathering a community of friends for a party guarantees that some who are unacquainted will meet, friends may become friends in a way that would never happen if the party were not held. Friendships that see the light of day in this way are reinforced by public affirmation. Friends are increasingly accountable to one another when it is known that they are friends *intending to be accountable*. It is that simple.

Of course I am not suggesting that every friendship be celebrated publicly, nor that so-called sacramentalizing is magic. I am simply observing that public acknowledgement adds something essential that should not be reserved only for marriages, much less only for Catholics. To repeat, sacramentalization is too powerful to be given over to religions that use it sparingly. It belongs to the created order.

In urging the sacramentalization of friendship I am not arguing for more sacraments in the Catholic Church. I do not expect to live to see such a sensible expansion of its sacramental system. I am suggesting that religious traditions have a good relational intuition at work when they provide a forum for persons to express their commitment in a public and religious setting. That forum, sadly, is circumscribed by some religions' own strictures (e.g., in the Catholic tradition a denial of that forum to persons who are divorced, to persons who are in same-gender relationships, to those who choose to marry a non-Catholic without dispensation). Still this secular sense of sacrament is a good idea that others can take up and use.

The act of taking public responsibility for relationships is useful. It is good to acknowledge and celebrate love for its own sake. Other groups could fruitfully follow the churches' lead and teach them something in the process about the almost limitless possibility of friendships.

My suggestion is that friends take ourselves and one another seriously enough to develop such public expressions. I say that mindful of the fact that many of us are finally more private than such extroverted expressions allow. But the point is that we, too, need some ways to tell one another, ourselves, and the world at large whom we love and that it is good. We need ways to express what it means to be friends. We need gestures, rituals, ceremonies that are not now second nature in the way that heterosexual rites of commitment have become. If the exclusive hold of marriage is to be broken, then society must find and/or develop ways to express other forms of commitment. Such ceremonies help to orient people, at least symbolically, in an evolving relational order. Besides, the lack of imagination, both relational and ceremonial, in evidence at most public rituals of commitment is so embarrassing as to beg for improvement.

Some ceremonies exist and have been a part of Western Christian life for centuries. Not surprisingly, they have been kept under wraps in recent times. John Boswell's research proves that their expressions are remarkably varied and widespread.[11] Early findings in his research indicate that the existing sources are mainly ceremonies for two friends, often something like a same-sex marriage ceremony, which is now drawing increasing attention especially in the Episcopal Church.[12] Professor Boswell's research helps to show the link between current desires to affirm same-sex relationships and past commissionings of friends who went forth to spread the Christian Gospel. Affirmation of friends who committed their lives to one another in concrete work was something that a community could do easily. Why not revive some semblance of this as one among many ways to celebrate the generative qualities of friendship?

Few of these ceremonies stress friendship outside of the one-to-one model that mimics the heterosexual configuration. I do not mean to inspire the alternative, promiscuity, nor the unrealistic position argued for by some religiously committed celibates that they, like Christ, are to love everyone. Such foolishness is easily read as encouragement for a lack of commitment (sometimes found in the whimsical maxim "celibacy means you do not have to be monogamous"). Rather, I am suggesting that coupled and uncoupled alike should be thinking about community. Nothing is gained simply by adding same-gender friends to the existing marriage model. Why celebrate at all if only to stress another twosome to the exclusion of a larger community? Why mimic a marriage model that does not work for many heterosexuals? Why have a ceremony that makes more people feel left out or uncommitted? Better to stay home and keep things quiet.

My own view of celebration is that since celebrations of friendship are almost nonexistent, then any new celebrations ought to be occasions for stressing the communal nature of friendship. Every opportunity to lift to public expression the efforts people are making, however unsuccessful, to love well deserve attention. Several approximations of this new approach come to mind.

Greta's fiftieth birthday was an occasion for gathering friends from a variety of sectors for a weekend in the country. Rather than receiving gifts, Greta made clear that she was giving her friends reminders of how important they were in her life. Each one was different, a token of a shared memory, something the friend liked, a reminder of an activity they enjoyed together. It was a simple but provocative shift in power dynamics, bringing friends together to meet and get acquainted through their common source, Greta.

Another example is the annual women's music festivals, which are a time to gather friends. One of the ways in which to celebrate and reinforce friendships is by making attendance a priority. Ethnic groups gather in the same way for German Days, Irish picnics, Latina fiestas. Extended families have reunions in backyards and parks as ways to catch up and move along together. Whatever the occasion, these are ways to attend to friendship.

Anniversaries, usually reserved to heterosexual couples, are something that friends are gradually adapting for their own use. When same-sex couples mention theirs, the first question that arises is, "But what do you celebrate?" There are plenty of things to celebrate: a first sexual experience, meeting, a phone conversation that changed things. Imaginations are the limit. The important thing is that people see that friendship, like marriage, takes attention. Celebrating it once a year using whatever milestone as an excuse is very little to ask.

Some groups of friends find that certain holidays, for example, Thanksgiving in my culture, provide natural times for making explicit references to their friendships. Whatever the form, the content of public coming together by groups of friends is powerful. It need not replace family ties and gatherings, but it certainly complements them in an increasingly important way as family ties become all the more complicated due to divorces, blended families, and new reproductive technologies.

I leave additional rituals for later exploration and developments by friends. They are, after all, the "experts" in this field since it is a challenge to develop ceremonies that convey friendship without sentimentalization, that express affection without romanticizing human possibility.

In fact, much ritual is accomplished one to one, over dinner, or in bed, or with a small group in the natural unfolding of life together. But bringing these events to community attention, sacramentalizing them, is a way of filling in the blanks for those who cannot imagine new ceremonies, much less new relationships. It is this lack of imagination, both relational and ceremonial, that can only be addressed in communities of friends to which we will turn our attention shortly.

In fact, of seven billion greeting cards sold annually, almost two billion are considered "nonoccasion" cards, intended obviously to fill in the blanks. I suggest that the "relationship without rules" or fierce tenderness is as common as "a common loaf of bread" (Judy Grahn). Little ceremonies are often sufficient, but making them public helps the rest of us.

A Holocaust survivor, married to another Holocaust survivor, tells of their frequent nightmares. When one of them wakes up screaming from a nightmare about the most heinous crime in our time, the other gets up too. They make tea for one another, regardless of the hour. They have drunk a lot of tea in fierce tenderness. Their simple celebration underscores the way in which friends help one another to survive. How generous of them to share this with a larger circle of friends.

· 6 ·

Justice-seeking Friends in Unlikely Coalitions

We'll weave a love that opens our eyes
    to see one another beyond all disguise
Where trust like water will wash away lies
    Together my friend we'll weave on,
        we'll weave on

We'll weave a love that holds the despised,
    the stranger who wanders the focus of lies
We'll stand sure as mountains with Earth's victimized
    Together my friends we'll weave on,
        we'll weave on

—Carolyn McDade
"Song of Community"

Many parents express deep emotion when explaining away their "thirtysomething" unmarried daughter and her male companion by sighing, "Oh, they're just friends," when asked about their daughter's prospects for marriage. Equally, many a daughter has despaired of weaning her parents from this heterosexist response especially when she and her *compañero* enjoy one another's company.

"Just friends" is a phrase that haunts. It connotes the reality, disappointing to some, that most friendships do not come to fruition in marriage. Nor should they. For a parent wanting grandchildren this is a source of chagrin, but for the world at large it is a happy fact of life. It is about time that theology caught up with this reality instead of pretending otherwise. Then perhaps some adequate and meaningful ways of evaluating and encouraging "right relations" can emerge.

An even happier fact that I want to highlight, if it is not already obvious from experience, is that maybe, just maybe "just friends" is really an abbreviation for "justice-seeking friends." At least exploring the possibility will open new relational horizons and provide constructive ways to understand the variety of friendships that are written off as "just friends." In fact I seek a world in which the phrase "just friends" will be shorthand for the fact that friendship is the pinnacle of human relating.[1]

The phrase "just friends" conveys exactly how a heterosexist, patriarchal society treats friendship. The opposite is not "friends," as in "we're real friends," but marriage partners. The disappointment in the parents' voices is not due to the quality of the daughter's friendship with her *compañero*, but to the fact that the daughter is not about to marry him. She is not about to move from friendship to spouse, from at least theoretical equality to theoretical inequality in a patriarchal culture. She is not about to forsake her interdependence for socially-enforced dependence (legal, economic, and other structures that limit married women's rights, e.g., to credit in their own names). Admittedly this view emerges from a white middle-class context. Marriage for women in African American communities, for example, can mean increased support for dependent children, access to financial resources that may spell the difference between life and death. But for many women the institution of marriage, like the institution of motherhood, has not changed sufficiently in the last two decades of feminist activism to guarantee a qualitatively different experience.

The fact that U.S. society is constructed to favor rigid family ties and not in favor of nurture, commitment, and mutual responsibility where they exist plays itself out on the other side as well. Women who are prevented from receiving government support if they are married to a man whose pay check will not stretch far enough and elderly people who are encouraged not to remarry because they will lose retirement benefits both point out the absurdity of the situation. In short, legal, social, and theological changes are needed to take account of changing mores. Then the moves toward forming friendships and not necessarily familial bonds will come more easily. Perhaps things are further along than I perceive when eighty-year-olds say, "To hell with marriage," if it will be too costly for them. Economics is a major factor in the formation of any relationship.

Lillian Rubin uses the phrase "just friends" to distinguish friends from blood relatives.[2] Her example of attending the wedding of a close friend's child and being consigned to a middle pew while blood relatives, regardless of their closeness to the family, were in the front makes clear the priority that is placed on family over friends in the most inappropriate ways. "Just friends" is a way of saying that some folks do not quite measure up relationally. It is to miss a big point, namely, that having friends is a great asset. There is no reason to apologize for friends nor to consign them to a lesser place than family. To do so is to reinforce the same cultural norm that brings us domestic violence, incest, and other unhealthy family patterns. These emerge in a society that has few if any alternatives for caring, nurturing constellations of people. This is especially problematic for women who, while typically holding the family together, for better or for worse, bear the fallout of the overused and ineffective family patterns.

Martha Ackelsberg makes this important point with regard to women: "families have *not* been the only sources of nurturance within most social systems...." She goes on to say that "while families may serve as institutions that nurture *men*, women have received much of *their* nurturance from extra-familial friendship ties."[3] In fact most women find more support from their neighbors and their co-workers than from their husbands.

This is not a phenomenon of late twentieth-century life, but something that has characterized Western society for generations. Carroll Smith-Rosenberg's look at nineteenth-century friendships, for example, makes clear that women relied extensively on one another for survival and pleasure. She concludes: "...the supposedly repressive and destructive Victorian sexual ethos may have been more flexible and responsive to the needs of particular individuals than those of the mid-twentieth century."[4] Her research came as something of a surprise to scholars in the early 1980s who had thought of their Victorian forbearers as the guarantors of family life, only to discover that we are guarding the pen that the animals left some while ago.

The larger methodological implication of Professor Smith-Rosenberg's project bears on our concern for developing a new moral norm for relationships:

> To ignore women is not simply to ignore a significant subgroup within the social structure. It is to misunderstand and distort the entire organization of that society. Incorporating women's experiences into our social analysis involves far more than adding another factor to our interpretation and thus correcting an admittedly glaring oversight. It forces us to reconsider our understanding of the most foundational or-

dering of social relations, institutions and power arrangements within the society we study.[5]

This is never more profoundly true than in religious ethics, where the systematic ignoring of women's experiences has meant that a powerful ethical system predicated on men's experiences holds sway to the exclusion of any female-based mores. That is why a norm based on friendship may be written off cavalierly even though significant data show that women's experiences of friendship are foundational. The most heinous approaches have been certain psychological theories of arrested development and prolonged adolescence for those who do not mate heterosexually "on time." These have been picked up uncritically by some Christian ethicists to explain the stages of human development and their parallel ethical mandates. The inevitable result is marriage, with divorce and/or life-long celibacy variously allowed as exceptions. As the limited (male) experiential base on which such an ethic is predicated becomes clear along with the role of friendship as the formative relational experience, ethical systems based on inadequate foundations need to be replaced.

Feminist Foundations for Ethics

The so-called First Wave of feminism, like the so-called Second Wave, was rife with female friends encouraging one another to make change, beginning with the most foundational social unit, the family, and aiming at the still elusive Equal Rights Amendment. Rosemary Radford Ruether notes that part of what broke up the old feminist movement was a negative view of women bonding, a new active heterosexuality, thus a focus on relations with men rather than with women. Consciousness-raising groups, so characteristic of the early years of the Second Wave, were considered threatening as much because women became friends as because of the ideology that emerged.

Women friends have been instrumental in social change, sustaining and nurturing one another in the acts of "speaking the truth to power." Many women friends emerge in the history of social change, for example, Susan B. Anthony and Elizabeth Cady Stanton, Jane Addams and her Hull House colleagues, Angela Davis and the supporters who accompanied her throughout her trial, Dorothy Day and the Catholic Workers. In fact, it is hard to find an example of a woman who made social change apart from a group of friends.

This is especially true in the histories of female-founded religious orders, where the foundress frequently had a close companion with whom she headed out to save the world as well as a strong friendship circle of other members. These provide material for a separate study of women's friendships. Biographies reveal many intimate friends who undoubtedly sustained one another in the face of cultural (and ecclesiastical) resistance.

Women friends making change is not a new phenomenon. Calling it what it is and celebrating the creative model that it provides for society's moral norms is. By contrast, the male model of the "rugged individual" taking on society often obscures the equally present support group. If "the wife" is credited at all, she is praised for maintaining the home rather than for her public contributions. Or the female secretary, graduate student, or administrative assistant is mentioned by-the-by with no acknowledgement of her contribution, however substantial it may be. This pattern not only allows elitism to go unchallenged, but it distorts history.

Friends Survive

Women's friendships in a patriarchal context emerge as much out of necessity as out of attraction. This is not negative, as if the ideal were electromagnetic force that mysteriously glued people together in the manner that romantic novels, beauty magazines, and soap operas would have it. Rather, many women's friendships grow from the need to survive. Whether the conditions of their survival include bringing up children, getting through school, making it on a fixed income, talking every day with someone who says you're not crazy, or "making a way where there is no way," women friends help one another survive. Survival is never seen as simply an individual experience, but as a way in which a community for women makes it through.

Thus women's friendships have a social component to them almost implicitly. This is a different starting point than male-male or even female-male friendships. Male-male friendships typically have mutual enhancement as their *modus operandi*. Power meets power and produces more power. Female-male friendships are alleged to start with mutual attraction. That model takes the energy inward, usually resulting in an enhancement of power for the male and a diminution of power for the female. A careful look at this phenomenon is properly the subject of another study, and of course exceptions prove the rule. But in general this is the pattern, at least in the West, for many mixed-gender friendships. It is a contributing factor to why so many marriages flounder. In a patriarchal culture equality between female and male is chancy at best, given the myriad factors that structure inequality.

This built-in social component, the fact that survival depends on bonding and bonding facilitates survival, is why I choose women's friendships as the prototype of a new ethical norm. Many progressives who work toward structural change have passed over this crucial component, claiming that it is somehow "bourgeois decadence" to focus on the so-called private sphere of friendship. What they do at home is no one's business. But friendship, by its relational nature and public character, defies this split. Such rhetoric exposes the extent to which even the most "politically correct" have bought society's line that friendship is a privatized relationship. The more effectively that message can be spread the more firmly entrenched are patriarchal ethics.

Friendship is a political choice. It is what helps to break down the artificial distinction between personal life and political commitment, which most women experience as integrally bound together. Changes in friendship patterns, e.g., a female politician turning to her women friends for support, is not individual change only, but a form of social change as well. War-like behavior at the interpersonal level in the U.S. peace movement, for example, is a remnant of this archaic thinking. Starhawk and other feminist activists have tried to weave feminist relational patterns into the peace movement with varying degrees of success.[6] The point is that justice-seeking friends begin their search at home but it never ends there. "Justice-seeking friends" is redundant among those whose survival is at stake. The main insight into this reality is provided by womanist theologian Delores S. Williams. She defines womanist, after the fashion of writer Alice Walker, as a perspective that is "committed to survival and wholeness of entire people, male and female."[7]

Delores Williams goes on to say that the major concerns of womanist theology are survival and "community building and maintenance...[for] the entire Christian community and beyond that to the larger human community."[8] Note that a womanist theological perspective, while rooted in the Christian tradition, sees the whole human family as its proper context. Just as sacramentalizing can be secular, so too can feminist and womanist theologies be as useful in the secular arena as in the religious one. I daresay receptivity is often greater there than in Christian churches that find such insights threatening to their base. The context in which such work is done is "demonarchy," the expression of racism and class struggle that grounds a womanist approach in survival needs and thus sheds light on all women's experiences, different though they may be.[9] White feminists may not appropriate nor usurp womanist insights, but learn from them. As activists, especially Bell Hooks, have stressed, "Until all women are free no woman is free."[10]

Womanist insight into the demonic character of patriarchal society underscores the need for women, especially women who are exploited economically and discriminated against racially, to form bonds that will assure their survival. That they seek justice goes without saying. Their examples highlight the extent to which all women, though to varying degrees due to class, race, age, and sexual preference, struggle to survive. We all "get by with a little help from our friends," but some need and some give more than others.

Of necessity women's friendships are grounded in struggle. For some women this means the daily economic grind. For others it is the psychological battle for self-confidence and personal worth. Women struggle with all manner of issues in between: job, children, incest, rape, loss of memory, death of a parent, AIDS, boredom. As Ada Maria Isasi Diaz reminds, *"La vida es la lucha!"* (Life is struggle). In no way do I consider these struggles parallel. Women whose struggle involves food and shelter will simply not live long enough to experience the anxiety of their white upper-class oppressors. Urgency alone gives their concerns a moral priority. But in each instance women's friendships make a significant difference. Building bridges across class/race/national lines, to which I will refer shortly, is something for which friendship, though not sufficient, in the absence of other resources, is at least a start.

Equally important to a womanist perspective that helps to locate and analyze women's friendship is Delores S. Williams's insistence on "women's determination to love themselves," as an antidote to taking on too much of the community's burden. Professor Williams, following Alice Walker again, advises that "women can avoid this trap by connecting with women's communities concerned about women's rights and well-being."[11] Here the explicit connection to "black feminists like Sojourner Truth, Frances W. Harper, and Mary Church Terrell" paves the way for future womanist reflections on African American women's friendships as a resource for theology.[12]

The implications of this foundational work in womanist theology shape my claims about friendship from a feminist perspective. For a religious tradition like Christianity that is allegedly based on the good of the whole community, women's friendships deepen and extend the message. In fact, women's friendships challenge the adequacy of Christianity's central metaphor, the death and resurrection of a man who laid down his life for his friends. This is one reason why many feminist women find the Christian message so dubious.

Women friends surely would have seen to a woman's survival and not to her death. Some friends Jesus must have had! Granted friendship does not stop death, but the mystique of giving up life in order to find it again does not appeal as readily to those who are struggling to survive as it might to those who in a "survival of the fittest" contest consider themselves the fittest. A more apt metaphor from women's experience would be the triumph of a group of women over injustice without losing anyone. The mythical dimensions of the resurrection story are decidedly male in this respect. What meaning feminists find in the Christian tradition comes not so much from Jesus and his friends, but from the "Jesus movement," those who bonded together in reaction to loss.[13] I can only conclude (in the imaginative constructive mode of Elisabeth Schüssler Fiorenza) that the Jesus movement must have been made up of lots of women just as today's churches are held together by women's bonds.

Perhaps some of the feminist critique of the artistic rendering of a woman on the cross, "The Christa," is because we intuit that a woman savior would have been significantly different. A more authentic possibility would have been, at the very least, several women killed together for something they believed in. A better image would be a group of women refusing to hand over any one of their own to be killed. Their triumph would be as powerful as any resurrection story to instill hope and sustain memory. How different the Christian tradition would be if either of these were the dominant symbols.

I do not mean to romanticize women's goodness, nor to suggest that women friends cannot destroy one another with unspeakable acts of betrayal. History is full of examples. I am simply painting with a wide theological brush in order to point out how deeply ingrained the normativity of individual male experience is in the Christian tradition. Whether it can be modified enough in this regard to warrant women's continued adherence is an open question.

Rather than answer that question prematurely, or be sidetracked into rebutting a male-based tradition, I suggest three elements of women's friendships that have broad ethical significance. Then I will turn to what groups of justice-seeking friends ought to be, i.e., what religious communities (in the broad sense of church as well as in the narrow sense in which the term is now used to connote canonical and noncanonical groups) could be if an ethic of fierce tenderness and not a patriarchal one were to hold sway.

Elements of Female Friendship

It is virtually impossible to survey with any accuracy the myriad female friendships so as to construct an archetype. Prototypes work better for conveying the dynamic nature of the experience. However, literary, anthropological, psychological, and sociological data permit a feminist theological analysis that begins with three common themes in women's friendships that converge on a single unifying factor. They are attention, generativity, and community. They converge on justice.

Let me mention each one, then illustrate them more aptly by using the six case studies of women's friendships. It will become obvious why justice-seeking friends is such a rich, descriptive phrase, such a laudable and attainable ethical goal.

Attention, as mentioned earlier, is essential to the development and nurture of friendship. More than trust or attraction, more than admiration or nurture, attention is the factor that holds friends together. Even in times of petty disagreement and substantive difference, the commitment to slog on with a friendship, to attend to it even when it is not pleasant, is something that women seem to do. Sometimes we hang on too long, but usually the instinct to keep at it pays off. Women are not particularly apt at putting differences aside and moving on as if such differences did not matter because in fact they do. Men's seeming "ability" in this regard, while enviable at times when it proves expedient, is finally, not that at all. Rather, it is often a way of keeping what is painful at a distance so as not to upset the status quo. The problem is that it prevents the kind of deepening that comes with working through problems even at the risk of losing a friend.

Attending to the little things is characteristic of women friends. One woman, recently divorced and experiencing her first love affair with a woman, was asked by her teenage child why she had received flowers. "Because Kate is a nice person," was the mother's reply. Apparently her child was not used to such simple attention during the marriage. It is hard to get too much attention from friends, and the little things add up.

Generativity is even harder to define but just as obvious. Generativity means making something new, literally creating out of whole cloth what would not be there if the good energy of the friendship did not exist. Society teaches that love generates babies and little else. It takes a discerning eye, a feminist hermeneutic, and often a lesbian one as well, to perceive properly, to be able to see what else women's friendships generate. One thing that is generated is the protective space, both psychic and physical, to survive. Beyond survival, women's friendships generate music, poetry, gardens, woodworking, sewing, sports, home repairs, literature, even theology all inspired by muse-like women friends who call forth truths and talents that might have been left hidden without their beckon.

Community is similarly amorphous but just as common. If friendships come in plural, then their actual configuration is more like a community than a couple. While this may seem overwhelming — why can't we just be friends and be left alone? — the fact is that attention to friends generates community. This is more than a trite phrase; it is more like a law of relational physics. Simply put, people like to be around people who love well. There are people who have lots of friends; others who complain about a lack of social life. This is not coincidental, although I have claimed with equal conviction that there is some luck and circumstance involved. It is contingent on the time, energy, and hard work that make friendships possible.

A sense of community cannot be forced. It does not emerge just because people are in the same closed room or have made vows in the same fashion. It emerges slowly as a network grows between friends who share similar values and who nurture one another. Religious communities are common; some people who share beliefs, commitments, and praxis are bound to become friends.

Communities of resistance and struggle abound; having a common goal that demands action is a galvanizing force. Just as common are local, grassroots groups of friends who gather without determined goals but because they enjoy one another's company. All of these groups have reason enough to be. Their being points in the direction of justice. Let me review the cases before illustrating this conclusion.

Justice-seeking Friends

Attention is a clear dimension of each of the friendships. Recall that Deborah and Sandra were on a trip abroad together, taking time to nurture their friendship. Coca and Julia rarely left each other's sight, and certainly Julia would not let Coca meet with a group of strangers unaccompanied. Likewise Susan and Adrian were forever enjoying the outdoors together. It was their time together and their way of relating physically.

Catherine attended to others so much that it is not clear that she took sufficient care of herself. Some would say that she made a choice, but all would agree that she attended and attended and attended. Peg, Jane and Karen certainly attended to one another on an annual basis. Little is said about the quality of their interaction during the rest of the year, but setting aside a week to be together is more attention than some friends get in a year. Kathy and Dawn lost their friendship because one chose not to attend to the other and the other felt the loss.

In all of these examples it was an unspoken but implicit assumption that attention is a legitimate expectation in a friendship. It is expected that friends will take time and give attention to one another. Without attention, as Kathy and Dawn exemplify, the friendship is doomed. But with it, there are an infinite variety of ways that people can actualize the potential for friendship that is part of the human condition. There are of course equally many ways of thwarting that potential, beginning with unjust social structures (racism, class stratification, gender discrimination, heterosexism) and continuing with inattentive behavior.

Generativity takes many forms in the examples cited. Deborah and Sandra meet new people and build new bridges between their country and Latin American women. They generate a renewed sense of family as well. Coca and Julia build bridges too between their community and women who are very different from them. Without their friendship, without Julia's support, Coca would never do it alone. They generate new possibilities for their children, opening paths for them in parts of their own country beyond their immediate neighborhood.

Susan and Adrian generated more than their share of risk. Their own love was so surprising that they could hardly contain it, yet they knew the disastrous consequences that would have followed. Adrian's children could have been taken away from her; Susan's religious congregation might have dismissed her. Still they were able to generate good energy for the children and an even deeper sense of love in community out of their brief but powerful friendship.

Catherine built more than bridges. She generated committees and coalitions, subgroups, affinity groups, and every other human bonding imaginable to get the job done, the job for women that she defined as developing economic power and preventing burnout. As she pounded many a table to make her point she birthed and midwived programs, projects, and publications that other people usually completed. That is generativity and it can be exhausting.

Peg, Jane, and Karen generated energy and enthusiasm for their work. As physicians they experienced burnout from long hours, sometimes routine work, and the thankless schedules that left them few holidays and evenings for themselves and their families. Without their annual respite to sit back and take a long look at the year gone by and the year ahead they would have almost no opportunities for reflection.

Kathy and Dawn knew the difference once their friction started. They were used to creating art together and to critiquing each other's work. Their students became an extension of themselves as they formed a new generation of artists. When their rift came and they were only sparking each other's tempers instead of each other's creativity, it was perhaps the wisest decision to move apart, especially for their students' sake. Things could have gotten worse.

In each of these examples the next analytic step is asking why the friendships produce the explicit justice dimension. It is, after all the task of theology to explore meaning and value. It will be all the more obvious in the context of community in each instance.

Deborah and Sandra named their friendship in the context of a community of women from various countries. Other friends at the meeting who were engaged in social change work were like a mirror held up to them in which they recognized their own friendship for what it was. Coca and Julia obviously came from a community — their families and neighbors — and automatically expected some sense of community with the strangers with whom they met although they maintained a critical distance at the outset. It was exciting to realize that people with their narrow but deep experience of human community in a poor *barrio* could transfer it so effectively as to draw the best out of the group gathered.

Susan and Adrian had plenty of community, perhaps too much to have time and conditions for nurturing their own friendship. This can happen. Between a family and a religious order there is little psychic room to be two adults in the midst of fresh love. If anything, they needed less community, or at least a different community, for example, a strong feminist community in which to be affirmed for who they are and whom they love. They needed to find role models, other women who have had the same experience, lived through it, thrived even, to let them know that it can be done. But this was not to be in their case. Now their love simply instructs others to love well without delay.

Catherine had competing communities as well. Her religious order, while formative in her early years, simply did not keep pace with her ever expanding horizons. Luckily she found other people with whom to experience community, never forsaking her sisters, but always hoping that they would share her with the many poor, struggling, feisty people with whom she cast her lot on a regular basis. That they did is proof of community.

Peg, Jane, and Karen found that if two is a couple than three is community. They each came from different living situations and groups of friends, but all of their "significant others" (including Peg's fiancé who finally got the message) realized and respected the three's privacy. Similarly, when they got together they left the phone number only for the direst of emergencies and made sure that competent colleagues were covering their practices. Little interfered with their community time.

Kathy and Dawn, having known something about being friends in a community of other artists and teachers, chose to give that up. The breakup of their friendship meant that their friends had to redraw their own relational lines with each of them. Friends had to learn what they could say and not say depending on which of them was present. Some looked back and said that their breakup marked a turn in the road for their artistic medium with two competing schools emerging out of the one that they had shared. Such is the impact of a breakup on a closely knit community.

In each example the cumulative effect of attention, generativity, and community (as well as the impact of the lack of any or all of these) hints at justice. Deborah and Sandra realized the drastic class, economic, and racial differences that separated them from their friends in the south. They realized that a similar (though by no means comparable) gulf stood between them if they permitted the family tie to take precedence over their friendship. Justice is justice.

Coca and Julia were friends in the struggle for social change. Despite their ability to interact with other women, their primary responsibility was to the women of their own *barrio*. Justice means water, electricity, garbage pickup, a food co-op, child care, and these will not be achieved talking with anthropologists. But if those same anthropologists can be enlisted in the work at hand, and if the work is always primary, then these friends had reason for hope.

Susan and Adrian's friendship points the way to justice — to limitless possibilities of love for women with women. It became obvious to them that neither of them had made a real choice for her present situation as long as loving a woman had not been an option for her. Of course it was an option, but they agreed that the price seemed so high — the loss of respect for being a lesbian, the almost certain rejection twenty years before by a religious order, most of whose members could not have spelled the word, and the limited possibilities to have children — that it was a price neither of them considered paying. Justice was served by their simple act of loving.

Justice is frequently linked with Catherine's name. It is hard to imagine a friend whom she had not met at or cajoled into some social change activity. From civil rights marches to Central American trips, from women's ordination to reproductive rights she was a name people knew, a body they could expect to be there. Her friends came to realize that they would have to be right next to her if they wanted time with this justice-seeker. It always seemed like the connections between/among issues were clearest at her side.

Peg, Jane, and Karen sought justice for themselves. Frankly, this is unusual for women, and is often looked upon as solipsistic, as if women are only to look outward and at macro structures for justice. But this is something that friends teach us, that justice begins with oneself, treating oneself and one's friends at least as well as one would treat those who struggle for justice. This lesson has been lost on many feminists who have been so busy saving the whales that sometimes, at least momentarily, they have forgotten to do justice for themselves.

Kathy and Dawn illustrate how justice can be thwarted. It is not clear that the students involved will ever really be evaluated fairly by their teachers. How much will their own competitiveness show up, however inadvertently, in their reactions to the other students' art? Nor is it certain that the two will be able to collaborate in the future on the kinds of projects that had attracted them to one another in the first place — political art in the antinuclear movement. But that justice work will simply have to be borne by others, in justice to Kathy and Dawn.

Justice-seeking friends are more than Aristotle's image of "civic friendship" implies. Characteristically, he puts the emphasis on the good of the *polis*, expecting virtue by men without paying sufficient attention to the persons (especially women), their situations, and their power relationships. While his insight may have served well in his moment, women's friendships today provide a so much more complete, well rounded, nothing-wasted approach that I daresay Aristotle's version pales by comparison.

Bertha Conde observed that

> the ties of friendship are more potent in fashioning the wills of individuals than the bonds of blood. One never knows where the life of love

will lead.... The peace of the world will in the end depend upon our capacity for friendship and willingness to use it.[14]

I quite agree that justice-seeking friends are a powerful force that can effect widespread change. However, friendship bonds are not made willy nilly without regard for the real differences between and among women.

Structural Enemyhood and the Work of Justice

In each case studied a common thread of justice runs through these women's friendships. But so too does the structural enemyhood that places people at odds with one another in an unjust world. This will not be overcome easily. Understanding attention, generativity, and community as common elements of friendships on the micro level is useful for strategizing for social/structural change.

The hope is in the formation of unlikely coalitions of justice-seeking friends. This strategy takes seriously that women of all racial/ethnic, economic, age, and sexual preference groups will bond more naturally with one another than with women from other such groups. Likewise, it takes account of the fact that privileged women, whether white, wealthy, heterosexual, able bodied, and/or living in a so-called First World country have the demands of justice embedded in their friendships just as much as their disadvantaged sisters.

Building coalitions across the lines of structural enemyhood is very difficult. But it is one of the few and most promising strategies for making social change. There are likely and unlikely coalitions because both are necessary. We need the people like us with whom we can be at home without explaining presuppositions at every turn. But we also need to become friends with people who are quite different. Justice demands a reallocation of scarce resources, a redistribution of goods and property, a rethinking of old prejudices, and a reordering of priorities to reflect inclusivity. This cannot be done without many different voices participating in the conversation.

This reallocation sets the ethical agenda for people of good will, especially for Christians, for generations to come. It is overwhelming on the face of it. But broken down into the formation of unlikely coalitions of justice-seeking friends for specific tasks, for limited periods of time, for achievable goals, it is at least a start. It is because of experiences of this sort with friends, like my Argentine, Uruguayan, and Chilean friends, that I have even dim hope. As I have mentioned, I collaborate with these women in an ongoing project, "Women Crossing Worlds," an effort to share resources, exchange personnel, and "promise a permanent presence" as Latin and North American women.[15] While the program has achieved certain educational and liturgical goals, the hardest thing to convey but the most meaningful dimension of it is the bonds that have been forged among women. Friendship permits, nay demands, honest conversation, critical commentary, and pointed suggestions. Moreover, it is a privilege to accompany each other as friends through the ups and downs of governments, children, churches, and selves. Each sees her own setting differently because of cross-cultural friendships. Motivation for social change work comes from the knowledge that crossing worlds means doing justice.

This strategy of female friendship needs more exercise. It means listening to and appreciating on their own terms women whose racial/ ethnic identity is African American, Asian, Latin American, African. It means letting diversity show, expressing particularity without watering it down. Diversity can mean division; particularity does mean difference.[16] Feminist women are at the very earliest stages of learning how to share power, how to handle respective histories of injustice without dishonoring the roots that have nurtured other women.[17]

Womanist theology raises the question of whether African American women will choose to define themselves as feminist at all, and whether white women ought to refer to their perspective as womanist. Historical differences attend both of those words. To use them interchangeably is simply unacceptable. Still there are consequences for the use of each. Will womanist be acceptable in circles where feminist is a dirty word? Will feminist work suddenly seem establishment while womanist perspectives are left aside? Perhaps for now the most that can be hoped for is to avoid being set in opposition to one another. That in itself will be an accomplishment. Friends will try to see to it.

These are important questions and heady times for which only "unlikely coalitions" are sufficient to keep the conversation going. In many instances it is literally only because women of different racial groups are friends, and because they have developed some trust for one another over a long period of time, that difficult conversations can go on that will generate new insights.[18]

Once again Martha Ackelsberg's insightful comments are helpful. Friendship, she writes, can be "the basis for radical political association."[19] She continues,

although the roots of the women's movement are to be found in friendships, feminists and others have not thought seriously enough about
friendship as an alternative social model, as a ground from which to
respond to claims about the need for more communitarian and less
individualistic values in contemporary life.[20]

This insight bolsters the need to begin to think structurally about
friendship, about how unlikely coalitions of justice-seeking friends
can best work for social change and modify deeply entrenched views
and structures without being destroyed in the process. The sinister
genius of such unfriendly institutions is to set friends against one
another. It is as much a danger in the theological world as elsewhere.

For white women the temptation to brush aside differences in an
effort to resolve problems is strong. While so-called unlikely coalitions
may form, they cannot obscure the fact that justice-seeking friends are
still friends, demanding of each other attention to difference, generating new ways of dealing with it, and building communities of struggle
to do so. To call another "sister" uncritically is to betray lingering alle-
giances to the structures of inequality that the family metaphor keeps
alive. It will take longer to be able to say "friend," but doing so is a
step toward justice and therefore worth the wait.

The Ekklēsia of Justice

Theological ethics have traditionally been connected to a religious
tradition, embedded in the dogma and doctrine of a faith community.
One of the insights of religious feminists (and for me as a Catholic
it is especially powerful) is that just as women are said to have no
country, neither do many experience having a church. Discrimination
and our personal integrity lead to distancing from those institutions
that malign whatever good news they may once have had to offer by
refusing to abandon the obviously inadequate ways of their fathers.

Thus feminist religious ethics must construct a new meaning of
"church" or "ekklēsia" in order to contextualize its content. Or, à la
Mary Daly, women will move beyond the boundaries to the "New
Space" and "New Time" where the connections to patriarchal poli-
ties are severed once and for all. Mary Daly's approach has much to
recommend it. First, it leaves theology aside for the allegedly more
open philosophy, though I think it can be argued that philosophy is
finally just as tainted as theology. Second, it changes the intellectual

milieu by ignoring the trappings of religious belief, e.g., connection to a faith tradition, emphasis on worship/liturgy where most people meet religion (rather than on speculative writing), and focusing on immediate experience. Third, it is an attractive move because the audience is far broader and the implications for ethical work farther reaching. It is finally to leave aside most of what Western people know to be religious in order to begin anew from women's experience.

Problems notwithstanding, Mary Daly's strategy is far more effective for accomplishing my ethical agenda than any I have seen in the various reformist schools of Christian churches. Still I think another equally ambitious and ultimately just as challenging approach is to reconstruct the understanding of church that prevails in order to locate feminist religious ethics in a fresh context.

I do this using the concept of women-church that I have described earlier. Rather than simply insisting that women's experiences be taken seriously within the Christian framework, not unlike trying to adjust the understanding of wife without tinkering with the concept of husband, the women-church approach involves fundamental change in the context of Christian self-understanding both for individuals and for groups.

Women-church is made up of at least three central components. First, it is the historical development of women's base communities, small groups that gather in the homes of the members for worship, social change, and community building.[21] These groups of justice-seeking friends call themselves church. They link with one another through informal and formal networks; they connect to those parts of the Christian tradition that take women seriously, and they reject those that discriminate.[22] Solidarity and sacrament characterize these groups as church though they have much in common with other women-spirit groups from other traditions that are growing as well.

Second, women-church implies a theological commitment to develop a "discipleship of equals," an ekklēsia of "self-identified women and women-identified men."[23] This traditionally rooted and feminist-inspired theological approach sums up the goal and strategy of the women-church movement. Women were not included in the early Greek understanding of *ekklēsia*, a civil model that permitted only "free male citizens" to vote for the whole.[24] So much for women and other marginalized people who were not meant from the beginning to be a part of decision making, to have full participation.

The texts of the Christian community, with a lot of help from Elisabeth Schüssler Fiorenza's imaginative reconstruction, clearly indicate that women and men make up the community. Historical encrustations of patriarchy have robbed women of the self-understanding and men of the woman-identification necessary to embody this in contemporary churches. Thus only by calling attention to it, making the place of women (and by inference other marginalized people as well) explicitly equal to that of men, can there be any hope of fulfilling the potential of the Jesus movement.

In this sense the women-church movement represents a religious safe place for women who have been spiritually abused in patriarchal churches. Likewise, it represents theological insurance against cooptation for women who find a place, however small and tentative, within their religious communities.

Third, women-church is an example of religious agency. By religious agency, as mentioned earlier, I mean the ability to name one's own religious experience, to make decisions on the basis of it, and to live out those decisions in a community that holds one accountable and provides support. Religious agency is what I as a Catholic woman, for example, have never experienced within my church, but what I as a participant in the women-church movement experience all the time.

Being a religious agent means taking new responsibility, for example, in worship. It means working through ethical issues that were previously decided by fiat. It means providing pastoral support for one another in the absence of a well-developed structure to do so. Religious agency is time and energy consuming. Justice-seeking friends aid one another in assuming more and more agency as part of women-church.

Religious agency comes in a variety of packages of which women-church is but one. Thus my starting point for religious ethics in women-church is not meant in any way to be normative for others. For example, African American women whose historical, theological, and personal experience does not make women-church their context have no obligation whatsoever to adopt the term. Nor should white women, struggling to make sense of structural enemyhood, rush to convey honorary or anonymous women-church status on those who do not embrace it for themselves.

The point is that women are religious agents in a variety of historically conditioned ways. Building unlikely coalitions across those gaps while respecting the integrity of the religious experience involved is part of the task at hand. This is what friends do as individuals and what friendly religious communities can do in the feminist ecumenism of the twenty-first century.

Partners, Friends, or Truth?

Women-church is not the only context in which friendship is being explored. The institutional Roman Catholic Church has picked up on the idea in the second draft of its proposed pastoral letter on women. Mention of this dubious move will illustrate how important a renewed context is to a renewed understanding of the concept of friends. It is also a warning to women about how quickly patriarchal religious institutions will coopt feminist-sounding language without attending to the substantive structural changes that will give appropriate context to such words.

In the much criticized first draft of the letter, *Partners in the Mystery of Redemption*, the word "partner" was objected to strenuously by readers.[25] Apart from the outrageous effort to have male bishops presume to write on women, and the embarrassing fact that the principal drafter of a statement by the bishops on women was actually a woman (whose name will soon be forgotten in favor of the bishops), the notion that women were partners simply did not wash. Women have no experience of partnership in the Roman Catholic Church. It is not a "discipleship of equals." Women cannot be ordained to the priesthood, nor participate in decision making. Women are not religious agents but the unwilling recipients of the spiritual largesse of men if and when any participation is permitted.

Women are used and abused in the stopgap attempts to shore up a hierarchical model of church by appointing women pastors of so-called priestless parishes. Women are insulted by the influx of ordained, married male Episcopalian/Anglican priests, another desperate attempt to keep a sinking ship afloat. Women are prohibited from teaching, preaching, and ministering in ways that differ from the establishment line. Women would be ill advised to seek partnership with persons who carry out such policies with impunity.

Instead of internalizing the critique, stopping the process, and practicing equality so as to have something to write about, the drafting committee skipped blithely to the notion of friends. The working title for the second draft is "I Call You Friends," a scriptural reference to Jesus' disclaimer about servants, his insistence that he called his followers friends. This is a nice idea, of course, but set in a patriarchal church "friends" has even more potential for insult and injury than "partners." The actual title of the second draft is "One in Christ: A Pastoral Response to the Concerns of Women for Church and Society." While it is decidedly worse than the first in its dogmatic insistence on status quo theology and polity, at least the bishops did not profane the word "friend" by building a letter on it.

I can only speculate as to what friendship might mean to the bishops. From a feminist perspective friendship means attention, generativity, and community building all aimed at justice. The contrast is vivid. In the patriarchal mindset of the Roman Catholic Church, even with the collective input of thousands of women who have talked with one another and been so gracious as to let an abusive institution in on their thinking, I shudder to think what would be implied by the use of the word "friends."

Attention would undoubtedly mean writing this one letter so as to get the monkey off the episcopal backs and return to business as usual, perhaps with a few compliant women to fill the clergy shortage. Generativity would probably take two forms. First, increased emphasis on women's "traditional call to motherhood" with attendant prohibitions on birth control, abortion, and lesbian sex would be obvious. Second, a subtle but not so thinly veiled invitation to women to generate energy for the church by increasing their participation in the helping roles while the institution maintains its customary ban on priesthood and de facto decision making would follow.

The community dimension of those who are called to be friends — and notice that the women friends do not do any calling — is of course the institutional church with its parish structure and hierarchy. Justice is entirely lacking in this approach. No substantive structural change is indicated that would set even the remotest preconditions for the possibility of friendship. The very use of the word "friends" in this context borders on theological pornography.[26] Like secular pornography, this misuse of persons objectifies women in a male-based understanding of friendship. It trivializes sexuality by passing over real differences. A serious analysis of the structural enemyhood that a feminist approach to church based on women's experiences demands is needed here. Finally, it leads to violence against persons by forcing women to leave their faith communities because their integrity will not permit them to participate in a lie.

Friendship for women, the fierce tenderness of justice-seekers, is simply too precious to be manipulated in this way. Of course it would be wonderful if friendship were a cure-all for centuries of discrimination. But it is not so easy and it degrades the very notion of friendship to presume that it is. Better to put the pens down for a bit, work at new relationships, and then, as an unlikely coalition of women and men, write something together. People might even become friends in the process, but at least they will not dishonor that experience by claiming it where it has little potential to be at the moment. Ironically, the bishops could learn a great deal from women friends that would be helpful in building new models of church.

· 7 ·

Fierce Tenderness in Deed

Every woman I have ever loved has left her print upon me,
where I have loved some invaluable piece of myself apart from
me — so different that I had to stretch and grow to recognize
her. And in that growing we came to separation, that place where
work begins.

—Audre Lord
Zami

A Theology of Friendship

I am wary of making too much of the friendship image, placing
more weight on it than any one concept can hold. But in the spirit
of theo-ethical analysis there are at least three obvious routes, the
divine, humanity, and the world, that invite exploration using this
material. These are not totally discrete categories, but they help to
organize insights for communal use. They are familiar to those who
do theology, and they are comprehensive in their scope. They expand the working definition of friendship in this book to one that
encompasses attention, generativity, community, and justice-seeking.
Friendship refers not simply to one-to-one human relationships, but
to much, much more.

165

Divine Friends

Imagining the divine as a friend is quite easy and rather pleasing. More than parent, spirit, and force, friend has the advantage of being widely available as a positive relationship, as one that is personal without being intrusive, powerful without being mystical. It is not perfect, but it works quite well in the absence of much competition.

The categories introduced earlier of attention, generativity, community, and justice provide a natural framework. Divine attention is expressed not only in the fact of creation, but in the abiding presence that religious people experience. God, the Goddess, the Holy, God/ess, et al. can be conceived of as an attentive friend.[1] This friend is waiting and cooperating creatively in the unfolding of history. This friend thinks of the smallest detail and permits the largest indiscretion without dominating or breaking the friendship.

A generative friend of the divine sort is equally compatible. Creation brims over with novelty; human beings are the proof of ongoing generativity. Art, music, and technology are open-ended expansions of the human horizon. A divine friend keeps on generating without end, so history overtakes and pushes into the future without apology. People go with that energy trusting that a divine friend is leading the way.

Human community flows from divine inspiration. People recognize common roots and celebrate the common condition as friends of the One who nurtures so many. This imagery is born out in the history of common suffering and promise that religious traditions have chronicled. Likewise it is useful for breaking down the particularities that set up hierarchies of privilege and dominance.

The justice dimension is equally obvious, especially when thought of with respect to the works of friendship. As argued earlier, the foregoing elements of attention, generativity, and community find their end in justice-seeking activities by justice-seeking friends. The God who is always on the side of the oppressed (Psalm 103:6) and the Goddess who stands with her people in the face of danger are obvious cases. Justice is no longer blindfolded. Justice stands with open arms and ample bosom ready to embrace and to nurture as necessary, to propel and encourage as appropriate. This is an image that women friends know and appreciate. The Pacha Mama, the Goddess of the earth in Latin America, is always connected with the harvest, the just production of the land tilled in right relation.

New images abound for a friendly divinity.[2] Like the figure of justice just described, the friendly companion divinity is a powerful possibility. She marches steadfastly "alongside" of her friends in the work of justice.[3] Like the Indian Weaver of Julia Esquivel's Guatemalan poetry, she beckons:

> Accompany us then on this vigil
> and you will know what it is to dream!
> You will then know
> how marvelous it is
> to live threatened with Resurrection!
> To dream awake,
> to keep watch asleep,
> to live while dying
> and to already know oneself
> resurrected![4]

Perhaps the most suggestive image for the divine that emerges out of women's friendships is not one divinity but many. Just as friends do not exist in the singular, neither is it feasible to imagine that something as complex and comprehensive as divinity could be singular either. There may even be a hint of this insight in the Christian trinitarian theologies, though I avoid the language of the hypostatic union. The point is that thinking of the divine as one friend reinforces a relationless content and minimizes the extent to which the divine, for all of its glory, is still more available through human imaginings.

Thus I conclude that "friend," while a relatively useful next step in articulating something about the divine, falls far short of the mark unless it is used in the plural. This polytheistic approach deserves more attention.[5] The point is that the notion of the divine as friend ought not to be plugged into the existing theological framework as if it were going to solve the problems that Father, Parent, Ground of Being, and other tried and untrue formulations have failed to solve. The fundamental problem is not so much with the image itself but with the context out of which it comes and in which it finds meaning.

Just as it is necessary to change the whole relational framework to make sense of women's friendships, so too is it necessary to revamp the theological landscape in order to use a new image for the divine. Communities of faith may find other ways to handle this problem. For example, they may stress their many relationships with the divine as a way to convey multiplicity. Or they may decide that the many different faith traditions, i.e., the many ways to be in a friendly relationship with the divine, are really diversity enough. In any case, the shifting is of the ground under the images as much as in the content of the images themselves. This is foundational theo-ethical work.

The concepts of plurality, polytheism, and diversity in relationship to the divine invite discussion. They challenge communities of friends to think anew, to discuss with one another what is ultimately meaningful and valuable. That is what theologizing means. The outcome is important of course, but in the long run on the issue of polytheism, for example, the important thing is to spark the religious imaginations of people who have probably never considered it before as a real option.

Nonetheless, there is plenty to recommend the divine as "friends" as a solution to the so-called problem of God-language. Diversity, complexity, and newness are all served. Lest premature enthusiasm lead anyone to regard this as *the* solution to the problem of God-language, it is important to note that at best this is a temporary solution to an unsolvable problem, not a final solution. After all, no language, however nuanced and metaphoric, is sufficient to name that which defies naming. That is the point. Theologizing just keeps going.

Still, "friends" serves an important purpose in theo-ethical reflection. It is not so much a name, which is after all only a placeholder in the language for that which has no proper name. It is a way to express at the limits of language what is ultimately most meaningful and valuable. In that sense, the use of "friends" is, I suggest, the best anthropomorphic choice since it represents the most accessible and at the same time most desirable *human relationship*, no more, no less.

"Friends," when used to speak of the divine, conjures up far more than parent or sibling, though it can include both of them. It announces relationship without having to say "we." It connotes co-responsibility, mutual influence and commitment on both sides of the divine-human equation. It is a voluntary relationship entered into with intention and maintained with love. It has an enduring quality that takes friends over time and into history. It is fierce and tender all at once and without explanation.

Sallie McFague makes the important observation that friendship is a relationship of "maturity."[6] This is a signal that the parent-child model on which most of Christian God-language has been based is finally inadequate to mature faith. Moreover, Joanne Brown and Rebecca Parker suggest that the Father-Child relationship expressed by the Christian doctrine of the Atonement may be the legitimation of divine child abuse, something that rampant child abuse in our society sadly renders plausible.[7]

"Friends" is a useful term in the language of prayer and worship. Friends speak to friends in terms of endearment; friends turn to each other in moments of need. Friends expect comfort and appreciate stimulation. "Friends" conveys a sense of trust and disappointment, of serendipity and betrayal. It is not just a happy word, but one that puts people in touch with personal and collective histories, both their positive and negative points.

While not wanting to overuse the concept, I conclude that "friends" is a rich and suggestive image that helps to explore and explain the many things that are meant by "divine." It is not perfect by any means, but then what friends are? It is used sparingly but enough to assess its "fit." Some communities may find it entirely inappropriate; others may call it the answer to problems long wrestled with and needing at least an intermediate solution.

Human Friends

This leads to the insights that friends provide for an understanding of humanity, the second standing category of theo-ethical analysis. Much of this has already been said on the basis of women's friendships with women. But it can and must be expanded to outline how other friendships work as well.

The fundamental categories of attention, generativity, community, and justice do not shift, but their content changes with explicit ethical claims for men, children, animals, and the earth. That is what it means to use a suggestive paradigm for the formulation of a new ethic. Of course the categories of experience never transfer precisely, but the overlap is sufficient to be suggestive.

Let me begin with men since it can be argued that feminist approaches leave them out. Nothing of the kind is going on here, though in a future volume, perhaps with a male collaborator, I might usefully employ female-male friendships as another starting point for theo-ethical reflection. In the Christian tradition it is highly unusual to single out female experience and make normative claims. When it is done it sometimes *feels* as if men have been passed over when in fact they have only been joined at the center of concern. They have inhabited that place alone for so long that it takes time for everyone to get used to sharing it.

The dynamic is usually that females appropriate male experience, fitting themselves, however awkwardly, into their mold. My proposal is not a turning of the tables; that would defeat the purpose. Rather, it is to suggest some parallels that might emerge if men were to take seriously that women's experiences participate in the larger rubric of human experience. The categories of attention, generativity, community, and justice-seeking are useful across the board, though not exhaustive.

Friendship between women and men provides additional clues to a constructive ethic. Attention needs to be shared. In a culture in which the needs of men have always been primary and in which women have been brainwashed into caretaking, this dynamic must even out for friendship to be possible. This requires both letting go of the need for the spotlight by men and a claiming of the legitimate place in the lights for women. Old patterns die hard.

Women's friendships model equality between equals, and in the case of structural enemyhood (i.e., race, class, differences), the need for justice between unequals until equality is achieved. This pattern begins in the reverse for female-male friendship. With equality between unequals as the starting point, the demands of justice are constant until equality is reached. This is both a case by case and a structural demand, an explanation for why so much frustration is built into female-male relationships. It often has less to do with the individuals themselves than with the structures of which they are a part. Many progressive women report this when they marry. For all of their good intentions, there are still people and institutions that do not respect their wishes, for example, to keep their own name or to continue their individual credit rating. They discover that structures rule.

Nonetheless, the insight here for an ethic of friendship is that justice-seeking must be a central activity. The very act of loving, of choosing to be friends in new ways, becomes part of the political order. No one wants to be calculating about friendship. People I want to be around do not subject their relationships to a standard of political correctness. We love as we love, or at least we like to think that we do. Still, it is naive to think that any friendship takes place beyond the boundaries of powerful social structures that determine and predetermine who will love and how.

Of course there are exceptions to this, both serendipitous ones and those that emerge from hard work at loving well. Everyone likes to think that theirs is the exception. But many of us have found ourselves sadly disappointed when the weight of patriarchy comes crushing down even on our best efforts. That is why personal efforts, my relationship with Bob, however wonderful, are never sufficient. If they were I would content myself with psychology and leave theo-ethical work aside. Attention to substantive structural change is necessary to make more and more female-male friendships approximate the quality that many women enjoy with one another.

Generativity takes many forms and the demands of "justice for all" go beyond simply a baby for every couple. The agony of people who cannot have children when they want them is a special pain, but one that is worsened by the pressure to procreate as if no other form of generative behavior were sufficient. If we cannot solve one part of the problem, i.e., infertility, we can at least lend a creative conceptual hand by unmasking the tyranny of an individualistic, "my baby" society that exploits prospective parents in unscrupulous "fertility" clinics. I advocate measures to help people with this painful problem of course, but I would insist that consideration be given to the many ways in which generativity takes place lest the agony of infertility be exacerbated by a one-track culture.

The countless other ways in which female-male friendships generate newness urge variety here. The mindset that controls contemporary ethical formulations is stuck on child-bearing as evidence of the pinnacle of human relating. Until this is undone, not simply for women friends but for women and men as well, there will be no friendly sharing of responsibility nor a full appreciation of generative powers. It is technically possible to "generate" children in a variety of ways because medical science has responded to human demand. Why not spend some money and energy exploring other options of justice-seeking generative action — housing for the homeless, meaningful work even if at lower pay, time for art and scholarship, forming international networks, or the many ways in which creative powers and society's resources could be put to use by female and male friends if the "heterosexual couple with 'our baby'" were not engraved in our psyches.

Community is equally challenging to mixed-gender friends. The powerful coupling of heterosexual patriarchy, the moves toward privatization of friendship, and the real limits on time and energy force the community dimension to fall away. Even parishes, congregations, and other local church groups are on the decline, raising the question where most people ever experience much community in heterosocial settings. The rise of Twelve Step programs like Alcoholics Anonymous, Gamblers Anonymous, Overeaters Anonymous, most of which are mixed gender (though they often have same-gender options such as women's A.A. groups), are evidence of the hunger that exists for community in general, for some form of communal accountability that also provides an equal measure of support.

Moreover, the most successful religious communities, namely, those that have withstood the rigors of a patriarchal church, have been made up of members of one gender. This was "logical" under patriarchy since it was presumed that mingling the genders would mean only one kind of generation. It never occurs to people that friends might generate art, scholarship, music, poetry or justice work, nor that single-gender groups would be just as sexually active with their own members. Mixed religious communities, though historically part of the scene (Quakers, Shakers, etc.), for the most part remain to be tried. Those experiments in intercommunity formation programs (for example, Franciscans or Dominicans, both women and men) are reported to be stimulating and successful.

All of these observations point to the need, in justice, for a wholesale rethinking of the ethical framework of adult women and men. Presuppositions based on outmoded data and prescriptions based on power-wielding protectors of virtue are simply inadequate for these complex relationships. While friendship is not a complete blueprint for just behavior, it provides enough clues to shape the parameters of justice-seeking actions.

Criteria of attentiveness, generativity, community-building, and justice-seeking are beginning points to use to assess the value of a friendship. There are many more possibilities once the theo-ethical strictures (such as compulsory heterosexuality, one marriage per person, no sexual experience outside of monogamous marriage, etc.) that Christian ethics has insisted upon are rethought. By adopting more open and realistic norms religious professionals and churches will regain credibility. In time religious professionals may even be seen again as a resource for discussing particular situations. Church communities may once again become a repository of the wisdom of those who have lived in right relation. For now, without substantial reshaping of theo-ethical foundations, these people and institutions in no way fulfill the function that therapists and informal support groups have taken on in their absence.

Friendship with children and between children raises other important factors. It is easy to romanticize children and their ways. But some guesses are better than others. One is that friendship is a learned activity as much as it is a potential with which people are born. As such it requires the careful nurture (attention) of adults who both model it in their own relationships and offer it as a possibility with children. Leery as I am about facile formulas that contend people learned everything they need to know in kindergarten (what about how to use a microwave oven and open a bottle of fine wine?) there is much to be said for early patterning.

Children make ethical mistakes all the time. Being their friends is a reminder of the need to forgive and forget just as quickly and move on to the next activity. They do this rather readily for the most part; a spat in the sandbox is all but forgotten when there is an extra cookie to share. They seem to generate reconciliation for practical reasons, not a bad model for adult friends. Children usually have high expectations of their friends. They do not give them up easily and move on to others when they detect value. It may only be a coveted toy or a favorite puzzle that holds their attention about another child. But I sense that they want community as badly as adults do. They are sometimes more willing to contain their egos than adults give them credit for when the good of their little group is at stake.

Children know about justice only what they are taught. It is not a nascent quality, but one that grows organically in communities that hold up certain values and struggle until they are achieved, passing on to children and the children's children the unaccomplished tasks as part of the challenge of right relation. The imperative of justice may be one of the most powerful gifts adults give children friends. Another is the assurance that they follow in a long tradition of justice-seeking friends.

Ecological Friendship

These same dimensions of friendship that apply to men and children can also be applied to the rest of the created order, to a way that humans interact with the world. In fact, ecology is not simply a word about the biosphere, but a shorthand way of speaking about friendship. A simple linguistic example will suffice to illustrate the point.

"Mother Earth" is a common expression that connotes a certain respect for the planet. But it also permits a certain cavalier distance. It is as if Mother has done her job by birthing the earth and she will grow old and die anyway. Why worry excessively about her ageing problems when in fact there is living to be done? By contrast, the earth as a friend expects the same attention, generativity, community, and justice that any other friend demands. "Friend earth" is in relationship but it is not modeled on the parent-child; it is an equal.

This semantic change signals a quite different, more mature relationship to the earth. Ecology is to the earth what friendship is to people. Friends of the Earth is a well chosen name for ecologists that religionists need to internalize as well.

The image and commitment shown to the earth can and must be extended to encompass animal life, too. Friends of animals are not simply those who work to stop cruel hunting, vivisection, and unnecessary animal experimentation. They are also those who take the time to attend to animals' well-being, to generate new ways to do the scientific work for which animals have been the prime sufferers, to explore and develop concepts and projects in which human and animal friends live in respectful community.

Friends of animals are those who extend the demands of justice to all of creation. This can be done without losing the limited but important prior claim that responsible humans have in the created order. This is not specism as much as an acknowledgement that humans are the animals who are charged with making difficult decisions for the whole of creation. That makes humans different.

These initial reflections on using aspects of women's friendships to illuminate relationships with men, children, the earth, and animals are meant to be suggestive and not exhaustive. They suggest the contours of an ethic that is at once attentive to particularity and generative of new norms as data dictate. This is an ethic located in communities of people who are held accountable for their actions and helped to live in right relation by one another. It is an ethic that is rooted in a commitment to justice-seeking activities that ground friendship.

Such an ethic may seem far from the norms of the communities in which most people live. The powers of prevailing mores being what they are, few will live to see the ethic actualized. But having articulated an ethic that emerges out of the experiences of women friends, experiences that are only now beginning to see the light of ethical day, I express hope that parts of it may eventually take root.

Extending the Ethical Umbrella

Much of the discussion on a friendship-based ethic is properly located in the domain of personal ethics. But it is applicable in the realm of social ethics as well. For example, the Christian imperative to go and make friends in all nations reflects a comprehensive understanding of friendship that personal ethics lacks. It implies that friendship is more than a privatized experience, something that can make a difference in the public forum. It functions on the macro level as well both as a metaphor and as a challenge.

Friendship is a metaphor that is used frequently in public foreign policy debates. Language is often hyperbolic and anthropomorphic. For example, the United States' relations to the nations of Central America can be characterized as friendly or unfriendly depending on the degree of cooperation they wrest from the respective governments. Unfriendly language about some small countries is prominent and used unabashedly as if there were no differences in power that mitigate circumstances in a decisive way.

A quick look at the model used to understand women's friendships, with certain modifications of course, makes it easy to see the root of the problem. Lack of respect for national sovereignty, much less love, is only the beginning. Grossly unequal power dynamics prevail. Serious threats to the embodiment of a people are daily occurrences. A callous disregard for the quality of life, its spirituality, complete a very unfriendly pattern. At the risk of simplifying a complex history and belaboring a complicated foreign policy matter, it is fair to say that if the language of friendship is to persist in the international realm, then some rigorous analysis of what it means is in order.

Components of the model could be modified to show how completely unfriendly the relationship is and to indicate justice-seeking work that can be done to remedy it. For example, humanitarian aid programs provide much-needed supplies that will improve the quality of life. This friendly gesture by committed friends means millions of dollars worth of much-needed equipment, medicine, and school supplies to our friends. It is a drop in the bucket by comparison with what is needed, but it is an important symbolic and real gesture in crisis.

Massive changes in the power equation and other structural modifications in the situation are necessary before the United States can even use the term "friend" to talk of countries toward which it has acted in unfriendly ways. But the example points out how the model offered in this book can shed light on some of the most complex and unjust situations in history.

The deeds of friendly justice-seekers make a significant difference in the world. This is the essence of religiously based social change movements, many of which are best described as unlikely coalitions of religious and nonreligious people who join forces to do the works of love and justice.

Women's friendships, fierce and tender, provide clues for reappropriating symbols for the divine, ethical norms with human beings, and appropriate codes of behavior toward animals and the earth. Most of all they provide the impetus for communities of justice-seeking friends to engage in active reflection and reflective action to create a friendly world.

Notes

Introduction

1. Sallie McFague, *Metaphorical Theology: Models of God in Religious Language* (Philadelphia: Fortress Press, 1982), 178.

Chapter 1/Fierce and Tender

1. Elisabeth Schüssler Fiorenza treats this topic in her forthcoming book *Claiming the Center*. This social dynamic for oppressed groups is explored by Bell Hooks in *Feminist Theory: From Margin to Center* (Boston: South End Press, 1984).

2. Carter Heyward explores "right relation" in *The Redemption of God: A Theology of Mutual Relation* (Washington, D.C.: University Press of America, 1982). She deepens her ethical analysis in *Touching Our Strength: The Erotic as Power and the Love of God* (San Francisco: Harper & Row, 1989).

3. Ada Maria Isasi-Diaz shared early thoughts on this issue in unpublished form. See also Carolyn Lehmann's reflections on friendship from her vantage point at the Casa Sofía in Santiago, Chile, "Where Wisdom and Friendship Dwell," November 1986, unpublished manuscript.

4. See my doctoral dissertation, "Feminist Liberation Theology: The Development of Method in Construction" (Berkeley, Calif.: Graduate Theological Union, 1980) for a fuller treatment of the genesis of this position.

5. See Mary E. Hunt, "Theological Pornography: From Corporate to Communal Ethics," in *Christianity, Patriarchy and Abuse: A Feminist Critique*, edited by Joanne Carlson Brown and Carole R. Bohn (New York: Pilgrim Press, 1989), 89–104.

6. Lillian B. Rubin, *Just Friends* (New York: Harper & Row, 1985); Letty Cottin Pogrebin, *Among Friends* (New York: McGraw-Hill Book Company, 1986); Luise Eichenbaum and Susie Orbach, *Between Women* (New York: Viking, 1987).

7. Janice Raymond, *A Passion for Friends* (Boston: Beacon Press, 1986).

8. Ibid., 205.

9. Beverly Wildung Harrison makes a persuasive case for women's moral agency in *Our Right to Choose* (Boston: Beacon Press, 1983). I believe this helpful concept can be extended to encompass women's religious and spiritual agency as well.

10. See Elisabeth Schüssler Fiorenza's now classic *In Memory of Her* (New York: Crossroad, 1983).

11. Alice Walker, *In Search of Our Mothers' Gardens* (San Diego: Harcourt Brace Jovanovich, 1983).

12. Delores S. Williams, "Womanist Theology: Black Women's Voices," *Christianity and Crisis*, March 2, 1987, 66–70. Other treatments of the issues include Katie Geneva Cannon, *Black Womanist Ethics*, American Academy of Religion Academy Series (Atlanta: Scholars Press, 1988), and Jacquelyn Grant, *White Women's Christ and Black Women's Jesus*, American Academy of Religion Academy Series (Atlanta: Scholars Press, 1989).

13. See Letty Russell, Kwok Pui-lan, Ada Maria Isasi-Diaz, Katie Geneva Cannon, editors, *Inheriting Our Mothers' Gardens: Feminist Theology in Third World Perspective* (Philadelphia: Westminster, 1988), for a variety of different approaches by women from different backgrounds.

14. Susan Brooks Thistlethwaite takes this seriously in her *Sex, Race, and God* (New York: Crossroad, 1989).

15. Simone Weil, *Waiting for God*, translated by Emma Craufurd (New York: G. P. Putnam's Sons, 1951), 75.

Chapter 2/The Power of Women's Friendships

1. Adele Logan Alexander, "'The Migs' of Dunbar High," *Washington Post*, May 26, 1988.

2. Holly Near, "Plain and Simple Love," recorded on *Don't Hold Back*, Oakland, Calif.: Redwood Records, 1987.

3. Gerda Lerner, *The Creation of Patriarchy* (New York: Oxford University Press, 1986). Charlotte Bunch, *Passionate Politics* (New York: St. Martin's Press, 1987). Rosemary Radford Ruether, *Sexism and God-Talk* (Boston: Beacon Press, 1983). Elisabeth Schüssler Fiorenza, *In Memory of Her* (New York: Crossroad, 1983).

4. Gerda Lerner, *The Creation of Patriarchy*, 239.

5. Ibid.

6. This is the subtitle of Charlotte Bunch's *Passionate Politics*.

7. Charlotte Bunch, *Passionate Politics*, 22.

8. Ibid., 253.

9. Ibid., 341.

10. Rosemary Radford Ruether, *Sexism and God-Talk*, 19.

11. Ibid., 22.

12. Ibid., 23.

13. Elisabeth Schüssler Fiorenza, *In Memory of Her*, 35.

14. Ibid., 34 and 36.

15. John Boswell laid the groundwork for much of the current work on homosexuality in the Christian tradition in his *Christianity, Social Tolerance and Homosexuality* (Chicago: University of Chicago Press, 1980). He makes no claim to treat women's experience exhaustively. In his forthcoming work he deals with same-sex commitment and marriage ceremonies that have been part of Christianity for centuries. But his useful discoveries about men's experiences of bonding will appear in forthcoming work.

Kevin Gordon tried to redeem "fraternity" as a way to describe male friendship. His clinical expertise on men's lives and his creative theologizing gave him the raw materials to do so. See his "The Sexual Bankruptcy of the Christian Traditions: A Perspective of Radical Suspicion and of Fundamental Trust," in *AIDS Issues: Confronting the Challenge*, edited by David G. Hallman (New York: Pilgrim Press, 1989), 169–212.

16. For example, John McNeill's *Taking a Chance on God* (Boston: Beacon Press, 1988), has the somewhat overwhelming subtitle "A Liberating Theology for Gays, Lesbians and Their Lovers, Families and Friends." While I find the book a useful exploration of what I can only imagine as men's spirituality, I would never cast such a wide net on the basis of female experience.

The methodological implication is not to encourage an equally general claim from the other side, but to suggest that writers limit their claims. Dialogue with women and joint publications by women and men are, in my judgment, sounder ways to achieve a more inclusive result.

17. Christine Downing, *Myths and Mysteries of Same-Sex Love* (New York: Continuum, 1989). See especially her chapter 12 "Woman-Loving Women," chapter 13 "Same-Sex Love among the Goddesses," and chapter 14 "Sappho" for insights into women's experiences and history.

18. Some of the most innovative research in the field has been presented at the Group on Lesbian Feminist Issues in Religion of the American Academy of Religion that convenes at the annual meeting of the AAR.

19. Adrienne Rich, "Compulsory Heterosexism and Lesbian Existence," *Signs: A Journal of Women in Culture and Society* 5, no. 4 (Summer 1980), 631–60.

20. See my essay, "Celibacy — The Case Against: Liberating Lesbian Nuns" in *Out/Look*, Summer 1988, 68–74. I apply Rich's insight to women in canonical religious communities, nuns who make a public vow of celibacy.

21. Charlotte Bunch, *Passionate Politics*, 162.

22. Ibid., 164.

23. Ibid., 176.

24. Ibid., 178.

25. Adrienne Rich, "The Images" (1976–78), in *A Wild Patience Has Taken Me This Far* (New York: W. W. Norton and Co., 1981), 3–5.

26. Gloria Naylor, *The Women of Brewster Place* (New York: Penguin Books, 1983).

27. Ibid., 130.

28. Isabel Carter Heyward, *Our Passion for Justice* (New York: Pilgrim Press, 1984), 47.

29. Ibid., 183.

30. See Carter Heyward and Mary E. Hunt, "Lesbianism and Feminist Theology," a round table discussion in *Journal of Feminist Studies in Religion* 2, no. 2 (Fall 1986), 95–99.

31. See Mary E. Hunt, "Lovingly Lesbian" in *A Challenge to Love*, edited by Robert Nugent (New York: Crossroad, 1983); "Loving Well Means Doing Justice" in *A Faith of One's Own*, edited by Barbara Zanotti (Trumansburg, N.Y.: Crossing Press, 1986); "Friends in Deed," in *Sex and God*, edited by Linda Hurcombe (London: Routledge and Kegan Paul, 1987).

32. See Judith Brown's *Immodest Acts* (New York: Oxford University Press, 1986), for the astonishing story of Benedetta Carlini and Bartolomea Crivelli, seventeenth-century nuns whose tales of romantic involvement and love making confirm the suspicions of many.

Likewise, Rosemary Curb and Nancy Monahan's *Breaking Silence: Lesbian Nuns* (Tallahassee, Fla.: Naiad Press, 1985), is an interesting, if uneven, collection of stories of women who were and/or are part of religious communities. The scandal that attended the publication of this volume was focused on the fact that the publisher sold parts of some of the articles to male pornography magazines.

I contend that an underlying reason for the violent outburst, even by some lesbians, was internalized homophobia. It decreases desire to have the facts on the table when it comes to the delicate matter of lesbian nuns. If "lesbian" were not somehow wrong, i.e., if heterosexist patriarchy were not so strong, I am sure that the reaction and attendant publicity would have been inaudible since, with all due respect, the book itself does not warrant such extravagant attention.

33. See Mary E. Hunt, "Celibacy — The Case Against: Liberating Lesbian Nuns" (note 20) for further nuances of the argument.

34. See Mary E. Hunt, "Valuing the Widow's Mite, in *More Light Update* 10, nos. 11–12 (June–July 1990): 1–9.

35. The term "hermeneutics of suspicion" has its roots in the work of Paul Ricoeur. The term has been used extensively by Latin American liberation theologians including Beatriz Melano Couch and especially Juan Luis Segundo in his *The Liberation of Theology* (Maryknoll, N.Y.: Orbis Books, 1976), to signal the fact that most theological work has not been done from the perspective of the oppressed. Careful, critical evaluation with the interests of marginalized people at the center is the emerging theological perspective of liberationists.

36. See Heyward and Hunt, "Lesbianism and Feminist Theology," 99.

37. Rosemary Radford Ruether in remarks made at the Christology Section at the annual meeting of the American Academy of Religion, Atlanta, November 1986.

38. Doris Grumbach, *Chamber Music* (New York: Fawcett, 1979), 203.
39. Janice Raymond, *A Passion for Friends* (Boston: Beacon Press, 1986), 11.
40. See Joan Nestle's powerful collection *A Restricted Country* (Ithaca, N.Y.: Firebrand Books, 1987), especially "Lesbians and Prostitutes: An Historical Sisterhood," 157–77.
41. See my "Political Oppression and Creative Survival" in *Women's Spirit Bonding*, edited by Janet Kalven and Mary I. Buckley (New York: Pilgrim Press, 1984), 164–72.
42. Anna Quindlen, "Between Women, Talk Is Digging for Buried Treasure," "Life in the 30's" series, *New York Times*, April 22, 1987.

Chapter 3/Friendship as Inspiration: A Study in Theo-Politics

1. Meg Greenfield, "Friendship in Washington," *Washington Post*, July 20, 1983.
2. See Linda Otto Lipsett, *Remember Me: Women and Their Friendship Quilts* (San Francisco: Quilt Digest Press, 1985). This is a beautiful volume that details the history of friendship quilts and contains stunning pictures of these beautiful designs.
3. Ibid., 21.
4. Ibid., 28–29.
5. Ibid., 30.
6. See Mary E. Hunt, "Feminist Liberation Theology: The Development of Method in Construction" (Berkeley, Calif.: Graduate Theological Union, 1980), for a modest example of such deconstruction.
   Elisabeth Schüssler Fiorenza's efforts to "decenter" biblical scholarship are an important part of this movement. See her brilliant essay "The Ethics of Biblical Interpretation: Decentering Biblical Scholarship," Society for Biblical Literature Presidential Address (December 5, 1987), *Harvard Divinity Bulletin*, Fall 1988, 6–9.
7. See Ada Maria Isasi-Diaz and Yolanda Tarango, *Hispanic Women: Prophetic Women in the Church* (San Francisco: Harper & Row, 1988).
   Elsa Tamez's interviews with male theologians of liberation in *Against Machismo* (Oak Park, Ill.: Meyer-Stone Books, 1987) are fascinating accounts of their various ways of approaching the issues. It is clear from these interviews that there is plenty of work yet to be done if liberation is to be achieved.
   Fortunately women in Latin America are developing their own liberation theology. Excellent examples include *Apuntes y aportes de la mujer ecuménica*, edited by Alieda Verhoeven, Mendoza, Argentina: Acción Popular Ecuménica Regional Cuyo, nos. 4, 5, 6, 1987. Also *El rostro feminino de la teología*, Elsa Tamez et al. (San José, Costa Rica: Departamento Ecuménico de Investigaciones [DEI], 1986). These contain essays that were originally delivered

as lectures for the Reunión Latinoamericana de Teología de la Liberación desde la Perspectiva de la Mujer, Buenos Aires, 1985. See Elsa Tamez, editor, *Through Her Eyes: Women's Theology from Latin America* (Maryknoll, N.Y.: Orbis Books, 1989).

8. See Marjorie Heins, *Cutting the Mustard: Affirmative Action and the Nature of Excellence* (Winchester, Mass.: Faber and Faber, 1987), for a full account of the firing of Nancy D. Richardson from Boston University School of Theology. The case of Elizabeth Bettenhausen was set in the same web of conservative theo-politics and power wielding.

9. For example, *With Passion and Compassion*, edited by Virginia Fabella and Mercy Amba Oduyoye (Maryknoll, N.Y.: Orbis Books, 1988), provides a look at Asian, African, and Latin American women's theological writings. European theologians like Marga Bührig, Catharina J. M. Halkes, Bärbel von Wartenberg-Potter are equally important. See Marga Bührig, *Die unsichtbare Frau und der Gott der Väter* (Stuttgart: Kreuz Verlag, 1987), and *Spät habe ich gelernt, gerne Frau zu sein* (Stuttgart: Kreuz Verlag, 1987). Among the many published works of Catharina J. M. Halkes see "Feministische theologie en bevrijding," in *Op zoek naar een Westeuropese bevrijdingstheologie*. Verslag kongresdag Kritische Gemeente Ijmond 1985, 6–18. See Bärbel von Wartenberg-Potter, *We Will Not Hang Our Harps on the Willows* (Bloomington, Ind.: Meyer-Stone Books, 1988).

10. Matilda Joslyn Gage, *Woman, Church and State*, copyright 1893, reprint edition (Watertown, Mass.: Persephone Press, 1980).

11. Elizabeth Cady Stanton and the Revising Committee, *The Woman's Bible* (New York: European Publishing Company, 1895; reprint, Seattle: Coalition Task Force on Women and Religion, 1974).

12. Ibid., 103.

13. Ibid., 184.

14. Valerie Saiving, "The Human Situation: A Feminine View," originally published in *The Journal of Religion*, April 1960; reprinted in *Womanspirit Rising*, edited by Carol P. Christ and Judith Plaskow (New York: Harper & Row, 1979), 25–43.

15. Saiving in *Womanspirit Rising*, 27.

16. Mary Daly, *The Church and the Second Sex* (Boston: Beacon Press, 1968), and *Beyond God the Father* (Boston: Beacon Press, 1973).

17. Mary Daly, *Beyond God the Father*, 115–78.

18. Mary Daly, *Gyn/Ecology: The Metaethics of Radical Feminism* (Boston: Beacon Press, 1978), and *Pure Lust: Elemental Feminist Philosophy* (Boston: Beacon Press, 1984).

19. Mary Daly, *Pure Lust*, especially chapters 10–12.

20. Ibid., 374.

21. Ibid.

22. Ibid.

23. Mary Daly, *Websters' First New Intergalactic Wickedary of the English Language* (Boston: Beacon Press, 1987), 176 and 163 respectively.

24. Beverly Wildung Harrison, "The Power of Anger in the Work of Love: Christian Ethics for Women and Other Strangers," in *Making the Connections*, edited by Carol S. Robb (Boston: Beacon Press, 1985), 3–21.

25. Ibid., 8.

26. Ibid.

27. Ibid., 18.

28. Ibid., 8.

29. Beverly Wildung Harrison, "Misogyny and Homophobia," in *Making the Connections*, 135–51.

30. Ibid., 151.

31. Ibid.

32. This happy phrase originates with J. Giles Milhaven in his article "Sleeping Like Spoons," *Commonweal*, April 7, 1989, 207. Sensual trust is what friends embody; fierce tenderness is sensual trust.

33. See my essay "Friends in Deed," in *Sex and God*, edited by Linda Hurcombe (New York: Routledge and Kegan Paul Inc., 1987), 46–54.

34. Sallie McFague, *Models of God* (Philadelphia: Fortress Press, 1987).

35. Quoted in ibid., 159, from C. S. Lewis, *Four Loves* (New York: Harcourt, Brace and Co., 1960), 88.

36. Ibid., 91.

37. See *Embodied Love: Sensuality and Relationship as Feminist Values*, edited by Paula M. Cooey, Sharon A. Farmer, and Mary Ellen Ross (San Francisco: Harper & Row, 1987).

38. Sheila Davaney, "Problems with Feminist Theory: Historicity and the Search for Sure Foundations," in ibid., Paula Cooey et al., 79–95, especially 92.

39. James B. Nelson, *The Intimate Connection: Male Sexuality, Masculine Spirituality* (Philadelphia: Westminster Press, 1988). This work stands in sharp contrast with other contemporary male theological treatments such a Bob Mesle's "A Friend's Love: Why Process Theology Matters," *The Christian Century*, July 15–22, 1987, 622–25, where the focus is, typically, on the implications for theology rather than for human conduct. Such efforts, while useful insofar as they take friendship seriously as the most adequate and meaningful way of talking about the divine-human relationship, are finally inadequate and relatively meaningless because they are abstract and because they objectify the matter at hand.

40. James B. Nelson *The Intimate Connection: Male Sexuality, Masculine Spirituality*, 49.

41. Ibid., 48.

42. Ibid., 66.

43. Judith Plaskow and Carol P. Christ, *Weaving the Visions: Patterns in Feminist Spirituality* (New York: Harper & Row, 1989).

44. See ibid., part 3, "Self in Relation," 171–266.

45. See Janice Raymond, *A Passion for Friends: Toward a Philosophy of Female Affection* (Boston: Beacon Press, 1986).

46. Ibid., 4.

47. See Elisabeth Schüssler Fiorenza, *In Memory of Her* (New York: Cross-road, 1983), and *Bread Not Stone* (New York: Boston: Beacon Press, 1984), 15–22 and chapter 5.

48. See Renita Weems, *Just a Sister Away* (San Diego: Lura Media, 1988).

49. Raymond, *A Passion for Friends*, 114.

50. Adele M. Fiske, *Friends and Friendship in the Monastic Tradition*, a doctoral dissertation presented at Fordham University, later published, Cuernavaca, Mexico: Centro Intercultural de Documentación, *CIDOC Cuaderno* no. 51, 1970. I am indebted to Virginia Anderson, M.D., for bringing this remarkable source to my attention.

51. Ibid., Introduction, 15.

52. Ibid., chapter 20, 2.

53. See *I Am the Way*, the Constitution of the Sisters of Loretto, approved by the General Assembly, 1984, 2.

54. Marian McAvoy, S.L., "President's Report," July 1984, 29.

55. Ibid.

56. Carolyn Lehmann, "Where Wisdom and Friendship Dwell," Santiago, Chile: Casa Sofía, November 1986.

57. Bibliography for a seminar on friendship taught by Ralph B. Potter, Harvard Divinity School, Harvard University, 1980. This was considered by many scholars to be a definitive listing on a topic that is treated very lightly in the theological literature. Several of the items listed by women involve sociological or other related materials. Of the more relevant theological materials is the work of Anne Therese de Marguent de Coucelles, Marquise de Lambert (1647–1733), *The Works of the Marchioness de Lambert*, 2 vols. (London: W. Owen, 1769), "A Treatise on Friendship," vol. 1, 140–75.

58. Rosemary Radford Ruether, *Sexism and God-Talk*, 258.

59. Anna Quindlen, "Between Women, Talk Is Digging for Buried Treasure," "Life in the 30's" series, *New York Times*, April 22, 1987.

60. The most comprehensive and convincing treatment of these issues is Carol J. Adams, *The Sexual Politics of Meat: A Feminist-Vegetarian Critical Theory* (New York: Continuum, 1989).

Chapter 4 / Fierce Tenderness: A Model for "Right Relation"

1. By "right relation" I mean what Carter Heyward spells out in *The Redemption of God: A Theology of Mutual Relation* (Washington, D.C.: University Press of America, 1982). In addition, I claim that right relation applies to the way in which we treat ourselves, animals, the natural order, and, especially in a nuclear age, our collective future.

2. See Mary E. Hunt, "Spiral Not Schism: Women-Church as Church," in *Religion and Intellectual Life* 7, no. 1 (Fall 1989), 82–92.

3. Eleanor Hume Haney, "What is Feminist Ethics? A Proposal for Continuing Discussion," *Journal of Religious Ethics* 8, no. 1 (1980) 115–24.

4. Letty Cottin Pogrebin, "Hers" column, *New York Times*, October 6, 1983.

5. Ibid.

6. Lois Kirkwood writes: "Liberative love/justice demands that we challenge dominant/subordinate relationships as they are currently institutionalized in the U.S. and all stratified societies where racism and other group oppressions are shaped and maintained by a complex spectrum of social structures" (excerpt from Introduction to "Enemy Love in Racial Justice: A Christian Social Ethical Perspective," forthcoming Ph.D. dissertation, Union Theological Seminary, New York).

7. Aristotle, *Nicomachean Ethics* (Harmondsworth, Middlesex, England: Penguin Books, 1953), see especially Book Eight, chapters 2 and 6.

8. Ibid., 233.

9. Ibid., 240.

10. See Edward Schillebeeckx, *The Church with a Human Face* (New York: Crossroad, 1985), 42.

11. The phrase was coined by Elisabeth Schüssler Fiorenza and is spelled out in *In Memory of Her* (New York: Crossroad, 1983).

12. Barbara Ehrenreich, "In Praise of 'Best Friends,'" *Ms.*, January 1987, 35.

13. Ibid., 36.

14. Delores S. Williams, "The Color of Feminism: Or Speaking the Black Woman's Tongue," *Journal of Religious Thought* 43, no. 1 (Spring–Summer 1986), 42–58.

15. Ibid., 52.

16. Ibid.

17. Mary McGrory, "Of Wit and Gallantry," *Washington Post*, October 15, 1983.

18. Ibid.

19. Ibid.

20. Ibid.

21. Dorothy Haecker, "Teacher to Student," in *Ms./Campus Times*, October 1985, 54.

22. Ibid.

23. Ibid.

24. See Marie Marshall Fortune, *Is Nothing Sacred?: When Sex Invades the Pastoral Relationship* (San Francisco: Harper & Row, 1989), for a treatment of the inappropriate sexual activity between clergy and parishioners.

25. Haecker, "Teacher to Student," 54.

26. Ibid.

27. See Marie Augusta Neal, *The Socio-theology of Letting Go: A First World Church Facing Third World People* (New York: Paulist Press, 1977).

She discusses the dynamics of relinquishment for wealthy and powerful countries in order to empower the rest of the world. Something of this dynamic takes place on the micro level as well.

28. See James B. Nelson, *Embodiment: An Approach to Sexuality and Christian Theology* (Minneapolis: Augsburg Publishing House, 1978). Nelson used the term helpfully in this book aimed at a mainstream theological audience.

Marilyn Thie, Professor of Philosophy and Religion at Colgate University, speaks about sexuality as "embodied energy." Writings in feminist spirituality and feminist psychology are full of references to our embodied being in the world. I use the term in the hope that it will so belabor the obvious as to make the point that our bodies are crucial to our self-definition and activity.

29. See J. Giles Milhaven, "Sleeping Like Spoons" *Commonweal*, April 7, 1989. Note his deep indebtedness to feminist writers including Susan Griffin, Audre Lorde, and Adrienne Rich, who have made similarly insightful observations on the nature and scope of the erotic.

30. Among the many useful sources on the topic are Kim Chernin, *The Obsession* (New York: Harper & Row, 1981). The general trend in eating disorders literature seems to be toward seeing them as a form of depression. With media standards set so viciously, and with such a clearly misogynist bias, it is a wonder that more such problems do not exist.

31. See the excellent publication *Media and Values*, no. 46 (Spring 1989), "The Birds, the Bees and Broadcasting: What the Media Teaches Our Kids About Sex," edited by Elizabeth Thoman, for a thorough treatment of sex and the media.

Chapter 5/The Limits of Friendship in Loss and Celebration

1. See Martha A. Ackelsberg " 'Sisters' or 'Comrades'? The Politics of Friends and Families," in *Families, Politics and Public Policies*, edited by I. Diamond (New York: Longman, 1983), 339–56, for an astute analysis of the language of family.

2. "Ordinary time" is a liturgical phrase that signals that part of the Christian church year that is not designated as one of the major seasons such as Lent, Advent, and so on. It is the time when things are rather routine. It is essential that some routine be built in if only to contrast with the specificity of the season, e.g., their colors, readings, special ceremonies.

3. May Sarton, *As We Are Now* (New York: W. W. Norton and Co., 1973).

4. See new theoretical work by Joan and Eric Erikson, reported in *New York Times*, June 14, 1988.

5. This is a line from the movie *Desert Heart*, based on the novel *Desert of the Heart* by Jane Rule. The gambler who utters the line is played by the

director of the film, Donna Dietch. This is one of her very few, but very memorable lines.

6. Literature abounds on adult children of alcoholics. Among the most helpful books are Claudia Black, *"It Will Never Happen to Me!"* (New York: Ballantine Books, 1981), and Janet Geringer Woititz, *Adult Children of Alcoholics* (Pompano Beach, Fla.: Health Communications Inc., 1983).

7. See "Death of God" theology, especially the work of Thomas J.J. Altizer, *The Gospel of Christian Atheism* (Philadelphia: Westminster, 1966); Paul van Buren, *The Secular Meaning of the Gospel* (New York: Macmillan, 1963); Gabriel Vahanian, *The Death of God* (New York: George Braziller, 1961).

8. Sheila G. Davaney, editor, *Feminism and Process Thought* (Lewiston, N.Y.: Edwin Mellen Press, 1980).

9. Barbara Cullom observed this with regard to Sisters Against Sexism (SAS), a women's worship group, Ocean City, Md., April 1988. I extend her insight because it is so compelling.

10. For example, Diann Neu has written the "Feminist Farewell: 'In Memory of Her'" liturgy on the occasion of the death of Mary O'Dwyer Flynn (*WATERwheel*, quarterly publication of the Women's Alliance for Theology, Ethics and Ritual [WATER], Silver Spring, Md., 1, no. 3 [Fall 1988], 4–5).

11. See John Boswell's work on same-sex marriages, a videotape entitled *1500 Years of the Church Blessing Lesbian and Gay Relationship: It's Nothing New*, copyright 1988, Integrity, Inc.

12. John Spong, *Living in Sin* (Nashville: Abingdon Press, 1988).

Chapter 6/Justice-seeking Friends in Unlikely Coalitions

1. Note that this is the title of Lillian Rubin's book on friends. She uses the phrase to underscore the need for friends.

Renita Weems uses it as the title for her article in *Essence* 20, no. 1 (May 1989), 60ff., to explore her feelings as a heterosexual woman about her lesbian friends. In this case there is a certain ambiguity in the use of the phrase, straddling as Renita Weems does the literary world where homosexuality is acceptable and the church world where it is usually anathema.

2. See Lillian Rubin, *Just Friends* (New York: Harper & Row, 1985).

3. See Martha A. Ackelsberg, "'Sisters' or 'Comrades'? The Politics of Friends and Families," in *Families, Politics and Public Policies*, edited by I. Diamond (New York: Longman, 1983), 343.

4. Carroll Smith-Rosenberg, "The Female World of Love and Ritual: Relationships Between Women in Nineteenth-Century America," originally published in *Signs* no. 1 (Summer 1980), 1–29, later published as part of her classic text *Disorderly Conduct: Visions of Gender in Victorian America* (New York: Alfred Knopf, 1985), 53–76, especially 76.

5. Ibid., 19.

6. Starhawk, a witch, has been actively involved in social change movements, especially the antinuclear movement, for many years. Her books *Dreaming the Dark: Magic, Sex and Politics* (Boston: Beacon Press, 1982 [1988]), and *Truth or Dare: Encounters with Power, Authority, and Mystery* (San Francisco: Harper & Row, 1987), are constructive efforts to use women's values and rituals to make peace peacefully.

7. Delores S. Williams, quoting Alice Walker from *In Search of Our Mother's Garden*, in "Womanist Theology: Black Women's Voices," in *Weaving the Visions: Patterns in Feminist Spirituality*, edited by Judith Plaskow and Carol P. Christ (San Francisco: Harper & Row, 1989), 179.

8. Ibid., 182.

9. Delores S. Williams, "The Color of Feminism: Or Speaking the Black Woman's Tongue," *The Journal of Religious Thought* 43, no. 1 (Spring–Summer 1986), 42–58, especially 52.

10. The work of Bell Hooks, *Ain't I a Woman: Black Women and Feminism* (Boston: South End Press, 1981), and especially *Talking Back: Thinking Feminist, Thinking Black* (Boston: South End Press, 1989), is crucial for understanding the complexity of the issues involved. Although she does not wholeheartedly embrace the term "womanist" (see "Black Women and Feminism" in *Talking Back*, 177–82), she does explore the issues in a very helpful way. I suspect that womanist theologians use the term in a way that she would applaud.

11. Delores S. Williams, "Womanist Theology," 182.

12. Ibid., 182.

13. Elisabeth Schüssler Fiorenza in *In Memory of Her* (New York: Crossroad, 1983), stresses the "Jesus movement" as the locus of the Christian tradition.

14. Bertha Conde, *The Business of Being a Friend* (Boston and New York: Houghton Mifflin, 1916), 31–32, quoted by Ackelsberg, "'Sisters' or 'Comrades'?" 344.

15. See my "Women Crossing Worlds — A Feminist Model of Mission," *WATERwheel* (Women's Alliance for Theology, Ethics and Ritual) 2, no. 1 (Winter 1989), 1–3.

16. See Maria C. Lugones and Elizabeth V. Spelman, "Have We Got a Theory for You! Feminist Theory, Cultural Imperialism and the Demand for 'The Woman's Voice'" *Women's Studies International Forum* 6, no. 6 (1983), 573–81, and Elizabeth V. Spelman's *The Inessential Woman: Problems of Exclusion in Feminist Thought* (Boston: Beacon Press, 1988), for a useful summary of the problems of ethnocentrism in feminist theory. No easy solutions are proposed but helpful suggestions for what not to do are a good start.

17. See Letty Russell, Kwok Pui-lan, Ada Maria Isasi-Diaz, Katie Geneva Cannon, editors, *Inheriting Our Mothers' Gardens: Feminist Theology in Third World Perspective* (Philadelphia; Westminster, 1988), and Mud Flower

Collective, *God's Fierce Whimsy* (New York: Pilgrim Press, 1985), the best examples of cooperative work with clear respect for difference.

18. I had one such conversation with Rev. Joan Martin, campus minister, University of Pennsylvania, as part of the program at the Tri-State Women-Church Conference, Portsmouth, N.H., April 1, 1989. Her clear articulation of her experience as an African American woman ordained in a predominantly white (Presbyterian) denomination was in sharp and instructive contrast to my own background as a white Irish Catholic. Naturally our relationships to the women-church movement are different. What the audience found so helpful was our clarifying that we did not need to become the other in order to support the other.

19. Martha Ackelsberg, "'Sisters' or 'Comrades'?" 351.

20. Ibid.

21. See Rosemary Radford Ruether, *Women-Church: Theology and Practice of Feminist Liturgical Communities* (San Francisco: Harper & Row, 1986).

22. See the directory of over one hundred women-church base communities, forthcoming, WATER (Women's Alliance for Theology, Ethics and Ritual) 8035 13th St., Silver Spring, MD 20910.

23. Elisabeth Schüssler Fiorenza spells out the implications of these insights in the Epilogue to *In Memory of Her*, 343–51.

24. See Edward Schillebeeckx, *The Church with a Human Face* (New York: Crossroad, 1985), 42.

25. *Partners in the Mystery of Redemption*, United States Catholic Bishops, April 1988; principal author is Susan Muto. See my response "Limited Partners," *Conscience*, May/June 1988, 6–10, and *WATERwheel* 1, no. 2, 1–3.

26. See Mary E. Hunt, "Theological Pornography," in *Christianity, Patriarchy, and Abuse*, Joanne Carlson Brown and Carole R. Bohn, editors (New York: Pilgrim Press, 1989), 89–104.

Chapter 7 / Fierce Tenderness in Deed

1. Rosemary Radford Ruether favors "God/ess," a nonsexist and unpronounceable formulation, in her book *Sexism and God-Talk* (Boston: Beacon Press, 1983), 68–71. It has been used widely by feminist theologians as a good compromise, though it is difficult to integrate into worship, as Professor Ruether acknowledges.

2. See my essay "Friends in Deed" in *Sex and God: Some Varieties of Women's Religious Experience*, edited by Linda Hurcombe (New York and London: Routledge and Kegan Paul, 1987), 46–54.

3. Ruth Page explains the value of "alongside" rather than a vertical relationship with the divine in "Human Liberation and Divine Transcendence,"

Theology 85 (1982), 184–90, quoted by Sallie McFague, *Metaphorical Theology: Models of God in Religious Language* (Philadelphia: Fortress Press, 1982), 183 and 221, n. 91.

4. The idea of accompanying one another in justice struggles is prevalent in Latin American liberation theology. It is expressed powerfully by Julia Esquivel in "They Have Threatened Us with Resurrection," in *Threatened with Resurrection* (Elgin, Ill.: Brethren Press, 1982), 63.

5. Naomi Goldenberg, *Changing of the Gods: Feminism and the End of Traditional Religions* (Boston: Beacon Press, 1979), is a stimulating treatment of feminism and pluralism. She argues, and I quite agree, that "it is not necessary for human beings to share the *same* myths, images and symbols. Instead it is more important that human beings share the *process* of symbol creation itself" (53).

6. Sallie McFague, *Metaphorical Theology*, 183.

7. Joanne Carlson Brown and Rebecca Parker, "For God So Loved the World?" in *Christianity, Patriarchy, and Abuse*, Joanne Carlson Brown and Carole R. Bohn, editors (New York: Pilgrim Press, 1989), 1–30.

Bibliography

Ackelsberg, Martha A. " 'Sisters' or 'Comrades'? The Politics of Friends and Families." In *Families, Politics and Public Policies*, 339–56. Edited by I. Diamond. New York: Longman, 1983.

Adams, Carol J. *The Sexual Politics of Meat: A Feminist-Vegetarian Critical Theory*. New York: Continuum, 1989.

Altizer, Thomas J.J. *The Gospel of Christian Atheism*. Philadelphia: Westminster, 1966.

Aristotle. *Nicomachean Ethics*. Middlesex, England: Penguin Books, 1953.

Boswell, John. *Christianity, Social Tolerance and Homosexuality*. Chicago: University of Chicago Press, 1980.

Brown, Joanne Carlson, and Carole R. Bohn, eds. *Christianity, Patriarchy, and Abuse*. New York: Pilgrim Press, 1989.

Brown, Judith. *Immodest Acts*. New York: Oxford University Press, 1986.

Bührig, Marga. *Spät habe ich gelernt, gerne Frau zu sein*. Stuttgart: Kreuz Verlag, 1987.

Bunch, Charlotte. *Passionate Politics*. New York: St. Martin's Press, 1987.

Cannon, Katie Geneva. *Black Womanist Ethics*. American Academy of Religion Academy Series. Atlanta: Scholars Press, 1988.

Chernin, Kim. *The Obsession*. New York: Harper & Row, 1981.

Christ, Carol P. *Laughter of Aphrodite*. San Francisco: Harper & Row, 1987.

Condren, Mary. *The Serpent and the Goddess*. San Francisco: Harper & Row, 1989.

Cooey, Paula M., Sharon A. Farmer, and Mary Ellen Ross, eds. *Embodied Love: Sensuality and Relationship as Feminist Values*. San Francisco: Harper & Row, 1987.

Curb, Rosemary, and Nancy Monahan. *Breaking Silence: Lesbian Nuns*. Tallahassee, Fla.: Naiad Press, 1985.

Daly, Mary. *The Church and the Second Sex*. Boston: Beacon Press, 1968.

———. *Beyond God the Father*. Boston: Beacon Press, 1973.

———. *Gyn/Ecology: The Metaethics of Radical Feminism*. Boston: Beacon Press, 1978.

———. *Pure Lust: Elemental Feminist Philosophy*. Boston: Beacon Press, 1984.

191

————. *Webster's First New Intergalactic Wickedary of the English Language.* Boston: Beacon Press, 1987.

D'Angelo, Mary Rose. "Women Partners in the New Testament." In *Journal of Feminist Studies in Religion* 6, no. 1 (Spring 1990): 65–86.

Davaney, Sheila G., ed. *Feminism and Process Thought.* Lewiston, N.Y.: Edwin Mellen Press, 1980.

√ Downing, Christine. *Myths and Mysteries of Same Sex Love.* New York: Continuum, 1989.

Ehrenreich, Barbara. "In Praise of 'Best Friends.'" *Ms.*, January 1987, 35.

Eichenbaum, Luise, and Susie Orbach. *Between Women.* New York: Viking, 1987.

Esquivel, Julia. *Threatened with Resurrection.* Elgin, Ill.: Brethren Press, 1982.

Fabella, Virginia, and Mercy Amba Oduyoye, eds. *With Passion and Compassion.* Maryknoll, N.Y.: Orbis Books, 1988.

Fiorenza, Elisabeth Schüssler. *In Memory of Her.* New York: Crossroad, 1983.

————. *Bread Not Stone.* Boston: Beacon Press, 1984.

————. "The Ethics of Biblical Interpretation: Decentering Biblical Scholarship." Society for Biblical Literature Presidential Address (December 5, 1987). *Harvard Divinity Bulletin,* Fall 1988, 6–9.

Fiske, Adele M. *Friends and Friendship in the Monastic Tradition.* CIDOC Cuaderno no. 51. Cuernavaca, Mexico: Centro Intercultural de Documentacíon, 1970.

Fortune, Marie Marshall. *Is Nothing Sacred?: When Sex Invades the Pastoral Relationship.* San Francisco: Harper & Row, 1989.

Gage, Matilda Joslyn. *Woman, Church and State.* Copyright 1893. Reprint edition: Watertown, Mass.: Persephone Press, 1980.

Goldenberg, Naomi. *Changing of the Gods: Feminism and the End of Traditional Religions.* Boston: Beacon Press, 1979.

Gordon, Kevin. "The Sexual Bankruptcy of the Christian Traditions: A Perspective of Radical Suspicion and of Fundamental Trust." In *AIDS Issues: Confronting the Challenge,* 169–212. Edited by David G. Hallman. New York: Pilgrim Press, 1989.

Grant, Jacquelyn. *White Women's Christ and Black Women's Jesus.* American Academy of Religion Academy Series. Atlanta: Scholars Press, 1989.

Greenfield, Meg. "Friendship in Washington." *Washington Post,* July 20, 1983, p. A23.

Grumbach, Doris. *Chamber Music.* New York: Fawcett, 1979.

Haecker, Dorothy. "Teacher to Student." In *Ms./Campus Times,* October 1985, 54.

Haney, Eleanor Hume. "What is Feminist Ethics? A Proposal for Continuing Discussion." *Journal of Religious Ethics* 8, no. 1, 1980, 115–24.

Harrison, Beverly Wildung. *Our Right to Choose.* Boston: Beacon Press 1983.

————. *Making the Connections.* Edited by Carol S. Robb. Boston: Beacon Press, 1985.

Heins, Marjorie. *Cutting the Mustard: Affirmative Action and the Nature of Excellence.* Winchester, Mass.: Faber and Faber, 1987.

Heyward, Carter. *The Redemption of God: A Theology of Mutual Relation.* Washington, D.C.: University Press of America, 1982.

————. *Our Passion for Justice.* New York: Pilgrim Press, 1984.

————. *Touching Our Strength: The Erotic as Power and the Love of God.* San Francisco: Harper & Row, 1989.

————, and Mary E. Hunt. "Lesbianism and Feminist Theology." *Journal of Feminist Studies in Religion* 2, no. 2 (Fall 1986): 95–99.

Hooks, Bell. *Ain't I a Woman: Black Women and Feminism.* Boston: South End Press, 1981.

————. *Feminist Theory: From Margin to Center.* Boston: South End Press, 1984.

————. *Talking Back: Thinking Feminist, Thinking Black.* Boston: South End Press, 1989.

Hunt, Mary E. *Feminist Liberation Theology: The Development of Method in Construction.* Berkeley, Calif.: Graduate Theological Union, 1980.

————. "Political Oppression and Creative Survival." In *Women's Spirit Bonding,* 164–72. Edited by Janet Kalven and Mary I. Buckley. New York: Pilgrim Press, 1984.

————. "Limited Partners." *Conscience,* May/June 1988, 6–10, and *WATERwheel* (Women's Alliance for Theology, Ethics and Ritual, Silver Spring, Md.) 1, no. 2: 1–3.

————. "Celibacy—The Case Against: Liberating Lesbian Nuns." *Out/Look,* Summer 1988, 68–74.

————. "Spiral Not Schism: Women-Church as Church." *Religion and Intellectual Life* 7, no. 1 (Fall 1989): 82–92.

————. "Women Crossing Worlds — A Feminist Model of Mission." *WATERwheel* (Women's Alliance for Theology, Ethics and Ritual, Silver Spring, Md.) 2, no. 1 (Winter 1989): 1–3.

————. "Valuing the Widow's Mite." *More Light Update,* nos. 11–12 (June–July 1990): 1–9.

Hurcombe, Linda. *Sex and God: Some Varieties of Women's Religious Experience.* New York and London: Routledge and Kegan Paul, 1987.

Isasi-Diaz, Ada Maria, and Yolanda Tarango. *Hispanic Women: Prophetic Women in the Church.* San Francisco; Harper & Row, 1988.

Jaggar, Alison M., and Susan R. Bordo, eds. *Gender/Body/Knowledge: Feminist Reconstructions of Being and Knowing.* New Brunswick and London: Rutgers University Press, 1989.

Keller, Catherine. *From a Broken Web.* Boston: Beacon Press, 1986.

Kirkwood, Lois. "Enemy Love in Racial Justice: A Christian Social Ethical Perspective." Forthcoming Ph.D. dissertation, Union Theological Seminary, New York.

Lehmann, Carolyn. "Where Wisdom and Friendship Dwell" (pamphlet). Santiago, Chile: Casa Sofía, November 1986.

Lerner, Gerda. *The Creation of Patriarchy*. New York: Oxford University Press, 1986.

Lipsett, Linda Otto. *Remember Me: Women and Their Friendship Quilts*. San Francisco: Quilt Digest Press, 1985.

Lugones, Maria C., and Elizabeth V. Spelman. "Have We Got a Theory for You! Feminist Theory, Cultural Imperialism and the Demand for 'The Woman's Voice.'" *Women's Studies International Forum* 6, no. 6 (1983): 573–81.

McFague, Sallie. *Metaphorical Theology: Models of God in Religious Language*. Philadelphia: Fortress Press, 1982.

McGrory, Mary. "Of Wit and Gallantry." *Washington Post*, October 15, 1983, C1.

McNeill, John. *Taking a Chance on God*. Boston: Beacon Press, 1988.

Mesle, Bob. "A Friend's Love: Why Process Theology Matters." *The Christian Century*, July 15–22, 1987, 622–25.

Milhaven, J. Giles. "Sleeping Like Spoons." *Commonweal*, April 7, 1989, 205–7.

Morton, Nelle. *The Journey Is Home*. Boston: Beacon Press, 1985.

Mud Flower Collective. *God's Fierce Whimsy*. New York: Pilgrim Press, 1985.

Naylor, Gloria. *The Women of Brewster Place*. New York: Penguin Books, 1983.

Neal, Marie Augusta. *The Socio-theology of Letting Go: A First World Church Facing Third World People*. New York: Paulist Press, 1977.

Nelson, James B. *Embodiment: An Approach to Sexuality and Christian Theology*. Minneapolis: Augsburg Publishing House, 1978.

———. *The Intimate Connection: Male Sexuality, Masculine Spirituality*. Philadelphia: Westminster Press, 1988.

Nestle, Joan. *A Restricted Country*. Ithaca, N.Y.: Firebrand Books, 1987.

Nugent, Robert. *A Challenge to Love*. New York: Crossroad, 1983.

Oduyoye, Mercy Amba. *Hearing and Knowing: Theological Reflections on Christianity in Africa*. Maryknoll, N.Y. : Orbis Books, 1986.

Plaskow, Judith. *Standing Again at Sinai: Judaism from a Feminist Perspective*. San Francisco: Harper & Row, 1990.

———, and Carol P. Christ, eds. *Weaving the Visions: Patterns in Feminist Spirituality*. New York: Harper & Row, 1989.

Pogrebin, Letty Cottin. "Hers" column. *New York Times*, October 6, 1983, C2.

———. *Among Friends*. New York: McGraw-Hill, 1986.

Porter, Roy, and Sylvana Tomaselli, eds. *The Dialectics of Friendship*. New York: Routledge, Chapman and Hall, 1989.

Quindlen, Anna. "Between Women, Talk Is Digging for Buried Treasure." *New York Times*, April 22, 1987.

Raymond, Janice. *A Passion for Friends: Toward a Philosophy of Female Affection*. Boston: Beacon Press, 1986.

Rich, Adrienne. "Compulsory Heterosexism and Lesbian Existence." *Signs: A Journal of Women in Culture and Society* 5, no. 4 (Summer 1980).

Rubin, Lillian B. *Just Friends.* New York: Harper & Row, 1985.

Ruether, Rosemary Radford. *Sexism and God-Talk.* Boston: Beacon Press, 1983.

———. *Women-Church: Theology and Practice of Feminist Liturgical Communities.* San Francisco: Harper & Row, 1986.

Russell, Letty, Kwok Pui-lan, Ada Maria Isasi-Diaz, Katie Geneva Cannon, eds. *Inheriting Our Mothers' Gardens: Feminist Theology in Third World Perspective.* Philadelphia: Westminster, 1988.

Saiving, Valerie. "The Human Situation: A Feminine View." Originally published in *The Journal of Religion*, April 1960. Reprinted in *Womanspirit Rising*, 25–43. Edited by Carol P. Christ and Judith Plaskow. New York: Harper & Row, 1979.

Sarton, May. *As We Are Now.* New York: W. W. Norton, 1973.

Schillebeeckx, Edward. *The Church with a Human Face.* New York: Crossroad, 1985.

Segundo, Juan Luis. *The Liberation of Theology.* Maryknoll, N.Y.: Orbis Books, 1976.

Smith-Rosenberg, Carroll. *Disorderly Conduct: Visions of Gender in Victorian America.* New York: Alfred Knopf, 1985.

Spelman, Elizabeth V. *The Inessential Woman: Problems of Exclusion in Feminist Thought.* Boston: Beacon Press, 1988.

Spong, John. *Living in Sin.* Nashville: Abingdon Press, 1988.

Stanton, Elizabeth Cady, and the Revising Committee. *The Woman's Bible.* New York: European Publishing Company, 1895; reprint, Seattle, Washington: Coalition Task Force on Women and Religion, 1974.

Starhawk. *Dreaming the Dark: Magic, Sex and Politics.* Boston: Beacon Press, 1982 (1988).

———. *Truth or Dare: Encounters with Power, Authority, and Mystery.* San Francisco: Harper & Row, 1987.

Tamez, Elsa. *El rostro feminino de la teología.* San José, Costa Rica: Departamento Ecuménico de Investigaciones (DEI), 1986.

———. *Against Machismo.* Oak Park, Ill. Meyer, Stone, 1987.

———, ed. *Through Her Eyes: Women's Theology from Latin America.* Maryknoll, N.Y.: Orbis Books, 1989.

Thistlethwaite, Susan Brooks. *Sex, Race, and God.* New York: Crossroad, 1989.

Thoman, Elizabeth, ed. *Media and Values.* "The Birds, the Bees and Broadcasting: What the Media Teaches Our Kids About Sex," no. 46 (Spring 1989).

Vahanian, Gabriel. *The Death of God.* New York: George Braziller, 1961.

van Buren, Paul. *The Secular Meaning of the Gospel.* New York: Macmillan, 1963.

Verhoeven, Alieda, ed. *Apuntes y aportes de la mujer ecuménica.* Mendoza, Argentina: Acción Popular Ecuménica Regional Cuyo, nos. 4, 5, 6, 1987.
von Wartenberg-Potter, Bärbel. *We Will Not Hang Our Harps on the Willows.* Oak Park, Ill.: Meyer, Stone, 1988.
Walker, Alice. *In Search of Our Mothers' Gardens.* San Diego: Harcourt Brace Jovanovich, 1983.
Weems, Renita. *Just a Sister Away.* San Diego: LuraMedia, 1988.
Weil, Simone. *Waiting for God.* Translated by Emma Craufurd. New York: G. P. Putnam's Sons, 1951.
Williams, Delores S. "The Color of Feminism: Or Speaking the Black Woman's Tongue." *The Journal of Religious Thought* 43, no. 1 (Spring–Summer 1986): 42–58.
———. "Womanist Theology: Black Women's Voices." *Christianity and Crisis,* March 2, 1987, 66–70.
Woititz, Janet Geringer. *Adult Children of Alcoholics.* Pompano Beach, Fla.: Health Communications, 1983.
Zanotti, Barbara, ed. *A Faith of One's Own.* Trumansburg, N.Y.: Crossing Press, 1986.

Index

Accountability, 13, 36, 113
  communal, 171
  increased, 81
Ackelsberg, Martha, 145, 158
Addams, Jane, 146
Adult Children of Alcoholics, 128
Affirmation, of friends, 139
African American women
  as feminists, 158
  power of friendships, 28
  struggle for survival, 20
  women-church concept and, 161
Ageism
  as part of power equation, 101
  stereotyping, 123
AIDS, 33, 44, 45, 116, 149
Alcoholics Anonymous, 171
Alexander, Adele Logan, 28
Alienation, 53, 81
Among Friends (Pogrebin), 15
Animals, friendships with, 83, 174
"An Observation" (Sarton), 24
Anthony, Susan B., 63, 146
Aristotle, approach to friendship,
  92–96, 156
As We Are Now, 123
Attention, 22, 151, 163
  content changes, 169
  divine, 166
  intensity of, 22
  justice-seeking friends and,
  152–53
  sharing, 170
  understanding, 157
Autograph books, 58

Backlash, 73
Beauvoir, Simone de, 66
Befriending, 66, 132

Beguines, 74
Benedict, Ruth, 74
Bennett, John C., 109
Best friends, 94, 95
Betrayal, 34, 39, 150, 169
Bettenhausen, Elizabeth, 62
Between Women (Eichenbaum and
  Orbach), 15
Beyond God the Father (Daly), 65
Biases
  anti-religious, 128
  ethnocentric, 41
Biblical studies, 75
Blood relatives, 36
Blood ties, 124
Body images, media standards of,
  104
Bonding, 157–58
  female, 29, 42, 49, 55, 77, 146
  male, 92
  powerful experiences of, 119
  survival and, 77, 148
Boswell, John, 45, 139
Briggs, Sheila, 46
Brown, Joanne, 168
Buber, Martin, 11, 78
Bunch, Charlotte, 40, 41, 46, 47, 77

Catholic women, history of, 49
Celebration(s), 18, 21, 135–41
  created by feminist groups, 137
  limits of friendship in, 115
  need for, 131
  value of, 125
Celibacy
  commitment to, 106, 139
  compulsory, 50
  life-long, 146
  vow of, 49

197